Infertility

**Perspectives from Stress and
Coping Research**

The Plenum Series on Stress and Coping

A CLINICAL GUIDE TO THE TREATMENT OF THE
HUMAN STRESS RESPONSE
George S. Everly, Jr.

COPING WITH NEGATIVE LIFE EVENTS
Clinical and Social Psychological Perspectives
Edited by C. R. Snyder and Carol E. Ford

DYNAMICS OF STRESS
Physiological, Psychological, and Social Perspectives
Edited by Mortimer H. Appley and Richard Trumbull

HUMAN ADAPTATION TO EXTREME STRESS
From the Holocaust to Vietnam
Edited by John P. Wilson, Zev Harel, and Boaz Kahana

INFERTILITY
Perspectives from Stress and Coping Research
Edited by Annette L. Stanton and Christine Dunkel-Schetter

INTERNATIONAL HANDBOOK OF TRAUMATIC STRESS SYNDROMES
Edited by John P. Wilson and Beverley Raphael

POST-TRAUMATIC STRESS DISORDER
A Clinician's Guide
Kirtland C. Peterson, Maurice F. Prout, and Robert A. Schwarz

THE SOCIAL CONTEXT OF COPING
Edited by John Eckenrode

STRESS BETWEEN WORK AND FAMILY
Edited by John Eckenrode and Susan Gore

WOMEN, WORK, AND HEALTH
Edited by Marianne Frankenhaeuser, Ulf Lundberg, and Margaret Chesney

Infertility

Perspectives from Stress and Coping Research

Edited by
ANNETTE L. STANTON
University of Kansas
Lawrence, Kansas

and
CHRISTINE DUNKEL-SCHETTER
University of California
Los Angeles, California

PLENUM PRESS • NEW YORK AND LONDON

Library of Congress Cataloging-in-Publication Data

Infertility : perspectives from stress and coping research / edited by
   Annette L. Stanton and Christine Dunkel-Schetter.
        p.   cm. -- (The Plenum series on stress and coping)
   Includes bibliographical references and index.
   ISBN 0-306-43844-5
   1. Infertility--Psychological aspects.   I. Stanton, Annette L.
II. Dunkel-Schetter, Christine. III. Series.
   [DNLM: 1. Adaptation, Psychological. 2. Infertility. 3. Stress,
Psychological.   WP 570 I43873]
RC889.I565 1991
616.6'92'0019--dc20
DNLM/DLC
for Library of Congress   91-3007
                                                                  CIP

ISBN 0-306-43844-5

© 1991 Plenum Press, New York
A Division of Plenum Publishing Corporation
233 Spring Street, New York, N.Y. 10013

Printed in the United States of America

Contributors

Antonia Abbey, Wayne State University and the Institute for Social Research, University of Michigan, Ann Arbor, Michigan 48106.

Glenn Affleck, Department of Psychiatry, University of Connecticut School of Medicine, Farmington, Connecticut 06032.

Frank M. Andrews, Institute for Social Research, University of Michigan, Ann Arbor, Michigan 48106.

Susan Miller Campbell, Department of Psychology, University of California, Los Angeles, California 90024-1563.

Leslie F. Clark, Department of Psychological Sciences, Purdue University, West Lafayette, Indiana 47907.

Val Davajan, Department of Obstetrics and Gynecology, University of Southern California School of Medicine, Los Angeles, California 90033.

Christine Dunkel-Schetter, Department of Psychology, University of California, Los Angeles, California 90024-1563.

L. Jill Halman, Institute for Social Research, University of Michigan, Ann Arbor, Michigan 48106.

Susan M. Henry, Department of Psychological Sciences, Purdue University, West Lafayette, Indiana 47907.

Robert Israel, Department of Obstetrics and Gynecology, University of Southern California School of Medicine, Los Angeles, California 90033.

Marci Lobel, Department of Psychology, State University of New York, Stony Brook, New York 11794.

Richard Mendola, Department of Psychiatry, University of Connecticut School of Medicine, Farmington, Connecticut 06032.

Letitia Anne Peplau, Department of Psychology, University of California, Los Angeles, California 90024-1563.

Anthony E. Reading, Center for Reproductive Medicine, Cedars-Sinai Medical Center, Los Angeles, California 90048.

Annette L. Stanton, Department of Psychology, University of Kansas, Lawrence, Kansas 66045-2160.

Donna M. Taylor, Department of Psychology, Memphis State University, Memphis, Tennessee 38152.

Howard Tennen, Department of Psychiatry, University of Connecticut School of Medicine, Farmington, Connecticut 06032.

Foreword

As a researcher whose work focuses largely on the causes and consequences of unwanted pregnancy, I may appear to be an unlikely candidate
to write a foreword to a book on infertility. Yet, many of the themes that
emerge in the study of unwanted pregnancy are also apparent in the study
of infertility. Moreover, this volume is an important contribution to the
literature on fertility, women's health issues, and health psychology in
general, all topics with which I have been closely involved over the past two
decades. Neither pregnancy nor its absence is inherently desirable: The
occurrence of a pregnancy can be met with joy or despair, and its absence
can be a cause of relief or anguish. Whether or not these states are wanted,
the conscious and unconscious meanings attached to pregnancy and infertility, the responses of others, the perceived implications of these states,
and one's expectations for the future all are critical factors in determining
an individual's response.

In addition, both unwanted pregnancy and failure to conceive can be
socially stigmatized, evoking both overt and subtle social disapproval. Further, they involve not only the woman, but her partner, and potentially the
extended family. Finally, both of these reproductive issues have been
poorly researched. Because both are emotionally charged and socially
stigmatized events, they are difficult to study. Much of the early literature
relied on anecdotal or case reports. Personal or theoretically based beliefs
about the psychology of women and the role of reproduction in a woman's
life at times engendered an exclusive focus on the more negative aspects
of these experiences. As a result, the literature on infertility has been
somewhat unbalanced and limited. A chance had been missed to contribute to understanding this prevalent and highly important reproductive
issue.

The current volume begins to right the imbalance in our understanding of infertility. In selecting contributors, the editors wisely chose experts who viewed infertility within broad conceptual frameworks. In the first chapter, Stanton and Dunkel-Schetter lay out a plan for the book that involves synthesizing past infertility work with current knowledge and methods from stress and coping frameworks. The plan of the book is unique in that, rather than the easier task of including reviews of the extant literature, the editors elected instead to attract chapters from those who are doing current and conceptually grounded work in the area. Davajan and Israel, leading physicians in infertility treatment, provide a valuable review of causal factors in infertility and of treatments that can be used to achieve conception given specific problems. As they note, a number of couples who are untreated will conceive, and conception is far from certain to result from treatment. The possibility for successful technological intervention provides hope for many couples and, at the same time, may render it difficult for couples to move forward in planning their lives should they be unable to conceive. The study of infertility thus provides an important case study for health psychology to examine the interface of new technologies and psychological responses.

In their excellent review of the literature on psychological adjustment to infertility, Dunkel-Schetter and Lobel note the substantial individual variability that is found in responses to the experience of infertility. Subsequent chapters provide theoretical backing for why particular variables should affect adjustment and functioning, as well as provide empirical evidence for the association of some of these variables with psychological outcome. The critical processes affecting adjustment to infertility that emerge from the research and theories covered in these chapters are causal explanations (Tennen, Affleck, and Mendola), appraisal of the experience and processes initiated to cope with it (Stanton), social support and marital conflict (Abbey, Andrews, and Halman), perceived control (Campbell, Dunkel-Schetter, and Peplau, as well as Tennen, Affleck, and Mendola), and evaluation of one's own parenting goals and how they can be met (Clark, Henry, and Taylor). Central to many of these variables is the meaning that infertility holds for the individual—how the person understands its causes, the extent to which it affects self-perceptions, and how it is linked to major life goals.

The processes described in the chapters of this book are critically important ones to understand and document. A number of interventions are suggested by them, and Reading specifically considers possible goals for intervention and the types of approaches that may be of value to infertile women and couples. The final chapter by Dunkel-Schetter and Stanton, as well as the other chapters in this volume, underlines the importance of using concepts and measures that cast the experience of infertility in relation to theory and research on other life events. In grounding research on infertility in broader stress and coping frameworks, as the authors in this volume have done, we can understand individual differences in response and discover the commonalities in responses to infertility and other difficult life experiences.

The experience of infertility is potentially one of the most painful events of life to which people must adjust. It is a complex experience affecting the woman, the man, and the couple. It is fraught with uncertainty and can lead to alternating hope and despair. It brings people into contact with the leading edge of biomedical technology, where uncertainties abound and procedures are costly, painful, and intrusive. Multiple losses can result. This volume provides an exceptional contribution to our understanding of infertility and is likely to shape the field for years to come. The authors of these chapters are doing the work that is needed to accumulate knowledge and develop interventions that can facilitate adaptation and growth in the face of this difficult experience. The chapters are thought-provoking and insightful, and we owe the authors and especially the editors our gratitude for having undertaken to bring together the theory of and research on this complex and important topic.

Nancy E. Adler

University of California, San Francisco

Preface

This book developed from our meeting in 1987 as chair and discussant for an American Psychological Association symposium on psychological concomitants of infertility. We soon discovered our striking agreement on a number of issues. First, we noted that infertility is an often neglected problem among social scientists and health care providers, as well as in the public realm. Although estimates suggest that over two million couples in the United States experience infertility, we each had observed that awareness of the problem seemed lacking, often resulting in infertile couples feeling isolated and unsupported. Second, our personal observations led us to believe that infertility frequently engenders significant alterations in the lives of individuals and couples. Couples told us of the challenges that infertility presented to their emotional balance, self-esteem, and perspectives regarding the controllability and fairness of life.

As researchers in psychology, we agreed that traditional psychological approaches to infertility were inaccurate or incomplete. Early suggestions that infertility resulted from psychopathology in the female were not validated by empirical tests. Further, they carried a component of blame that we thought destructive to women. The alternative conceptualization of infertility as a life crisis might capture the experience of some who experience infertility, but failed to account for the marked individual variability that we had observed in reactions to the experience. We agreed that recent theory and research in stress and coping offered a sound foundation for advancing our understanding of the infertility process. Although there exists no single stress and coping approach, the literature in this area provides many strong bases for identifying the conditions under which infertility might be perceived as most stressful and for specifying the factors that might facilitate or hinder adjustment to infertility. Thus, we expected that research stimulated by this literature would better account for individual variability in the experience of infertility and would aid in the identification of those at risk for greater distress during the infertility process. In turn, we anticipated that the study of individuals' and couples' experience with infertility would enrich the extant body of research and theory on stress and coping in general. Finally, we believed that, although the several sources that provide a clinical or personal vantage point on infertility furnish a rich characterization of commonly encountered issues and serve as a basis for generating hypotheses, rigorous empirical research is essential for advancing our knowledge regarding the process of adjustment to the inability to conceive. It was from these shared perspectives that our enthusiasm for this volume evolved.

We hope that this book accomplishes several goals. First, it is intended to offer the reader a background on infertility and the body of research regarding its psychological concomitants. Second, our authors provide theoretically grounded chapters that present the most recent investigations of psychosocial influences on adjustment to infertility. Thus, the chapters are intended to introduce a conceptually driven analysis of psychological processes involved in adjustment to infertility. Third, we seek to promote attention to infertility as a stressful life transition and to provide a framework for continued investigation in this area. We encourage other researchers and health care professionals to devote concentrated efforts toward understanding the experience of infertility. A final purpose is to promote application of research in infertility to the development of effective supportive interventions for those who confront fertility problems. Not everyone who encounters infertility will need or want aid in coping with its exigencies. Those who do, however, deserve the best that our empirical and clinical proficiencies have to offer. We hope that the suggestions for intervention offered in this book will prove valuable to practitioners and those whom they serve.

We extend our thanks to many who aided in the completion of this volume. First, we thank those who offered suggestions and encouragement regarding the book's development, content, and structure. These include Rick Snyder, Eliot Werner, who is executive editor at Plenum, and Don Meichenbaum, editor for the Plenum Series on Stress and Coping. We also are grateful to Andrea Martin, our production editor at Plenum, and to Elizabeth Soliday, Anne Rochleau, and Liana Blas, who provided valuable administrative and research assistance. We profited from our collaboration on infertility research with a number of colleagues and graduate students, including Susan Campbell, Leslie Clark, Marci Lobel, Peggy McFarland, Debbie McQueeney, Karen Patterson, Anne Peplau, Joel Pittard, Bridget Smith, and Howard Tennen. We also gratefully acknowledge the good will and perseverance of our chapter authors.

This book is the product of a long process of unusually effective collaboration, beginning with the initial inspiration to write such a volume. We each contributed in essential ways to the completion of this work, and this collaborative effort was most enjoyable. Professional acquaintances at the outset, we have grown to be good friends despite the fact that we have met face-to-face on only three occasions. The telephone companies and the postal service are to be thanked (and might wish to thank us) for their part in the success of this collaboration. Although co-authors typically do not thank one another, we want to express our mutual respect for and appreciation of each other. We also thank our husbands Sam Green and Charles Schetter. Finally, this book would not have been possible without the willingness of several hundred people confronting infertility to share their experience. We hope that this book gives them something valuable in return for what they have entrusted to us.

Annette L. Stanton
Christine Dunkel-Schetter

Lawrence, Kansas, and Los Angeles

Contents

PART II: APPLICATION OF CONCEPTUAL MODELS AND CONSTRUCTS IN PSYCHOLOGY TO THE STUDY OF THE INFERTILITY PROCESS

Chapter 7. Perceived Control and Adjustment to Infertility among Women Undergoing *In Vitro* Fertilization 133

Susan Miller Campbell, Christine Dunkel-Schetter, and Letitia Anne Peplau

Chapter 8. Cognitive Examination of Motivation for Childbearing as a Factor in Adjustment to Infertility 157

Leslie F. Clark, Susan M. Henry, and Donna M. Taylor

PART III: CURRENT STATUS AND FUTURE DIRECTIONS

Chapter 9. Psychological Intervention and Infertility 183

Anthony E. Reading

Chapter 10. Psychological Adjustment to Infertility:
Future Directions in Research and Application 197

Christine Dunkel-Schetter and Annette L. Stanton

I

An Introduction to the Infertility Process

1

Psychological Adjustment to Infertility

An Overview of Conceptual Approaches

ANNETTE L. STANTON and
CHRISTINE DUNKEL-SCHETTER

The great majority of young adults assume that their life course will include bearing and raising children (Regan & Roland, 1985; Zuckerman, 1981). Presuming fertility, couples often use contraceptive methods to prevent pregnancy until conditions in their lives are conducive to the achievement of this central goal. When pregnancy is attempted, however, some couples find that their goal of becoming a parent is beyond their control. Try as they might, an avenue they have expected to provide fulfillment in life remains out of reach.

Infertility is a problem well suited for the study of adjustment to negative life experiences. In addition, adjustment to infertility is a topic worthy of study in its own right. Clinicians (Mahlstedt, 1985; Menning, 1980) as well as infertile couples cite the need for psychological services in this area. In their first contacts with an infertility clinic, 97% of couples endorsed a need for psychological services, and over 50% said that they would use such services during the infertility workup (Daniluk, 1988). In this chapter, we will describe the scope and magnitude of the problem of

ANNETTE L. STANTON • Department of Psychology, University of Kansas, Lawrence, Kansas 66045-2160. **CHRISTINE DUNKEL-SCHETTER** • Department of Psychology, University of California, Los Angeles, California 90024-1563.

3

infertility, provide an overview of the approaches taken by behavioral and social scientists to understanding the psychological aspects of infertility, and introduce our approach to examining factors that help and hinder couples as they negotiate this process. This material sets the stage for understanding subsequent chapters.

INFERTILITY: SCOPE AND MAGNITUDE OF THE PROBLEM

Infertility is defined as the inability to conceive a pregnancy after one year of engaging in sexual intercourse without contraception (Mosher & Pratt, 1982; U.S. Congress, Office of Technology Assessment [OTA], 1988). Individuals with primary infertility are those who have never had a biological child, whereas those with secondary infertility have had at least one previous documented conception. Typically, infertility characterizes the couple who is attempting conception, for although one member may carry the medically diagnosed cause, both members of the couple experience the inability to realize their goal of having a child.

What is the likelihood that a couple will have a fertility problem at some point in their reproductive history? The most comprehensive data addressing this question come from national surveys conducted in 1965, 1976, 1982, and 1988 and compiled by researchers for the National Center for Health Statistics (Hirsch & Mosher, 1987; Mosher, 1985, 1988; Mosher & Pratt, 1982, 1990; OTA, 1988; Pratt, Mosher, Bachrach, & Horn, 1984). In these surveys, personal interviews were conducted with four nationally representative samples of women between the ages of 15 and 44. Excluding those who were surgically sterile, the overall incidence of infertility in married couples evidenced little change, ranging from 13.3% of couples in 1965 to 13.7% in 1988. Including the surgically sterile, 7.9% of married couples were infertile in 1988, and it was estimated that 2.4 million couples met the standard medical definition of infertility (Mosher & Pratt, 1990). Impaired fecundity, a broader concept which includes difficulty or danger carrying a baby to term as well as problems conceiving, affected approximately 4.9 million married and unmarried women (Mosher & Pratt, 1990). Of these women, approximately 45% had no biological children and 55% had one or more previous births.

Although the overall incidence of infertility is not increasing (Mosher & Pratt, 1990), the rate among women aged 20 to 24 rose significantly from 3.6% in 1965 to 10.6% in 1982, perhaps owing to the concomitant rise in sexually transmitted diseases in that age group (OTA, 1988). In addition, the number of couples with primary infertility doubled, increasing from 500,000 in 1965 to one million in 1988. One recent British study suggested that as many as 20% to 35% of couples take more than one year to conceive at some stage in their reproductive history (Page, 1989). Thus, infertility is a problem that many couples confront, although many also become pregnant eventually, and one that may be of increasing concern for young adults.

Blacks have been found to be at greater risk for infertility and impaired fecundity than whites. For example, the risk of infertility was 1.5 times greater for black than white couples in 1982 (OTA, 1988). Mosher (1988) suggested that this may in part be due to the finding that black women were nearly twice as likely as white women to have been treated for pelvic inflammatory disease (PID), a risk factor for infertility. Other factors thought to contribute to this difference include (OTA, 1988): (1) The higher rate of sexually transmitted diseases among blacks than whites, a difference which reflects the difference in other relevant demographic characteristics, such as urban dwelling (OTA, 1988, p. 51); (2) the greater use among blacks of intrauterine devices (IUDs) for birth control, which may increase the likelihood of PID; (3) greater exposure among blacks to environmental factors, such as occupational hazards, which may affect reproduction; and (4) greater likelihood in blacks of infections or complications following abortion or childbirth, which may lead to scarring and other structural damage. In addition, poorer access to health care for black women (Manley, Lin-Fu, Miranda, Noonan, & Parker, 1985) may contribute to the higher infertility rate. Identification of factors that confer risk for infertility and of infertility rates for minority groups requires further investigation.

A rapid increase in the use of medical services for infertility has occurred during the last two decades. The estimated number of visits to private physicians for infertility-related consultation rose from approximately 600,000 in 1968 to 1.6 million in 1984 (OTA, 1988), with females much more likely to seek services than males. Reasons for this increased demand include: (1) The greater number of couples with primary infertility, who are twice as likely as those with secondary infertility to seek services; (2) the greater availability of services for infertility; (3) advances in diagnostic and treatment techniques; (4) the decreased number of infants available for adoption in some states; and (5) a more conducive social milieu, in which individuals have a growing awareness of the new reproductive technologies and increasingly expect to be able to control their reproductive histories (Aral & Cates, 1983; Hirsch & Mosher, 1987; OTA, 1988). Currently, one in every six couples is likely to use medical services for infertility at some point (Hull, Glazener, Kelly, Conway, Foster, Hinton, Coulson, Lambert, Watt, & Desai, 1985; OTA, 1988).

Those who seek infertility services may confront a protracted and costly process. Americans spent approximately one billion dollars in 1987 on medical care for infertility (OTA, 1988). According to estimates from the Office of Technology Assessment (1988), a full diagnostic workup for infertility is likely to cost $2500 to $3000, and treatment costs range from $2000 to $8000, on the average. In the extreme, couples may spend over $22,000 on infertility-related intervention, only a portion of which is reimbursable by health insurance. When a couple with fertility problems seeks medical treatment, their chances of successfully achieving a viable pregnancy are approximately 50% (OTA, 1988). The probability of success varies as a function of the diagnosed cause of infertility, with treatment of ovulatory failure yielding higher conception rates than intervention for sperm dysfunction, for example (Hull *et al.*, 1985). Thus, infertile couples entering the medical system encounter numerous challenges, often including acquisition of a new medical vocabulary, participation in invasive and time-consuming diagnostic and treatment procedures, and assumption of financial burdens, all without the guarantee of success. Specific medical procedures which infertile individuals undergo are discussed in detail in the next chapter by Davajan and Israel.

APPROACHES TO THE PSYCHOLOGICAL ASPECTS OF INFERTILITY

Infertility as a Psychosomatic Illness

Interest in infertility by mental health professionals and social scientists originally centered on the search for etiological factors. As little as two decades ago, emotional factors were presumed causal in 30% to 50% of infertility cases (Mazor, 1984; OTA, 1988; Seibel & Taymor, 1982). This assumption was applied primarily to cases when no organic pathology was discovered. Furthermore, psychogenic causes for infertility frequently were assumed to reside in the female. Thus, researchers postulated such psychogenic mechanisms as conflict over the maternal role (Allison, 1979; Eisner, 1963), feminine sexual identity problems (Mai, Munday, & Rump, 1972), and female immaturity and neuroticism (Sandler, 1968). To illustrate, Sandler (1968) asserted:

> In many patients even superficial observation will show that it [infertility] is only one manifestation of a total disturbance of her personality . . . as Menninger said many years ago, "her illness represents a psychic conflict sailing under a gynaecological flag." (p. 51)
> Sterility can thus be a defence of the disturbed personality against the experience of pregnancy and motherhood . . . The story so often demonstrates the failure of

these women to adapt to the demands of a mature interpersonal relationship, not only in the sexual sphere but in every aspect of life. (p. 58)

Psychodynamic hypotheses such as these generated research designed to demonstrate personality or emotional differences between fertile and infertile women (e.g., Eisner, 1963; Mai et al., 1972), between women with unexplained versus organic infertility (e.g., Kipper, Zigler-Shani, Serr, & Insler, 1977; Piotrowski, 1962), and between infertile women who subsequently achieved pregnancy and those that did not (e.g., Garcia, Freeman, Rickels, Wu, Scholl, Galle, & Boxer, 1985). A much smaller number of studies focused on male samples (e.g., Abse, 1966). In general, reviewers of this literature on psychogenesis have concluded that the preponderance of studies reveals no consistent or striking evidence for psychological causes of infertility (Bents, 1985; Denber, 1978; Edelmann & Connolly, 1986; Noyes & Chapnick, 1964). In addition, the related hypothesis that adoption facilitates conception by relieving emotional stress has failed to receive support in several studies (Aaronson & Glienke, 1963; Edelmann & Connolly, 1986; Rock, Tietze, & McLaughlin, 1965; Seibel & Taymor, 1982; Tyler, Bonapart, & Grant, 1960). Seibel and Taymor (1982) concluded in their review that "statistical evidence is overwhelmingly against the relationship of adoption and subsequent conception" (p. 144). Thus, the hypothesis that psychopathology in infertile individuals prevents pregnancy has fallen into disfavor.

Concurrent with research that failed to support a psychogenic model for infertility, procedures for diagnosing biomedical causes of infertility improved. Currently, over 80% of infertility cases are found to have an organic cause (Mazor, 1984; OTA, 1988), and it is estimated that infertility may be attributable to stress or emotional factors in no more than 5% of cases (OTA, 1988). Finding an anatomical, physiological, or neuroendocrinological cause for infertility does not preclude the possibility that psychological factors also contribute. In particular, several researchers have discussed the mechanisms whereby stress may affect spermatogenesis and ovulation (Domar & Seibel, 1990; Edelmann & Golombok, 1989; Giblin, Poland, Moghissi, Ager, & Olson, 1988; Harrison, Callan, & Hennessey, 1987; Seibel & Taymor, 1982). Thus, stress is a possible interactive etiologic factor.

The postulation that stress may affect fertility differs from previous psychogenic models in that they targeted causative factors within the person, whereas newer formulations focusing on stress typically emphasize taxing environmental events. For example, Harrison, Callan, and Hennessey (1987) demonstrated that the stress of undergoing an *in vitro* fertilization cycle may impair the sperm quality of some men. Psychodynamic models have been criticized for placing the blame on the couple for their infertility. A positive aspect of the newer models is that the infertile individual is not deemed at fault, because infertility is attributed not to the individual's psychopathology but rather to physiological reactions to environmental challenges. However, research to date has not tested sufficiently the precise role of stress in impairing fertility. In addition, researchers in this area must remain aware of the negative consequences for couples of implying that their infertility has a psychological cause. Finally, because of their focus on causes rather than consequences of infertility, psychogenic models in general carry few implications for understanding how couples adjust to infertility.

Infertility as a Crisis

As medical diagnostics for infertility improved and interest in the psychogenesis of infertility waned, it became increasingly apparent that the heightened emotional distress experienced by many infertile couples may be more a consequence of infertility than a cause. With the primary goal of aiding infertile couples in managing their experience, practitioners began to conceptualize infertility as a major life crisis (e.g., Berger, 1980; Bresnick, 1981; Cook, 1987; Kraft, Palombo, Mitchell, Dean, Meyers, & Schmidt, 1980; McGuire, 1975; Menning, 1977, 1980). Menning (1977) was the pioneer in applying crisis theory (Caplan, 1964; Lindemann & Lindemann, 1979; Moos & Schaefer, 1986) to infertility.

As a life crisis, infertility is conceptualized as a currently unsolvable problem that threatens important life goals, taxes personal resources, and arouses unresolved major problems from the past. According to Menning (1977), this crisis is developmental in that infertility may impede the acquisition of generativity, a concern with establishing and guiding the next generation, which Erikson (1950) postulated as a central developmental task of adulthood. The period of emotional disequilibrium that comprises the crisis creates a push toward resolution, toward regaining homeostasis.

According to Menning (1980), the crisis of infertility carries the potential for either maladjustment or positive growth. The crisis evokes a predictable pattern of feelings, including surprise, denial, anger, isolation, guilt, and grief. Effective resolution requires that these feelings be "recognized, worked through, and overcome" (Menning, 1980, p. 317). Thus, a grief process is required, wherein the infertile couple mourns their often numerous losses, including losses of the child the couple might have had, self-esteem, a sense of control, and belief in the fairness of life (Kraft *et al.*,

1980; Mahlstedt, 1985; Menning, 1980; for elaboration, see Dunkel-Schetter & Lobel, this volume). Through the experience and expression of emotions involved in the grief process, the couple is thought to move toward an acceptance of their infertile state, engage in the exploration of alternative plans, and begin to move forward with their lives.

The conceptualization of infertility as a major life crisis is valuable, in that it helped to stimulate the development of support groups for infertile couples, engender an awareness among professionals of infertile patients' concerns, and legitimize adjustment to infertility as a problem worthy of empirical attention. In addition, a crisis model carries implications for understanding psychological adjustment, in that the experience and expression of emotions in the grief process is hypothesized to be essential for successful adjustment. The research that has accompanied this conceptualization, however, has not differed very substantially from that examining hypotheses regarding the psychogenesis of infertility. With the exception of a theory-driven longitudinal study examining early adulthood infertility and the development of males' midlife generativity (Snarey, Son, Kuehne, Hauser, & Vaillant, 1987), few studies have gone beyond the demonstration of differences and similarities between infertile and fertile subjects in the emotions postulated to accompany infertility.

To our knowledge, no study has evaluated Menning's proposal that individuals go through predictable stages of emotion during their experience of infertility. In addition, the hypothesis that emotional expression is necessary to successful adjustment has not been evaluated. Inherent in both of these hypotheses is an assumption that infertile couples are similar as a group and that those who adjust successfully engage in similar behaviors. These "homogeneity myths" (Kiesler, 1966) promote the sort of group difference research that has been conducted thus far. Such study may enhance our ability to predict the emotions that infertile couples may experience. However, individual variability in the infertility experience is minimized, and factors that help or hinder couples as they manage the hurdles of infertility are given little attention.

Writers discussing the putative emotional stages in the infertility experience typically acknowledge the potential for individual variability. For example, Cook (1987) commented that "Differences in the way individuals perceive, react to, and resolve their infertility are not well understood" (p. 468). Unfortunately, crisis theory and discussions of the grief process provide little direction for furthering our knowledge of systematic variability in adjustment. Further, the published literature to date has gleaned little from other psychological theories to enhance our understanding of adjustment to infertility (cf. Matthews & Matthews, 1986; McEwan, Costello, & Taylor, 1987). Application of the substantial body of theory and research regarding adjustment to negative life events to the study of adjustment to infertility is the next logical step in this area. Such application comprises a primary goal for this book.

Infertility as a Stressful Experience

Researchers and theorists have generated many formulations of stress. Stress has been conceptualized as a stimulus, with stressors including major life events or changes (e.g., illness, divorce) as well as daily hassles (e.g., getting stuck in traffic; Lazarus & Cohen, 1977). Stress also has been defined as a response. For example, Selye (1956) spoke of stress as a nonspecific response of the body to a demand. Lazarus and Folkman (1984) discussed these formulations and proposed a relational definition of stress, which involves a "relationship between the person and the environment that is appraised by the person as taxing or exceeding his or her resources and endangering his or her well-being" (p. 19). This definition is appropriate for our purposes, as it allows for individual variability in response. To illustrate, we would expect infertility to be perceived as stressful by those for whom parenthood is a central life goal, whereas those for whom parenthood is less important might not appraise infertility as particularly stressful and thus would be at less risk for maladjustment.

For those who desire children, infertility is likely to be characterized by just those dimensions that individuals are most likely to appraise as stressful (Lazarus & Folkman, 1984; Taylor, 1990): unpredictability, negativity, uncontrollability, and ambiguity. Those attempting conception are likely to be surprised when they have difficulty conceiving (Menning, 1980), to view their infertility as an unwanted and negative status (Miall, 1986), to believe that they have relatively little control over attaining the desired outcome (Campbell *et al.*, this volume; Stanton, this volume), and to be uncertain of the probability of attaining their goal eventually. Hence, infertility provides an excellent opportunity for application of theory on the stress process.

Several frameworks have been developed for understanding how individuals respond when facing a stressful encounter (e.g., Cronkite & Moos, 1984; Lazarus & Folkman, 1984; Moos & Billings, 1982; Pearlin, Menaghan, Lieberman, & Mullan, 1981). Taken together, these conceptualizations of stress have yielded a rich empirical literature on stress, coping, and adjustment. Researchers have posed several central questions. Perhaps the largest body of work has centered on investigating whether the experience of stress leads to negative adaptive outcomes. For example, does exposure to many versus few stressful encounters in a particular period confer differential vulnerability to physical and mental illnesses? Such questions engender continuing active debate (Glass, 1989; Maddi, Bartone, & Puccetti, 1987; Schroeder & Costa, 1984).

These questions in turn have stimulated attempts to specify the conditions under which stressful encounters have detrimental or salutory outcomes. To understand the factors that determine adjustment to stress, researchers have tapped such established frameworks in psychology as attribution theory (e.g., Taylor, Lichtman, & Wood, 1984), social comparison theory (e.g., Wills, 1987), and theories regarding control (e.g., Averill, 1973), as well as constructing their own comprehensive theories of adjustment to stressful experiences (e.g., Antonovsky, 1987; Hobfoll, 1989; Lazarus & Folkman, 1984; Taylor, 1983). Using these frameworks, researchers have sought to determine the adaptive consequences of manifesting particular personality attributes (e.g., Kobasa & Puccetti, 1983; Martin, Kuiper, Olinger, & Dobbin, 1987), initiating specific coping strategies (e.g., Revenson & Felton, 1989), having social support (e.g., Cohen & Wills, 1985), or encountering little opportunity for control (e.g., Affleck, Tennen, Pfeiffer, & Fifield, 1987). These and other factors have been shown to affect an individual's psychological adjustment under conditions of stress. This literature on stress and adjustment provides a guide for understanding the ways in which personal and situational factors might help or hinder the adjustment of infertile couples.

In investigating factors that determine adjustment to stress, one must consider how to conceptualize adjustment. What are the indicators of successful versus unsuccessful adjustment to infertility? Lazarus and Folkman (1984) suggest that researchers of stressful encounters should consider adaptive outcomes within three domains: morale, social functioning, and somatic health. Thus, when one confronts a stressful encounter, adjustment might be gauged by virtue of one's abilities to maintain well-being and a positive sense of self, to continue performance of social roles and sustain satisfying interpersonal relationships, and to sustain optimal physical health. Another approach poses five adaptive tasks (Moos & Schaefer, 1986), three of which correspond to those of Lazarus and Folkman: (1) To establish the meaning and personal significance of the situation; (2) to confront reality and respond to the requirements of the situation; (3) to sustain relationships with family members, friends, or others who may be helpful (i.e., social functioning); (4) to maintain a reasonable emotional balance (i.e., morale); and (5) to preserve a satisfactory self-image and sense of competence (i.e., morale). Thus, success in meeting both the intrapersonal and interpersonal demands of infertility may signal successful adjustment. Assessment of well-being and distress to signify adjustment has ample precedent in the literature on adjustment to various stressful experiences (e.g., Andersen, Anderson, & DeProsse, 1989; Folkman & Lazarus, 1988; Taylor *et al.*, 1984) and seems warranted in investigating adjustment to infertility. The infertile individual's abilities to maintain well-being and manage distress are primary indicators of adjustment in the research reported in this book.

An additional point regarding psychological adjustment deserves consideration. One might question specifically what constitutes a "reasonable emotional balance" in adjustment to infertility. Particularly in light of Menning's (1980) suggestion that psychological resolution of infertility requires the experience and expression of grief, self-reported depression might reflect such a "working through" and therefore indicate effective rather than ineffective adjustment. By contrast, we would suggest that as levels of distress approach clinical significance or persist over a long period, impairment in role functioning and in one's sense of worth may result. How are the intensity and duration of reported distress related to successful adjustment in the long run? This is a pressing issue for researchers studying infertility and stress processes in general. Particularly given the chronicity of many infertility cases, whether adjustment measured at one point in this process predicts long-term resolution is an important empirical question.

In sum, the literature on stress and coping holds promise for furthering our understanding of adjustment to infertility. First, it specifies the conditions under which infertility is likely to be perceived as stressful. Second, it points to factors that are likely to facilitate or impede adjustment in infertile couples. Finally, it serves as a guide for defining what constitutes successful psychological adjustment to infertility. This literature comprises the foundation underlying several chapters of this book.

PLAN OF THE BOOK

Along with this chapter, the other introductory chapters in this section are intended to provide a background on current knowledge regarding the medical diagnosis and treatment of infertility, as well as its psychological concomitants. The second section contains chapters in which the authors apply conceptual models and constructs in psychology to the study of infertility. Each of these chapters is organized around basic concepts which are known to be important in predicting adjustment to stressful events and which have clear applicability to infertility. Thus, a conceptually driven analysis of this process is provided by chapters on the roles of casual explanations, coping processes, social relationships, examination of child-bearing motives, and perceptions of control in adjustment to infertility. Through our focus on the application of established theory and related research to investigation of the infertility process, we hope to encourage a reciprocal interplay between theoretical and empirical advances in the general literature on stress and adjustment, on the one hand, and the growing body of knowledge regarding adjustment to infertility, on the other.

In the final section of the book, Reading provides an overview of the literature on psychological intervention with infertile individuals and sug-gestions for clinical treatment. We conclude with an overview of key con-ceptual and methodological issues in the study of psychological adjustment to infertility, as well as themes in clinical implications drawn from previous chapters. In addition, we discuss contributions of empirical and conceptual work on infertility to our knowledge of the stress process in general, and we suggest directions for future study. Our hope is that this book will serve both to encourage researchers to tackle the empirical and theoretical com-plexities of adjustment to infertility and ultimately to aid those who are facing its challenges.

REFERENCES

Aaronson, H. G., & Glienke, C. F. (1963). A study of the incidence of pregnancy following adoption. *Fertility and Sterility, 14*, 547–553.

Abse, D. W. (1966). Psychiatric aspects of human male infertility. *Fertility and Sterility, 17*, 133–139.

Affleck, G., Tennen, H., Pfeiffer, C., & Fifield, J. (1987). Appraisals of control and predic-tability in adapting to a chronic disease. *Journal of Personality and Social Psychology, 53*, 273–279.

Allison, J. R. (1979). Roles and role conflict of women in infertile couples. *Psychology of Women Quarterly, 4*, 97–113.

Andersen, B. L., Anderson, B., & DeProsse, C. (1989). Controlled prospective longitudinal study of women with cancer: II. Psychological outcomes. *Journal of Consulting and Clinical Psychology, 57*, 692–697.

Antonovsky, A. (1987). *Unraveling the mystery of health: How people manage stress and stay well.* San Francisco: Jossey-Bass.

Aral, S. O., & Cates, W. (1983). The increasing concern with infertility: Why now? *Journal of the American Medical Association, 250*, 2327–2331.

Averill, J. R. (1973). Personal control over aversive stimuli and its relationship to stress. *Psychological Bulletin, 80*, 286–303.

Bents, H. (1985). Psychology of male infertility—A literature survey. *International Journal of Andrology, 8*, 325–336.

Berger, D. M. (1980). Couples' reactions to male infertility and donor insemination. *American Journal of Psychiatry, 137*, 1047–1049.

Bresnick, E. R. (1981). A holistic approach to the treatment of the crisis of infertility. *Journal of Marital and Family Therapy, 7*, 181–188.

Caplan, G. (1964). *Principles of preventive psychiatry*. New York: Basic Books.

Cohen, S., & Wills, T. A. (1985). Stress, social support, and the buffering hypothesis. *Psychological Bulletin, 98*, 310–348.

Cook, E. P. (1987). Characteristics of the biopsychosocial crisis of infertility. *Journal of Counseling and Development, 65*, 465–470.

Cronkite, R. C., & Moos, R. H. (1984). The role of predisposing and moderating factors in the stress-illness relationship. *Journal of Health and Social Behavior, 25*, 372–393.

Daniluk, J. C. (1988). Infertility: Intrapersonal and interpersonal impact. *Fertility and Sterility, 49*, 982–990.

Denber, H. C. B. (1978). Psychiatric aspects of infertility. *Journal of Reproductive Medicine, 20*, 23–29.

Domar, A. D., & Seibel, M. (1990). The emotional aspects of infertility. In M. Seibel (Ed.), *Infertility: A comprehensive text* (pp. 23–35). Norwalk, CT: Appleton-Lange.

Edelmann, R. J., & Connolly, K. J. (1986). Psychological aspects of infertility. *British Journal of Medical Psychology, 59*, 209–219.

Edelmann, R. J., & Golombok, S. (1989). Stress and reproductive failure. *Journal of Reproductive and Infant Psychology, 7*, 79–86.

Eisner, B. G. (1963). Some psychological differences between fertile and infertile women. *Journal of Clinical Psychology, 19*, 391–395.

Erikson, E. (1950). *Childhood and society*. New York: W. W. Norton.

Folkman, S., & Lazarus, R. S. (1988). Coping as a mediator of emotion. *Journal of Personality and Social Psychology, 54*, 466–475.

Garcia, C., Freeman, E. W., Rickels, K., Wu, C., Scholl, G., Galle, P. C., & Boxer, A. S. (1985). Behavioral and emotional factors and treatment responses in a study of anovulatory infertile women. *Fertility and Sterility, 44*, 478–483.

Giblin, P. T., Poland, M. L., Moghissi, K. S., Ager, J. W., & Olson, J. M. (1988). Effects of stress and characteristic adaptability on semen quality in healthy men. *Fertility and Sterility, 49*, 127–132.

Glass, D. C. (Chair). (1989, August). Stressful life events: What do we know? Where do we go from here? Panel debate and discussion presented at the annual meeting of the American Psychological Association, New Orleans.

Harrison, K. L., Callan, V. J., & Hennessey, J. F. (1987). Stress and semen quality in an in vitro fertilization program. *Fertility and Sterility, 48*, 633–637.

Hirsch, M. B., & Mosher, W. D. (1987). Characteristics of infertile women in the United States and their use of infertility services. *Fertility and Sterility, 47*, 618–625.

Hobfoll, S. E. (1989). Conservation of resources: A new attempt at conceptualizing stress. *American Psychologist, 44*, 513–524.

Hull, M. G. R., Glazener, C. M. A., Kelly, N. J., Conway, D. I., Foster, P. A., Hinton, R. A., Coulson, C., Lambert, P. A., Watt, E. M., & Desai, K. M. (1985). Population study of causes, treatment, and outcome of infertility. *British Medical Journal, 291*, 1693–1697.

Kiesler, D. J. (1966). Some myths of psychotherapy research and the search for a paradigm. *Psychological Bulletin, 65*, 110–136.

Kipper, D. A., Zigler-Shani, Z., Serr, D. M., & Insler, V. (1977). Psychogenic infertility, neuroticism and the feminine role: A methodological inquiry. *Journal of Psychosomatic Research, 21*, 363–369.

Kobasa, S. C., & Puccetti, M. C. (1983). Personality and social resources in stress resistance. *Journal of Personality and Social Psychology, 42*, 168–177.

Kraft, A. D., Palombo, J., Mitchell, D., Dean, C., Meyers, S., & Schmidt, A. W. (1980). The psychological dimensions of infertility. *American Journal of Orthopsychiatry, 50*, 618–628.

Lazarus, R. S., & Cohen, J. B. (1977). Environmental stress. In I. Altman & J. F. Wohlwill (Eds.), *Human behavior and the environment: Current theory and research.* New York: Plenum.

Lazarus, R. S., & Folkman, S. (1984). *Stress, appraisal, and coping.* New York: Springer.

Lindemann, E. (1979). *Beyond grief: Studies in crisis intervention.* New York: Jason Aronson.

Maddi, S. R., Bartone, P. T., & Puccetti, M. C. (1987). Stressful events are indeed a factor in physical illness: Reply to Schroeder and Costa (1984). *Journal of Personality and Social Psychology, 52,* 833–843.

Mahlstedt, P. P. (1985). The psychological component of infertility. *Fertility and Sterility, 43,* 335–346.

Mai, F. M., Munday, R. N., & Rump, E. E. (1972). Psychiatric interview comparisons between infertile and fertile couples. *Psychosomatic Medicine, 34,* 431–440.

Manley, A., Lin-Fu, J. S., Miranda, M., Noonan, A., & Parker, T. (1985). Special health concerns of ethnic minority women. Commissioned paper in *Women's Health: Report of the Public Health Service Task Force on Women's Health Issues,* Volume II (pp. II-35–II-37). Washington, D.C.: U.S. Department of Health and Human Services (DHHS Publication No. (PHS) 85-50206).

Martin, R. A., Kuiper, N. A., Olinger, L. J., & Dobbin, J. (1987). Is stress always bad? Telic versus paratelic dominance as a stress-moderating variable. *Journal of Personality and Social Psychology, 53,* 970–982.

Matthews, R., & Matthews, A. M. (1986). Infertility and involuntary childlessness: The transition to nonparenthood. *Journal of Marriage and the Family, 48,* 641–649.

Mazor, M. D. (1984). Emotional reactions to infertility. In M. D. Mazor & H. F. Simons (Eds.), *Infertility: Medical, emotional, and social considerations* (pp. 23-35). New York: Human Sciences Press.

McEwan, K. L., Costello, C. G., & Taylor, P. J. (1987). Adjustment to infertility. *Journal of Abnormal Psychology, 96,* 108–116.

McGuire, L. S. (1975). Psychologic management of infertile women. *Postgraduate Medicine, 57,* 173–176.

Menning, B. E. (1977). *Infertility: A guide for the childless couple.* Englewood Cliffs, NJ: Prentice-Hall.

Menning, B. E. (1980). The emotional needs of infertile couples. *Fertility and Sterility, 34,* 313–319.

Miall, C. E. (1986). The stigma of involuntary childlessness. *Social Problems, 33,* 268–282.

Moos, R. H., & Billings, A. G. (1982). Conceptualizing and measuring coping resources and processes. In L. Goldberger & S. Breznitz (Eds.), *Handbook of stress: Theoretical and clinical aspects* (pp. 212–230). New York: Free Press.

Moos, R. H., & Schaefer, J. A. (1986). Life transitions and crises: A conceptual overview. In R. H. Moos (Ed.), *Coping with life crises: An integrated approach* (pp. 3–28). New York: Plenum.

Mosher, W. D. (1985). Reproductive impairments in the United States, 1965–1982. *Demography, 22,* 415–429.

Mosher, W. D. (1988). Fecundity and infertility in the United States. *American Journal of Public Health, 78,* 181–182.

Mosher, W. D., & Pratt, W. F. (1982). *Reproductive impairments among married couples: United States.* Hyattsville, Maryland: U.S. Department of Health & Human Services, Office of Health Research, Statistics, and Technology, National Center for Health Statistics.

Mosher, W. D., & Pratt, W. F. (1990). Fecundity and infertility in the United States, 1965–1988. *Advance Data From Vital and Health Statistics,* no. 192. Hyattsville, MD: National Center for Health Statistics.

Noyes, R. W., & Chapnick, E. M. (1964). Literature on psychology and infertility: A critical analysis. *Fertility and Sterility, 15*, 543–558.

Page, H. (1989). Estimation of the prevalence and incidence of infertility in a population: A pilot study. *Fertility and Sterility, 51*, 571–577.

Pearlin, L. I., Menaghan, E. G., Lieberman, M. A., & Mullan, J. T. (1981). The stress process. *Journal of Health and Social Behavior, 22*, 337–356.

Piotrowski, Z. A. (1962). Psychogenic factors in anovulatory women. II. Psychological evaluation. *Fertility and Sterility, 13*, 11–19.

Pratt, W. F., Mosher, W. D., Bachrach, C. A., & Horn, M. C. (1984). Understanding U.S. fertility: Findings from the National Survey of Family Growth, Cycle III. *Population Bulletin, 39*, 3–40.

Regan, M. C., & Roland, H. E. (1985). Rearranging family and career priorities: Professional women and men of the eighties. *Journal of Marriage and the Family, 47*, 985–992.

Revenson, T. A., & Felton, B. J. (1989). Disability and coping as predictors of psychological adjustment to rheumatoid arthritis. *Journal of Consulting and Clinical Psychology, 57*, 344–348.

Rock, J., Tietze, C., & McLaughlin, H. B. (1965). Effect of adoption on infertility. *Fertility and Sterility, 16*, 305–312.

Sandler, B. (1968). Emotional stress and infertility. *Journal of Psychosomatic Research, 12*, 51–59.

Schroeder, D. H., & Costa, P. T. (1984). Influence of life event stress on physical illness: Substantive effects or methodological flaws? *Journal of Personality and Social Psychology, 46*, 853–863.

Seibel, M. M., & Taymor, M. L. (1982). Emotional aspects of infertility. *Fertility and Sterility, 37*, 137–145.

Selye, H. (1956). *The stress of life.* New York: McGraw-Hill.

Snarey, J., Son, L., Kuehne, V. S., Hauser, S., & Vaillant, G. (1987). The role of parenting in men's psychosocial development: A longitudinal study of early adulthood infertility and midlife generativity. *Developmental Psychology, 23*, 593–603.

Taylor, S. E. (1983). Adjustment to threatening events: A theory of cognitive adaption. *American Psychologist, 38*, 1161–1173.

Taylor, S. E. (1990). Health psychology: The science and the field. *American Psychologist, 45*, 40–50.

Taylor, S. E., Lichtman, R. R., & Wood, J. V. (1984). Attributions, beliefs about control, and adjustment to breast cancer. *Journal of Personality and Social Psychology, 46*, 489–502.

Tyler, E. T., Bonapart, J., & Grant, J. (1960). Occurrence of pregnancy following adoption. *Fertility and Sterility, 11*, 581–589.

U.S. Congress, Office of Technology Assessment. (1988). *Infertility: Medical and social choices,* OTA-BA-358. Washington, DC: U.S. Government Printing Office.

Wills, T. A. (1987). Downward comparison as a coping mechanism. In C. R. Snyder & C. E. Ford (Eds.), *Coping with negative life events: Clinical and social psychological perspectives* (pp. 243–268). New York: Plenum.

Zuckerman, D. M. (1981). Family background, sex-role attitudes, and life goals of technical college and university students. *Sex Roles, 7*, 1109–1126.

2

Diagnosis and Medical Treatment of Infertility

VAL DAVAJAN and ROBERT ISRAEL

In recent years, those who seek medical treatment for infertility often attempt to assimilate a great deal of information regarding diagnostic and treatment procedures. In order to provide support for infertile couples undergoing such procedures and to investigate this process adequately, therapists and researchers who study psychological adjustment to infertility require a working knowledge of its causes, diagnosis, and treatment. The present chapter is intended to provide an overview of current knowledge in this area. In addition, a description of the optimal approach to the infertility evaluation is offered. An infertile couple who receives less than optimal evaluation and treatment is likely to experience even greater distress than that arising from their inability to conceive.

INCIDENCE OF INFERTILITY

As discussed in the previous chapter, it has been estimated that between 10% and 15% of married couples in the United States are infertile. Although the exact incidence of infertility among childless women of dif-

VAL DAVAJAN and ROBERT ISRAEL • Department of Obstetrics and Gynecology, University of Southern California School of Medicine, Los Angeles, California 90033. Portions of this chapter have been adapted from Davajan, V., & Israel, R. (1989). Infertility: Causes, evaluation, and treatment. In L. J. DeGroot (Ed.), *Endocrinology* (2nd ed., Vol. 3, pp. 1969–1981). Philadelphia: W. B. Saunders.

ferent ages is unknown, data from several sources indicate that fertility declines as a woman ages. Data obtained from the National Survey of Family Growth were used to calculate the percentage of currently married women who would conceive during 12 months of unprotected intercourse. These pregnancy rates declined from 86% for women aged 20 to 24 years to 52% for women aged 35 to 39 years (Hendershot, Mosher, & Pratt, 1982). Studies of fertility rates in populations of women who do not practice contraception also reveal a substantial decline in fertility after age 30, with a greater decline after age 35 (Tietze, 1957). Although viable sperm production also declines with age in males (Johnson, Petty, & Neaves, 1984), the effect of this decline on fertility remains unknown (U.S. Congress, Office of Technology Assessment [OTA], 1988).

CAUSAL FACTORS IN INFERTILITY

The etiology of infertility can be divided into four major categories: (1) The female factor, (2) the male factor, (3) combined male and female factors, and (4) infertility of undetermined cause. It is difficult to assign exact percentages to each of these categories. It is reported that approximately 40% of infertility is due to a female factor and 40% to a male factor, and in 2% to 15% no diagnosis can be made after a complete investigation (Speroff, Glass, & Kase, 1983). It also has been reported that in as many as 35% of patients, the infertility may be of multiple origins (Behrman & Kistner, 1975).

DIAGNOSIS OF INFERTILITY

The Initial Consultation

Ideally, the diagnostic evaluation of infertility should be through and should be completed as rapidly as possible. At the initial interview, diagnostic tests and the reasons they are performed should be explained to patients. Available therapies and prognoses for the various factors of infertility should be discussed. The couple should know that after a complete diagnostic evaluation, the etiology for infertility still cannot be defined in about 10% of cases. For the latter patients, the incidence of spontaneous conception is stated to be only 3% (Warner, 1962). This direct approach to the initial consultation may prevent the frustrations that arise when patients instead are subjected to a protracted and repetitive evaluation with little information to guide them.

All couples should have complete histories and physical examinations. A sexual history should be obtained with special emphasis on the frequency and timing of intercourse and on the use of lubricants during intercourse. Not infrequently, an infertile couple will be found to be abstaining from intercourse and having only one "timed" intercourse in the middle of the cycle. For men with normal sperm counts, there is no evidence that "storing up" sperm increases the chances of conception. In fact, decreasing the number of exposures per week seems to be related to infertility.

Each couple should be instructed as to the optimum time for conception and should be encouraged to have frequent intercourse. With the introduction of the urinary luteinizing hormone (LH) detection kits for home use, it is now possible accurately to time intercourse based on the LH surge rather than relying on a basal body temperature (BBT) alone. Unless the husband has oligospermia, no abstinence should be recommended. In addition, some of the chemical lubricants used to improve coital satisfaction may interfere with sperm transport and thus should not be used. Certainly, "prescribed" intercourse may decrease sexual pleasure and result in sexual difficulties for some couples. In such cases, the couple should be informed of the optimum time for conception, but without strict instructions regarding the specific days or time for intercourse. The couple also can be told that among fertile couples, there is only a 20% chance of conceiving in each ovulatory cycle.

The Diagnostic Workup

The initial infertility evaluation typically can be performed within two to three months. If an abnormality is found in one of the first (noninvasive) steps, it should be treated before proceeding with the more costly and invasive procedures. For example, if the woman does not ovulate each month, and if the semen analysis is normal, ovulation should be induced before performing the other diagnostic measures.

Examination of Semen. About 30% to 40% of infertility is associated with such problems in the male reproductive system as oligospermia (scarcity of sperm in the semen), azoospermia (absence of sperm in the semen), high viscosity of semen, low sperm motility, and low volume of semen. Thus, the examination of semen is an integral part of the clinical investigation of infertility. In fact, because obtaining a specimen and performing a routine semen analysis is relatively easy, it should be the first step in the investigation of the infertile couple. The collection of the semen specimen is best done at home and, ideally, should be obtained by masturbation into a clean, wide-mouthed jar. Because most of the spermatozoa are found in the first milliliter of the ejaculate, the man should be instructed to take precautions not to spill any portion of the specimen. Examination of the semen should be performed within the first hour after collection. A normal semen analysis can be defined as one that has a volume of two to five milliliters, a count of at least 20 million sperm per ml, a motility of at least 50%, and 50% normal morphology (size and shape). More recently, the hamster egg human sperm penetration, test has become available in the evaluation of the male. This test assesses sperm penetration, but its exact role in the investigation of and prognosis for the infertile man is unclear.

If the semen analysis is significantly abnormal, an endocrine evaluation is conducted to examine hormone production. If the male has azoospermia and normal follicle-stimulating hormone, as assessed by a serum assay, a testicular biopsy can be conducted to determine whether the problem lies in the sperm-conducting system or in lack of sperm production by the testes. Performed under local or general anesthesia, a small sample of testicular tissue is obtained through an incision in the scrotum. This tissue is examined microscopically to identify any sperm cells at different stages of development.

Documentation of Ovulation. In some 10% to 15% of women, the infertility is due to failure of ovulation. An infertile women who has regular monthly menstrual cycles is probably ovulating. Nevertheless, ovulation should be documented in the workup by the following methods: (1) Basal body temperature (BBT); and (2) detection of urinary LH surge with a home monoclonal antibody test. Information from both can be used to instruct the couple about the optimal time for intercourse. The BBT is less costly than the LH detection methods but is less accurate. The patient records her BBT upon taking her temperature each morning prior to getting out of bed. Under the influence of circulating progesterone, the BBT shifts to a higher temperature in the luteal phase of the menstrual cycle. An average increase of at least 0.4 over the preovulatory phase temperature is considered normal. Ovulation most often takes place 24 to 72 hours after the nadir. In anovulatory cycles, there is no recognizable shift in temperature.

Obtained in the late luteal phase, the endometrial biopsy, in which a sample of cells is obtained from the lining of the uterus, and the mid-luteal serum progesterone test, in which a progesterone level is assessed from a blood sample, are tests that document ovulation. Transvaginal ultrasound performed at midcycle also can be used to determine follicular growth and corpus luteum development. If the patient is not ovulating, but has normal serum levels of estrogen and prolactin, ovulation-inducing drugs can be administered.

Postcoital Test. The exact incidence of infertility caused by abnormal mid-cycle cervical mucus-spermatozoa interaction is unknown but has been reported to be 10% to 30% (Davajan & Kunitake, 1969). The existence of this factor is based on the finding that in certain infertile couples, the microscopic examination of mid-cycle cervical mucus after the couple has had intercourse reveals poor mucus or good mucus with very few or no sperm, or in some cases only immobilized sperm. If the postcoital test is abnormal, the infertility is said to be caused by a "cervical factor," although the problem may lie with either the male or the female.

In the evaluation of infertility, the postcoital test (PCT) is the only routinely performed *in vivo* test that brings together both partners in a testing system. As ovulation approaches, the couple is asked to abstain from intercourse for two days prior to the planned test. The examination should be scheduled two days prior to the expected rise in the BBT or on the LH surge day. The couple is instructed to have intercourse within three hours of arriving at the physician's office. A catheter is then used to obtain samples of mucus from the cervical canal, and these are examined for mucus quality and motile sperm.

Investigation of the Female Upper Genital Tract. Along with the male factor, pelvic abnormalities (tubal occlusions, adhesions, and endometriosis) account for the majority of infertility. In most clinics, 30% to 40% of infertility can be attributed to a pelvic factor. The diagnostic techniques for evaluating tubal function, and the pelvis in general, have become more sophisticated. However, they still indicate only tubal patency (no obstruction), obstruction, or distortion, and fail to indicate the degree of physiologic impairment that exists. The capability for reproductive function remains unmeasured. To avoid X-ray exposure of a fertilized ovum, all tests for tubal abnormalities should be performed in the follicular phase of the menstrual cycle.

Hysterosalpingography involves instilling radio-opaque dye through the uterus into the fallopian tubes under X-ray fluoroscopy visualization. When the dye moves into the fallopian tubes, occlusions or other abnormalities can be seen. If the fallopian tube is open, the dye fills the tube and spills from the end of the tube into the abdominal cavity. The procedure typically takes no more than 15 or 20 minutes and can produce cramps, although typically the pain is no greater than that from a moderate menstrual cramp.

If the hysterosalpingogram is abnormal, laparoscopy should follow in the next menstrual cycle. Laparoscopy, an integral part of the infertility investigation, allows direct visualization of the female reproductive anatomy to detect endometriosis (presence of endometrial tissue outside the uterus), pelvic adhesions, and other structural abnormalities. While the woman is under general anesthesia, the laparoscope, a long, narrow telescopic instrument, is inserted through the navel to view the surface of the ovaries, uterus, and fallopian tubes. A small incision is made above the pubic bone to allow manipulation of the internal structures by a palpating probe. Discrepancies in results have been reported between hysterosalpingography and laparoscopy up to 25% of the time (Israel & March, 1976). Therefore, the hysterosalpingogram cannot be accepted as the final picture. However, if it is entirely normal, other diagnostic procedures can be carried out or appropriate medical therapy pursued, e.g., induction of ovulation, before laparoscopy is carried out.

The decision to proceed with conservative infertility surgery is made at the time of laparoscopy. Therefore, prior to laparoscopy, all possible findings and surgical risks are explained to the couple. Thus, if pelvic pathology is found, the patient is prepared to undergo corrective surgery immediately, utilizing the same anesthetic either by laparotomy or, in skilled hands, by operative laparoscopy.

Evaluation for Other Factors. In approximately 2% to 15% of couples, no abnormalities can be found after establishing the fact that ovulation is occurring, obtaining a semen analysis, performing a postcoital test, and investigating the upper female genital tract with a hysterosalpingogram and laparoscopy. Because a large percentage of couples do fall in this category of "unexplained" infertility, several additional investigations may be performed. Tests may be conducted to investigate whether infertility is secondary to immunologic incompatability between partners, genital ureaplasm infection, primary hypothyroidism, or inadequate luteal phase, as determined by inadequate progesterone production and "lag" in the histological maturation of the endometrium. The previously noted sperm penetration assay is usually performed in this phase of the workup. Other tests for male infertility include vasography and vesiculography, in which radio-opaque dye is used to perform X-ray examination of the sperm transport ducts.

TREATMENT OF INFERTILITY

Treatment follows from identification during the diagnostic process of specific impediments to fertility. Several of the more frequent treatments are described in this section.

Induction of Ovulation

Ovulation disorders include conditions such as amenorrhea (absence of menstruation) or oligomenorrhea (infrequent menstruation). However, ovulatory dysfunction can occur even when the menstrual cycle appears normal. Of course, treatment selection depends on identification of the specific origin of the dysfunction. Drug treatment is the most common, with clomiphene citrate (Clomid, Serophene) being the most frequently prescribed, and Pergonal (human gonadotropin) prescribed when Clomid fails to induce ovulation, or in more severe cases. Patients being treated with ovulation-inducing drugs should be informed fully of the incidence of multiple pregnancies, development of ovarian cysts, and fetal anomalies. Rates of potential consequences as well as success rates are given in Table 1.

Patients receiving Clomid should have a pelvic exam at monthly intervals before taking the next dose. The couple should try to achieve a pregnancy for at least three ovulatory cycles before instituting any further diagnostic procedures. Eighty percent of the patients treated with clomiphene who get pregnant do so within three cycles of therapy. If no conception occurs after three ovulatory cycles, the postcoital test and hysterosalpingogram should be performed. If these tests are normal, the patient should be allowed at least six ovulatory cycles before undergoing a laparoscopy. If the patient successfully ovulates with clomiphene and if no other factors for infertility can be found, the patient should be continued on this drug for as long as she desires. One patient in our clinic was treated for 29 ovulatory cycles before conception occurred.

Table 1. Side Effects of Clomid and Pergonal Therapy: Summary of Results from the Los Angeles County-University of Southern California Endocrine-Infertility Clinic

Side effects	Clomid (%)	Pergonal (%)
Multiple pregnancies	5	8–22
Ovarian cysts	5–10	6–15
Fetal anomalies	2–3	2–3
Ovulation	60–92	85–100
Term pregnancies	70–80	65–70
Spontaneous abortions	20–25	30–35

Treatment of Male Infertility

In general, treatments for male infertility are fewer than for female infertility and their efficacy less well documented. Several different hormonal and other therapies have been used to treat male infertility. Numerous agents, such as human gonadotropin, clomiphene citrate, testolactone, testosterone, corticosteroids, vitamins C and E, and anti-prostaglandins, have been prescribed. The efficacy of these treatments is not clear (OTA, 1988). Antibiotics have been used successfully to treat male reproductive tract infections which may impair fertility.

Surgical treatments for male infertility also have been developed. One of the most common is for repair of a varicocele, a dilated varicose vein in the testes. Between 10% and 20% of all men and between 20% to 40% of infertile men have a varicocele. Varicoceles may impair fertility by increasing scrotal blood flow which produces a concomitant increase in temperature, interfering with sperm production (Rothman, Newmark, & Karson, 1981). Rates of success for surgical repair of the varicocele in improving fertility have been variable (Dubin & Amelar, 1976; Silber, 1980). Microsurgery to correct blockage of sperm transport through the ducts of the male reproductive tract also may be performed to improve fertility (Silber, 1984). More recently, most male factor infertility problems are being managed by intrauterine insemination (IUI).

Treatment of Cervical Factor Infertility

An abnormal postcoital test points to the possibility of several factors, including anatomic defects of the cervix, abnormal cervical mucus, faulty coital technique, difficulties in sperm production, and immunologic factors. Depending on the differential diagnosis, interventions may include surgery, drug treatment, and review of coital technique. IUI also is performed, using motile sperm separated from immobilized and defective sperm, white blood cells, and seminal plasma debris (Percoll technique) or sperm "washed" with Ham's F-10 solution (an electrolyte and amino acid solution) or human tubal fluid-like solution. At our medical center, IUI led to a 45% conception rate among infertile women for whom the diagnosis of abnormal cervical mucus production was the cause of the abnormal postcoital test.

Treatment of Pelvic Factor Infertility

Surgical Correction of Tubal Abnormalities. Surgical correction is considered when investigation of the upper female genital tract indicates an abnormality. When it is found that adhesions are isolating the tubes and ovaries impeding ovum pickup by the fallopian tubes, surgical lysis (salpingolysis) of these peritubal and/or pelvic adhesions may be performed. Success of the surgery depends on the extent and type of adhesions, and whether they re-form postoperatively. The pregnancy rate resulting from this surgery has been reported to range from 40% to 70%, with 70% to 90% of the pregnancies going to term.

Salpingostomy, the opening of distal tubal occlusions (blockage at the distal point of the tube), is the least successful type of tubal surgery. Although the surgeon may be able to open the tube and have it remain open, anatomic and physiologic damage to the remainder of the tube only rarely supports the numerous normal reproductive processes necessary to achieve a successful pregnancy. Overall, pregnancy rates following salpingostomy have been reported to range from 10% to 40%.

The most successful primary tubal surgery is correction of mid-tubal occlusion resulting from previous tubal sterilization. Following end-to-end tubal reanastomosis, the pregnancy rate ranges from 60% to 80%.

Treatment of Endometriosis. Although several theories have been advanced regarding the causes of endometriosis (presence of endometrial tissue outside the uterus), the specific etiology of this disorder remains undetermined. Because ovarian steroids must be present for endometriosis to develop, its occurrence generally is confined to the reproductive years, with the peak incidence in the fourth decade of life. It has been found that 30% to 40% of patients with endometriosis have concomitant infertility (Buttram, 1988), although in many instances the endometriosis does not appear to be interfering with the normal reproductive processes. Sperm ascension, ovulation, and ovum transport can all take place, but the presence of even minimal pelvic endometriosis may cause infertility.

The symptomatology associated with endometriosis is quite variable. Over 50% of patients report dysmenorrhea (painful menstruation). Dyspareunia (painful intercourse) and dyschezia (painful bowel movements) also may be reported. However, even with extensive endometriosis, pain may not be significant. On the other hand, incapacitating pain may be associated with minimal amounts of active endometriosis. Thus, the degree of endometriotic involvement and spread bears no constant relationship to the presence or absence of subjective discomfort. Abnormal uterine bleeding (e.g., premenstrual spotting) may occur. Anovulation is not uncommon. Although diagnosis may be suggested by symptoms or pelvic examination, only laparoscopy can yield a definitive diagnosis of endometriosis.

Although controversy continues regarding the etiology, symptomatology, and detection of endometriosis, more uniformity in thinking exists regarding therapy for endometriosis in the infertile woman. Hormonal suppression and/or conservative surgery are the available therapeutic modalities. However, hormonal suppression eliminates ovulation, so surgical therapy is the predominant choice in infertility associated with endometriosis. At the time of laparoscopic diagnosis, surgical therapy can be carried out via fulguration or laser in cases of mild or moderate disease. When moderate endometriosis is associated with significant adhesions or severe pathology is present, laparotomy, with a short course (two to three months) of preoperative or postoperative hormone suppression will be necessary. Pregnancy rates after reconstructive surgery should be in the area of 50% for moderate endometriosis and 25% to 30% at best for severe endometriosis. After conservative surgery, endometriosis recurs in 5% to 25% of patients. Today, the drug therapy utilized would be a gonadotropin-releasing hormone agonist (Lupron, Synarel) that results in a menopausal-like condition during treatment by "down-regulating" pituitary gonadotropins.

Other Treatments

Several other treatments have been used for specific diagnoses, including clomiphene and/or progesterone treatment for inadequate luteal phase, antibiotic treatment for seminal fluid and cervical infections, and condom or glucocorticoid therapy for immunological disorders. Treatments which involve transfer of sperm, oocytes, or embryos also have been developed.

Assisted reproductive technologies (IVF, in vitro fertilization; GIFT, gamete intrafallopian transfer; ZIFT, zygote intrafallopian transfer) may be attempted when there is irreparable tubal damage or after unsuccessful tubal repair (IVF), after unsuccessfully treated and/or severe endometriosis (IVF), oligospermia (ZIFT), or unexplained infertility (GIFT, ZIFT). These procedures involve recovering mature oocytes via laparoscopy or ultrasound-guided transvaginal needle aspiration and exposing them to sperm for direct transfer into the tube (GIFT) or laboratory fertilization with subsequent transfer into the tube (ZIFT) or uterus (IVF). The Medical Research International and the Society for Assisted Reproductive Technology of The American Fertility Society reported on IVF/GIFT/ZIFT success rates in the United States from 163 clinics in 1989. The overall live delivery rates were 14% for IVF (in 15,392 oocyte retrievals), 23% for GIFT (in 3,652 retrievals), and 17% for ZIFT (908 retrievals).

In addition to learning about available treatments, couples may want to explore other alternatives, including such possibilities as adoption, surrogate motherhood, and choosing not to become parents. Obviously, given the range of possible diagnoses, treatments, and alternatives, the processes of making decisions and pursuing goals may hold many challenges.

RATES OF SUCCESS AND SPONTANEOUS CONCEPTION

Couples should be informed of the prognosis for their particular cause of infertility. Among 493 couples who were followed for one to two years, the chances of becoming pregnant were greater in women younger than 30 (52%) than in women older than 30 (37%) (Kliger, 1982). In addition, the success rate was higher in couples who had tried to conceive for less than three years prior to evaluation (63%) than in those who had tried for more than three years (34%). Of the patients who conceived, 90% of the pregnancies occurred within one year of the initial visit and 96% before the second year. Thus, if a patient does not conceive within two years of the initial infertility evaluation, the chances of becoming pregnant are poor.

As reported in 1983, 1,145 infertile couples were followed for two to seven years (Collins, Wrixon, Janes, & Wilson, 1983). For the 597 couples treated for infertility, 246 (41%) pregnancies occurred, whereas 35% pregnancies occurred in a group of 548 untreated couples. However, 31% of the 246 pregnancies in the treated group occurred at least three months after the last medical treatment or more than twelve months after adnexal surgery. If these pregnancies are combined with those that occurred without treatment, 61% of all the pregnancies occurred independently of treatment. Overall, 266 (23%) of the 1,145 infertile couples had a treatment-independent pregnancy. Thus, the chance that a spontaneous pregnancy will occur in an infertile couple is relatively high, and studies using untreated control groups, where ethically acceptable, must be done to evaluate the effectiveness of all treatment modalities, especially those used to treat cervical factors, endometriosis, partial tubal disease, and moderate sperm defects. The Collins *et al.* (1983) study reported that more than 50% of the pregnancies in couples with those diagnoses occurred without treatment. In contrast, couples with anovulation and total tubal occlusion had higher fertility rates in the treated group. Nevertheless, until such controlled studies are performed, we recommend treatment for all couples with infertility.

REFERENCES

Behrman, S. J., & Kistner, R. W. (1975). *Progress in infertility.* Boston: Little, Brown.

Buttram, V. C., Jr. (1988). Endometriosis. In S. J. Behrman, R. W. Kistner, & G. W. Patton, Jr. (Eds.), *Progress in infertility* (3rd ed., pp. 273–332). Boston: Little, Brown.

Collins, J. A., Wrixon, W., Janes, L. B., & Wilson, E. H. (1983). Treatment-independent pregnancy among infertile couples. *New England Journal of Medicine*, 309, 1201–1206.

Davajan, V., & Kunitake, G. M. (1969). Fractional in-vivo and in-vitro examination of post-coital cervical mucus in the human. *Fertility and Sterility*, 20, 197–210.

Dubin, L., & Amelar, R. D. (1976). Varicocelectomy as therapy in male infertility: A study of 504 cases. *Fertility and Sterility*, 26, 217–220.

Hendershot, G. E., Mosher, W. D., & Pratt, W. F. (1982). Infertility and age: An unresolved issue. *Family Planning Perspectives*, 14, 287–289.

Israel, R., & March, C. M. (1976). Diagnostic laparoscopy: A prognostic aid in the surgical management of infertility. *American Journal of Obstetrics and Gynecology*, 125, 969–975.

Johnson, L., Petty, C. S., & Neaves, W. B. (1984). Influence of age on sperm production and testicular weights in men. *Journal of Reproductive Fertility*, 70, 211–218.

Kliger, B. E. (1982). Evaluation, therapy, and outcome in 493 infertile couples. *Fertility and Sterility*, 41, 40–46.

Medical Research International and the Society of Assisted Reproductive Technology, The American Fertility Society. (1991). In vitro fertilization/embryo transfer (IVF-ET) in the United States: 1989 results from the IVF/ET Registry. *Fertility and Sterility*, 55, 14–23.

Rothman, C. M., Newmark, H., & Karson, R. A. (1981). The recurrent varicocele: A poorly recognized problem. *Fertility and Sterility*, 35, 552–556.

Silber, S. J. (1980). *How to get pregnant*. New York: Warner Books.

Silber, S. J. (1984). Microsurgery for vasectomy reversal and vasoepididymostomy. *Urology*, 23, 505–524.

Speroff, L., Glass, R. H., & Kase, N. G. (1983). *Clinical gynecologic endocrinology and infertility*. Baltimore: Williams & Wilkins.

Tietze, C. (1957). Reproductive span and rate of reproduction among Hutterite women. *Fertility and Sterility*, 8, 89–97.

U.S. Congress, Office of Technology Assessment. (May, 1988). *Infertility: Medical and social choices*, OTA-BA-358. Washington, DC: U.S. Government Printing Office.

Warner, M. P. (1962). Results of 25 year study of 1553 infertility couples. *New York State Journal of Medicine*, 62, 2663–2673.

3

Psychological Reactions to Infertility

CHRISTINE DUNKEL-SCHETTER and MARCI LOBEL

PSYCHOLOGICAL REACTIONS TO INFERTILITY

Like many other life stresses, infertility is not a discrete event but an unfolding process. The beginning of the process is frequently marked by the passing of a year attempting to conceive without success, and by entry into medical treatment, although many couples begin to worry and seek treatment sooner. For some, a medical condition necessitates treatment such as the surgical removal of reproductive organs that suddenly impairs fertility. Thus, many events may signify the beginning of the infertility process, a process that often continues over a long period of time as individuals contend with the prospect of being unable to conceive. Indeed, in most cases, it is the possibility rather than the reality of infertility that is at issue, because there is some degree of ambiguity about the outcome. This situation initially involves a threat rather than a loss (Lazarus, 1966; Lazarus & Launier, 1978; Lazarus & Folkman, 1984). As time passes without conception, the situation is gradually transformed into one of loss.

What are the reactions of women and men who suspect or learn that they are unable to have children biologically? How do individual reactions vary? Do they change over time? Are there gender differences? Our goal in this chapter is to summarize what is known about these issues by pro-

CHRISTINE DUNKEL-SCHETTER • Department of Psychology, University of California, Los Angeles, California 90024-1563. MARCI LOBEL • Department of Psychology, State University of New York, Stony Brook, New York 11794.

viding an overview of the available research on psychological reactions to infertility. We draw from both the published descriptive work and the empirical research in doing so. Although there are methodological limitations of the research, a clear picture on the psychological response to infertility is beginning to emerge.

METHOD OF OUR REVIEW

Our literature search on this topic uncovered 6 review articles, more than 30 descriptive or anecdotal articles, and 25 empirical research articles. We distinguished a source as empirical versus descriptive on the basis of whether any data were collected and whether quantitative results were presented. The descriptive literature provides a rich source of information about clinically observed reactions to infertility. The empirical research literature provides a scientific basis for evaluating these observations and themes. In the sections below, we consider each literature to assess the prevalence of specific psychological reactions to infertility. Review articles are also cited where they mention the themes discussed (e.g., Cook, 1987; Edelmann & Connolly, 1986; Pantesco, 1986).

OBSERVED EFFECTS OF INFERTILITY

The effects of infertility mentioned most frequently in the descriptive literature are emotional reactions, feelings of loss of control, effects on self-esteem, identity, and beliefs, and effects on social relationships.[1] These can be further differentiated and elaborated as illustrated in Table 1. For example, social effects include effects on social network interactions, on marital satisfaction, and on sexual functioning. The available descriptive articles were reviewed to determine the proportion that report each of the categories of reactions to infertility listed in Table 1.

Emotional Effects

Five emotional responses are recurrent themes: (1) Grief and depression, (2) anger, (3) guilt, (4) shock or denial, and (5) anxiety. The order in

---

[1]A small number of descriptive articles refer to what might be labeled cognitive effects of infertility, including ruminations and obsessive thought, inability to concentrate, and feelings of confusion and disorganization. Inasmuch as these were mentioned rarely and seemed to be confounded with other constructs such as emotions and coping, we did not treat them separately in this review.

Table 1. Observed Psychological Effects of Infertility

A. *Emotional effects*
   1. Grieving/depression
   2. Anger/frustration
   3. Guilt
   4. Shock/denial
   5. Anxiety

B. *Loss of control*
   1. Loss of control over activities, body, emotions
   2. Inability to predict and plan future according to life goals

C. *Effects on self-esteem, identity, beliefs*
   1. Loss of self-esteem, feelings of inadequacy
   2. Identity problems or shifts
   3. Changes in worldviews

D. *Social effects*
   1. Effects on marital interactions and satisfaction (positive and negative)
   2. Effects on sexual functioning
   3. Difficult social network interactions, changes in relationships with network members, loneliness, embarrassment

which these emotional responses are listed in Table 1 corresponds to the frequency with which they appear in the anecdotal literature. Grief and depression are the most frequently cited emotional responses, reported in 77% of the articles, whereas anxiety, reported in 40% of the articles, is mentioned least often.

Authors use a variety of terms to describe the grief and depression experienced by infertile individuals. They describe mourning, sadness, disappointment, loss, disillusionment, and hopelessness. Consider the following description by an infertile women:

> A lot of people don't understand that infertility is very much like having a child die. You grieve for the baby who wasn't conceived this month, and for all the babies you'll never have. (Lasker & Borg, 1987, p. 20)

Several authors, including Menning (1980) and Mahlstedt (1985), comment that depression and grief are the most common reactions they observe in individuals after a diagnosis of infertility. Mahlstedt (1985) suggests that depression is caused both by the loss that infertile individuals feel as well as the chronic strains that are experienced during infertility diagnosis and treatment.

In addition to grief, the majority of studies mention anger and guilt, suggesting that these may also be common emotional responses to infertility (Cook, 1987). The intensity of anger or frustration, cited in 73% of the anecdotal articles, ranges from reports of unfairness or resentment (e.g., Mahlstedt, 1985; Sawatzky, 1981) to more intense embitterment or rage (e.g., Kraft, Palombo, Mitchell, Dean, Meyers, & Schmidt, 1980). Infertile individuals may direct anger toward their spouses, themselves, other family members or their friends, couples with children, their doctors, or toward society (e.g., Daniels, Gunby, Legge, Williams, & Wynn-Williams, 1984; Mazor, 1978, 1984; Spencer, 1987). One woman said:

> I find myself *hating* the pregnant women I see at school, in the grocery store, and even in church. I have never had such intense negative feelings toward others, and I despise myself for having them. (Mahlstedt, 1985, p. 339)

Feelings of guilt, self-blame, or personal responsibility are mentioned in 68% of the articles (e.g., Daniels *et al.*, 1984; Domar & Seibel, 1990; Fleming & Burry, 1988; McCormick, 1980; Rosenfeld & Mitchell, 1979; West, 1983). According to these authors, some individuals feel guilty because of prior sexual practices, contraceptive methods, or life-styles that they believe helped produce their infertility, or because they delayed trying to have children. Others feel guilt that has no specific source, or feel guilt over a previous transgression for which infertility is seen as the punishment. Kraft *et al.* (1980), for example, describe a woman who "felt that if she had just been a better person this would not have happened" (p. 622).

Although shock and denial are mentioned less frequently, 45% of the descriptive studies cite these as emotional responses to infertility (e.g., Kraft *et al.*, 1980; Mazor, 1978; Spencer, 1987; Wilson, 1979). As illustration, one woman described her state of mind while waiting for her appointment with an infertility specialist:

> I sat in the corner away from the other patients, who were probably infertile. In my mind, I was *not* one of them. (Mahlstedt, 1985, p. 338)

Denial such as this, and shock or surprise, tend to be cited as initial responses to the diagnosis of infertility. Thus, shock and denial are probably underreported in the literature because individuals may no longer be experiencing them by the time they are in treatment or counseling.

Anxiety, worry, anguish, or desperation are reported in 40% of the anecdotal articles (e.g., Sawatzky, 1981; Spencer, 1987; Valentine, 1986; Walker, 1978). As West (1983) describes:

> Infertile people do feel anxious. Watching others crack the jackpot, often unintentionally, while their libidos revolve unsuccessfully around the bedroom thermometer, is apt to cause concern that something is amiss. (p. 40)

Infertile men and women may be anxious about the treatments they are undergoing, and particularly about whether or not they will be successful in becoming parents. Several authors observe that infertile people are also anxious about their body image, their sexual adequacy, or about the status of their marital relationship (e.g., Kraft *et al.*, 1980; Mazor, 1978; Woollett, 1985). Some report monthly cycles of anxiety or anticipation surrounding ovulation, followed by disappointment and depression when pregnancy is not achieved (e.g., Honea-Fleming, 1986; Kraft *et al.*, 1980; Mahlstedt, 1985; Valentine, 1986). These changes have been referred to by some (e.g., Honea-Fleming, 1986) as the "roller coaster" of hope and despair.

Several of the descriptive accounts and reviews on infertility mention a sequence or stages of emotional reactions that are observed among infertile individuals over time (e.g., Clapp, 1985; Griffin, 1983; Menning, 1980; Matthews & Matthews, 1986a; Williams & Power, 1977). The stages are typically surprise/shock, denial, anger, isolation, guilt, grief/depression, and acceptance or resolution. Because these stages of emotional response are often an assumption underlying the descriptive research, they are important to note.

Loss of Control

> We can't conceive; my wife is depressed; I'm sick with disappointment; and I can't do a thing about any of it. Nothing I have said or done has made a difference. (Mahlstedt, 1985, p. 343)

There are two responses to infertility which involve loss of control. One concerns control over events that are current, including a loss of control over one's daily activities, bodily functions, and emotions. The second concerns control of the future, specifically the ability to predict or plan the future, and to meet life goals. Although some articles mention a loss of both types of control, the two types appear to be distinguishable.

Fifty-four percent of the authors observe that infertility is accompanied by a real or perceived loss of control over the present (e.g., Daniels *et al.*, 1984; Griffin, 1983; Mahlstedt, 1985; McCormick, 1980; Valentine, 1986; Williams & Power, 1977). For example, because of the chronic stress associated with infertility, some individuals feel that they are unable to control their emotions and some complain of mood lability (McCormick, 1980; Mazor, 1978; Spencer, 1987). Infertility treatment may dictate the scheduling of work-related or social activities and thereby individuals may feel they have surrendered control over these domains as well (Mahlstedt, 1985; Spencer, 1987). Couples in treatment may also feel that they lose control over their sexual relationship and privacy because they must report many details to their physician and because treatment typically involves "assignments," such as when and how often to have intercourse (e.g., Daniels *et al.*, 1984; Kraft *et al.*, 1980; Mahlstedt, 1985, Matthews & Matthews, 1986b). One woman said:

> I bring my charts to the doctor like a child bringing home a report card. Tell me, did I do well? Did I ovulate? Did I have sex at all the right times as you instructed me? (Menning, 1980, p. 315)

In addition to losing control over these aspects of the present, 40% of the anecdotal articles report that infertile people experience a profound sense that they have lost control over their future (e.g., Griffin, 1983; Honea-Fleming, 1986; Kraft *et al.*, 1980; Mazor, 1978; Mazor, 1984; Sandelowski, 1987; Spencer, 1987; Woollett, 1985). Infertility eliminates the ability to initiate pregnancy and parenthood, which are often central to one's life goals (see Clark, Henry, & Taylor, this volume). Infertility treatment alone may disrupt career progress, by delaying relocations or promotions, for example. Because primary life decisions about marriage and career are often tied to having a child, the loss of control experienced due to infertility may be particularly distressing. Infertility for some couples brings about a radical change in their perspective of the future and in their perception that life goals are under individual control.

> It is the end of the Bowes family and the Bowes family name. It dies with us because of me. My husband is the last of the male children in his family . . . it is the death of a dream . . . (Menning, 1980, p. 317)

Effects on Self-Esteem, Identity, and Beliefs

Nearly 60% of the anecdotal articles suggest that the diagnosis of infertility threatens self-esteem or engenders feelings of failure and inadequacy (e.g., Fleming & Burry, 1988; Mahlstedt, 1985; Matthews & Matthews, 1986b; Rosenfeld & Mitchell, 1979; Spencer, 1987; Williams & Power, 1977; Wilson, 1979; Woollett, 1985). Many of these articles add that feelings of low self-worth are not limited to reproductive function, but they extend to "sexual function and desirability, physical attractiveness, performance, and productivity in other spheres as well" (Mazor, 1984, p. 27). One woman explained:

> [W]hen I discovered I was infertile, I felt damaged. Why couldn't I accomplish something as "natural" as conceiving a baby? Suddenly my sense of self-worth was shaken. I felt defective and very much a failure. Infertility was more than a medical problem. It was an attack on my self-esteem. (Mahlstedt, 1985, p. 338)

In addition to reduction in self-esteem, extended infertility produces identity changes or changes in the self-concept. Nearly 70% of the descriptive articles include reports of individuals questioning their gender identity (e.g., Daniels *et al.*, 1984; Honea-Fleming, 1986; Kraft *et al.*, 1980; Mazor, 1984), their role performance and role expectations (e.g., Valentine, 1986), or their specific identity as spouses or parents (e.g., Mahlstedt, 1985; Rosenfeld & Mitchell, 1979). Some infertile people also mention difficulty incorporating infertility into their self-view (e.g., Sandelowski, 1987), and some articles report negative body images held by individuals who are infertile. These persons say their body is defective, unfamiliar, or ugly (e.g., Mazor, 1978; Spencer, 1987; Williams & Power, 1977), as the following quotations demonstrate:

> I feel empty. It's like within me, where a uterus ought to be, there is a "black hole" of space. I feel mutilated. (Mazor, 1978, p. 148)

> It is more than I can bear to think of myself as barren. It's like having leprosy. I feel "unclean" and defective. (Mazor, 1978, p. 148)

By comparison to the number reporting effects on self-esteem and identity, fewer articles (32%) mention changes in worldviews following infertility (e.g., Honea-Fleming, 1986; Matthews & Matthews, 1986b; Sandelowski, 1987; Woollett, 1985). For example, Matthews and Matthews (1986b) as well as Clark, Henry, and Taylor, this volume, describe a major "reconstruction of reality" that takes place following infertility. This reconstruction can involve the meaning of marriage, parenthood, and existence itself. Some articles report that by examining their motives for pregnancy and parenthood, infertile individuals are led to question societal views of children, particularly the presumed idealization of parenting. According to one article (Woollett, 1985), some persons search for the reasons that infertility exists in our world at all.

Social and Relationship Effects

There are several ways in which infertility is reported anecdotally to have social and relationship effects. Effects on marital interaction and satisfaction are reported in 50% of the descriptive articles, effects on sexual functioning appear in 65% of the articles, and effects on social network interactions or feelings toward network members arise in more than 80% of the articles. Effects on marital interaction and satisfaction appear to be of four varieties. First, some people report increased anger, hostility, or resentment toward their spouse which may result from blaming a partner or feeling blamed, from feeling a lack of spousal understanding or emotional support, or feeling that one's spouse is not equally committed to having children (Mahlstedt, 1985; Mazor, 1978; Spencer, 1987; Wilson, 1979; Woollett, 1985). One woman explained:

> When we start to talk to each other we end up yelling. We resolved that by talking only
> very briefly . . . I know he feels terribly guilty because it is his infertility problem.
> (Lasker & Borg, 1987, p. 141)

Second, some spouses are anxious about the status of their relationship
and they occasionally report fears of abandonment or breakup (Mahlstedt,
1985; Mazor, 1978; Mazor, 1984; Williams & Power, 1977). Third, some
articles report that individuals feel unable to disclose their feelings to a
spouse, increasing a sense of isolation from their partner (e.g., Mahlstedt,
1985; West, 1983).

The fourth type of effect on marriages is positive as opposed to negative. Several articles describe individuals who feel increased closeness,
love, and support from their partners (Fleming & Burry, 1988; Honea-
Fleming, 1986; Mazor, 1984; Menning, 1980; Woollett, 1985). For some
couples, the crisis of infertility has brought them closer together and led to
mutual support during a period of strain or an opportunity to reflect on
the attachment to their partner.

> It's very difficult for me to imagine that anything else could happen that would
> require more of us than what we've been through over these last five years. We found
> out just how much we need each other. We are a team. Our marriage is strong . . .
> (Lasker & Borg, 1987, p. 138)

In contrast to there being both positive and negative effects of infertility on marital relationships, virtually all of the anecdotal articles which
discuss infertility's sexual ramifications describe these as negative (e.g.,
Elstein, 1975; Kaufman, 1969). Many individuals report a loss of sexual
desire, pleasure, or spontaneity (e.g., Kraft et al., 1980; Rosenfeld & Mitchell, 1979; Valentine, 1986; Williams & Power, 1977; Woollett, 1985).
Some report sexual dysfunction (e.g., Spencer, 1987; Walker, 1978; West,
1983). Individuals sometimes attribute these effects to their fears of sexual
inadequacy and to the fact that infertility treatment results in a loss of
privacy, control, and the reduction of intercourse to a clinical act of reproduction. Consider the following description:

> My wife was scheduled to have a postcoital test late one afternoon. Because of our
> work schedules and a 30-mile distance between our home and the doctor's office, we
> met at a motel close to the doctor's office to have sexual intercourse. At first, I could
> not maintain an erection, and when I finally achieved that, I could not ejaculate. We
> tried everything we knew, and after no success, we dressed, checked out, and went
> home . . . where we tried unsuccessfully again. This whole charade was so humiliating
> and painful for me that I could not imagine attempting such a thing again. (Mahlstedt,
> 1985, p. 337)

Most of the anecdotal articles report difficulties in social interactions
and relationships within the social network (82%). One type of difficulty

involves feeling socially unworthy or isolated (e.g., Cook, 1987; Daniels *et al.*, 1984; Domar & Seibel, 1990; Fleming & Burry, 1988; Mahlstedt, 1985; Mazor, 1978; West, 1983; Woollett, 1985). Said one woman:

> I do believe it lessens you in some people's eyes, makes you different and possibly even morally suspect like God is punishing you or something. Somehow infertility lessens your accomplishments for some people. (Miall, 1985, p. 395)

According to the descriptive literature, some men and women who are infertile report feeling unaccepted or scorned by others and feeling pressured by the expectations of their family, friends, or society in general. Many do not feel understood by their friends or family and therefore express an inability to disclose their feelings to others. Some withdraw from these relationships completely.

A second difficulty in social interactions involves feelings of jealousy, rivalry, resentment, and envy of people with children (e.g., Honea-Fleming, 1986; Mazor, 1984; Rosenfeld & Mitchell, 1979; Spencer, 1987; Valentine, 1986; Wilson, 1979). According to the descriptive literature, such feelings are often directed toward other family members. That may be true because family members are biologically similar and yet able to have children. Spending time around people with children may be uncomfortable because infertile people are probably making comparisons during these interactions (Taylor & Lobel, 1989).

> I feel like I don't belong, like a second-class citizen with no place to go. Without a child, I don't belong in the group with kids who play in the park. Without a child, my husband and I don't fit in with our friends. (Mahlstedt, 1985, p. 338)

Conclusions from the Descriptive Reports

As the foregoing summary and quotes demonstrate, individuals are described as responding to infertility with a range of responses. Grief and depression, and difficulty in social interactions are the responses reported most frequently, but other reactions such as loss of control and sexual difficulties are commonly cited as well. Overall, there is greater focus on the emotional effects of infertility than on loss of control, changes in identity or esteem, or social effects. This may indicate that emotional effects are more common, or it may reflect greater clinical interest in the topic of emotional responses to infertility. The descriptive literature characterizes infertile people as a group in substantial distress. However, it is important to note that the individuals portrayed in the descriptive articles are a select sample; they represent mainly those who have decided to pursue infertility treatment or who are receiving counseling.

Although the psychological effects of infertility are separable into the categories used in this review, there are probably some relationships between these effects. Depression, for example, may be a function of the loss of control that is experienced by many. Sexual difficulties may strain marital relationships. Lowered self-esteem may contribute to feelings of jealousy toward others with children. It may therefore be useful for future research or clinical intervention to consider the psychological effects of infertility as a web of interrelated reactions, rather than as distinct or independent responses.

EMPIRICAL RESEARCH ON EFFECTS OF INFERTILITY

Characteristics of the Studies

Twenty-five empirical articles were located on the psychological effects of infertility, all published between 1963 and 1988. Fewer than 25 investigations are involved because, in some cases, more than one article was published based on a particular study. The studies vary widely in research design and quality, as well as in their results. Most investigators sampled couples (sample sizes range from 20 to 300), although a sizable number studied only women, and a few involved male and female subjects who were not couples (18 to 150 individuals). As some reviews point out (Domar & Seibel, 1990; Pantesco, 1986), infertile men have been understudied relative to infertile women.

The empirical articles were evaluated based on two features of their research designs. First, we were interested in whether the study used a control group for comparison with the infertile group. This feature is important in addressing whether the psychological conditions studied are truly associated with infertility or whether they exist in fertile people to a similar degree. Even with a control group, it is impossible to determine whether the observed conditions are caused by infertility, but stronger inferences are possible than when no comparison groups exist.

The second feature we considered in examining research designs was whether the investigators employed standardized tests or scales, which have multiple advantages. Because standard scales have established reliability and validity, such measures more powerfully and accurately test the questions and hypotheses of interest. Also, standard scales usually have published norms available for comparing infertile subjects to other distressed and nondistressed groups.

The 25 articles were sorted into four categories on the basis of these two design features: (1) Designs with a control group and standard measures (7 articles); (2) designs with standard measures but no control group (11 articles); (3) designs with a control group but no standard measures (5 articles); and (4) designs with neither a control group nor standard measures (2 articles). Articles in the last two categories (lacking standard measures) are similar to the descriptive articles discussed earlier, except that they contain quantitative data on the prevalence of various patterns of behavior, rather than general impressions and descriptions. The 25 empirical articles are reviewed within the four categories of design below, after which general conclusions are drawn.[2]

Studies with Control Groups and Standard Measures

The studies with this design are outlined in Table 2 in approximate order from strongest to weakest. Two of the articles pertaining to the same study are reviewed together, that is, there is a total of six investigations of this type. Most of the studies have relatively large sample sizes (up to 150 subjects), although two use fairly small samples (15 to 25 subjects). Of the six investigations outlined, two report no significant differences between infertile and control groups, one reports very few differences, two report mixed results, and one reports mostly significant differences between infertile and control groups.

Paulson, Haarmann, Salerno, and Asmar (1988) found no differences between 150 women in infertility treatment and 50 control women on measures of anxiety, personality, depression, self-concept, and locus of control. This study utilized the largest sample in this group of studies. Similarly, no differences between two samples of infertile women (153 total) and 141 controls were found on several measures of emotional distress or personality in the study by Freeman, Garcia, and Rickels (1983). Nor were there differences between 103 infertile men and women and 61 fertile men and women on marital adjustment, self-esteem, psychiatric symptoms, body image, or sex roles in the study by Adler and Boxley (1985).

Of studies reporting differences, 53 infertile women in IVF treatment had significantly lower satisfaction with some aspects of life, such as self and life-style, but higher satisfaction with other aspects, such as their friendships and time for relaxation than did control groups (Callan, 1987; Callan & Hennessey, 1988). O'Moore, O'Moore, Harrison, Murphy, and Carruthers (1983) found 15 infertile women were more anxious than 10 control women on three of four anxiety measures, but their partners did

[2]Articles with samples of less than 20 in control and/or infertile groups and weaker measures were dropped from the review (e.g., Brand, 1982; James & Hughes, 1982; Slade, 1981). It should be noted that results of these studies are consistent in general with the conclusions of this review. For example, James and Hughes (1982) found that infertile women were equally happy on various measures regardless of whether clomiphene treatment had been successful or not.

Table 2. Designs with Control Groups and Standard Measures

Authors	Sample/control groups	Standard measures	Results
Paulson et al. (1988)	150 women referred for infertility treatment 50 matched controls	16 Personality Factor Scales (16 PF) IPAT Anxiety & Depression Subscales Tennessee Self-Concept Scale I-E Locus of Control	No between-group differences.
Freeman et al. (1983)	49 women starting treatment for anovulation 104 women in treatment for infertility from other causes 141 fertile women	Hopkins Symptom Checklist (HSCL-90) Eysenck Personality Inventory (EPI) Langner Psychiatric Symptoms Mood Analog Scale MMPI Semantic Differential procedure	No differences between the two infertile groups and the fertile controls on standard measures, except infertile women rated selves as less potent than partner, mother, or father. All group means in normal range.
Callan (1987) Callan & Hennessey (1988)	53 infertile women in IVF treatment 32 voluntary childless women 50 mothers 24 mothers with secondary infertility	Andrews Quality of Life Scale Bradburn Morale Scale Spanier Dyadic Adjustment Scale	Infertile women in IVF reported significantly lower life satisfaction on some dimensions (e.g., with self, life-style) and well-being than control groups, but also reported greater marital satisfaction and greater satisfaction in other areas of life (relaxation, friendship) than controls. No differences in affect between groups.

Study	Sample	Measures	Findings
Adler & Boxley (1985)	46 infertile men 57 infertile women 20 fertile individuals 41 formerly infertile individuals	Locke-Wallace Marital Adjustment Scale Rosenberg Self-Esteem Scale Langner Psychiatric Symptoms Behavior Check List Body Cathexis Scale Personal Attributes Questionnaire	No differences between infertile and fertile groups detected.
O'Moore *et al.* (1983)	15 infertile couples undergoing autogenic stress reduction training 10 control couples	Spielberger State & Trait Anxiety inventories (STA) Taylor Manifest Anxiety Inventory (MAS) Eysenck Personality Questionnaire (EPQ) 16 Personality Factor Scales (16 PF)	Women in infertile couples had higher trait anxiety, manifest anxiety, and EPQ anxiety scores than control women. No differences between female groups found in state anxiety or 16 PF. Men in infertile couples higher on EPQ lie scale and 16 PF distortion scales than male controls, but not on other variables.
Platt *et al.* (1973)	25 infertile couples seeking treatment as private patients 15 control couples (11 with children, 4 using contraception)	I-E Locus of Control Semantic Differential procedure Group Personality Projective Test (GPPT)	Infertile couples viewed events in their lives as more externally caused, felt present selves were less similar to ideal selves and to same-sex parent compared to controls. Also, infertile women had significantly greater disturbance on the GPPT than control women.

not differ in anxiety as a function of fertility status. In a third study, 25 infertile couples viewed their lives as more externally controlled and felt their "present selves" were less similar to their ideals on the Semantic Differential procedure than 15 control couples (Platt, Ficher, & Silver, 1973). This study also found infertile women more emotionally disturbed than controls but there were no differences between male groups. Freeman *et al.* (1983) also found differences on the Semantic Differential procedure between infertile women and fertile controls. Infertile women rated themselves as less potent than partner, mother, or father.

The dominant pattern across investigations is of no difference between fertile and infertile groups on most dimensions, with the possible exception of anxiety and emotional distress for women. Results on these variables are more equivocal. Two studies found infertile women more anxious or disturbed than fertile women, and four did not. Furthermore, the studies reporting significant differences for women are generally weaker in design, whereas those showing no differences are stronger methodologically. In addition, two studies report consistent differences between infertile and fertile women in perceptions of self relative to others, with infertile women showing less favorable self-perceptions.

Studies with Standard Measures But No Control Groups

The eleven studies are outlined in Table 3, beginning with the strongest and most relevant, and ending with the least relevant and weakest. These studies are quite diverse in design characteristics and quality. Four of them examine individuals undergoing IVF treatment. Two studies involve assessments of variables on more than one occasion, which is desirable for inferring changes over time, but there are other methodological weaknesses of this group of studies. Sample sizes vary from two investigations having samples of over 200 couples to three studies with samples of less than 25 couples. Measures are generally strong in these studies, although a few of them employed very few measures, and some use a combination of unvalidated and validated measures. Two studies were not conducted for purposes of examining the psychological effects of infertility, as indicated below, although they include some information on this.

Of the eleven studies, six report normative or predominantly normative patterns in infertile samples. In a few of the six, results suggest infertile samples were functioning more (rather than less) favorably than normative estimates on some dimensions. Three studies report poorer functioning than normative levels on some measures, and in two studies, the results are unclear or difficult to interpret.

Hearn, Yuzpe, Brown, and Casper (1987) report normative levels of

Table 3. Designs with Standard Measures But No Control Group

Authors	Sample	Standard measures	Results
Hearn *et al.* (1987)	300 married couples awaiting IVF treatment	Family Environment Scale (FE) Personality Research Form-E Quality of Life Questionnaire Life Satisfaction Questionnaire Life Appraisal Inventory Inventory of Socially Supportive Behaviors (ISSB) Ways of Coping Checklist Spielberger State and Trait Anxiety Inventories (STAI) Beck Depression Inventory (BDI)	Normative levels of life satisfaction, affect, well-being, coping, social support, and anxiety.
Freeman *et al.* (1985)	200 couples entering IVF treatment	MMPI	Scores were in the normal range.
Fagan *et al.* (1986)	45 couples undergoing IVF treatment	Derogatis Sexual Functioning Inventory (DSFI) Brief Symptoms Inventory (BSI)	Scores were in the normal range.
Dennerstein & Morse (1985)	30 couples before starting IVF treatment (half with unknown cause and half with known causes)	Eysenck Personality Inventory (EPI) Spielberger State and Trait Anxiety Inventories (STAI) Rosenberg Self-Esteem Scale Spanier Dyadic Adjustment Scale Bem's Sex-Role Identity Scale	Scores on anxiety, self-esteem, and identification with female role were higher than norms. Organic-cause cases lower than norms in neuroticism; unknown-cause cases higher than norms.

(continued)

Table 3. (*Continued*)

Authors	Sample	Standard measures	Results
Daniluk (1988)	63 couples in infertility treatment in a clinic	Measured at 4 timepoints (before treatment, 4 weeks later during treatment, within a week of diagnosis, 6 weeks post-diagnosis): SCL-90-R Index of Sexual Satisfaction from Clinical Measurement Package (CMP) Locke-Wallace Marital Adjustment Scale Relationship Change Scale	Mean distress, sexual satisfaction, and marital adjustment scores in the normal range at all timepoints. Distress highest at intake. Women more significantly distressed than men at diagnosis. Relationship changes either positive or nonexistent.
Link & Darling (1986)	43 couples 17 women recruited from private physicians and ads	Clinical Measurement Package (CMP) measures of general contentment and depression, marital satisfaction, sexual satisfaction	Norms not provided. Percentages of men and women above clinically significant cutoffs on all three scales described as "notable."
Lalos et al. (1985a)	24 couples undergoing female tubal microsurgery for infertility	Measured at 2 timepoints (1 month before and 2 years after surgery): Eysenck Personality Inventory	Women and men did not differ from norms at either time.
McEwan et al. (1987)	Clinic samples of: –45 infertile men –65 infertile women	General Health Questionnaire (GHQ) Social Adjustment Scale (SAS-SR) Derogatis Sexual Function Inventory (DSFI) Quantity-Frequency Alcohol Use (Q-FAU)	Purpose of study was to predict adjustment. Norms on scales given only for GHQ. 40% women and 13% men experienced severe distress on the GHC (scored above norms).

Study	Sample	Measures	Findings
Garcia et al. (1985)	49 anovulatory infertile women in a clinical drug trial	SCL-90 MMPI Eysenck Personality Inventory Langner Psychiatric Symptoms Mood Analog Scale Semantic Differential procedure Social Adjustment Scale Derogatis Sexual Functioning Mooney Problem Checklist	Nonpathological levels of anxiety, depression, and changes in marital and sexual function.
Bell (1981)	10 infertile couples starting treatment 10 couples in treatment	Sexual Experiences Scale Delusions-Symptoms-States Inventory (DSSI) measures state anxiety and depression Social Adjustment Scale (revised SAS-SR) Work, Leisure, & Family Life Questionnaire	Slightly higher than normative rates of emotional disturbance were observed. Marital, sexual, and social adjustment scores are not compared to norms, but appear slightly low.
Wiehe (1976)	22 couples applying for adoption	Adjective Checklist (ADL)	No means presented.

life satisfaction, affect, well-being, coping, social support, anxiety, and depression in 300 married couples awaiting IVF treatment. They also report more favorable family functioning in the couples, and they observed some atypical personality patterns in women such as higher-than-average need for harm-avoidance and nurturance. Freeman, Boxer, Rickels, Tureck, and Mastroianni (1985) found scores on the MMPI and Taylor Manifest Anxiety Scale to be in the normal range for 200 couples entering IVF treatment. Likewise, Fagan, Schmidt, Rock, Damewood, Halle, and Wise (1986) found normal sexual functioning and normal levels of distress in 45 couples currently in IVF treatment. Distress, sexual satisfaction, and marital satisfaction scores were in the normal range among 63 couples in infertility treatment in a fourth study by Daniluk (1988). Relationship changes, such as changes in trust, communication, or intimacy were either nonexistent or positive in this study. Also, women were significantly more distressed than men at the time of diagnosis. Fifth, Garcia, Freeman, Rickels, Wu, Scholl, Galle, & Boxer (1985) found nonpathological levels of anxiety and depression, and changes in marital and sexual functioning among 49 anovulatory infertile women in a clinical drug trial. Scores on the Eysenck Personality Inventory were normal for 24 couples undergoing female tubal microsurgery for infertility in the final study (Lalos, Lalos, Jacobsson, & von Schoultz, 1985a).

Forty percent of infertile women ($n = 65$) and 13% of infertile men ($n = 45$) experienced severe distress using normative cutoffs on the General Health Questionnaire in a study on predictors of adjustment to infertility (McEwan, Costello, & Taylor, 1987). In a study by Dennerstein and Morse (1985), scores on anxiety, self-esteem, and identification with the female role were higher than norms among 30 couples ready to start IVF treatment. Slightly higher than normative rates of emotional disturbance were observed by Bell (1981) among 10 infertile couples starting treatment and 10 couples in treatment. Twenty-three percent in the sample were distressed versus 5% in the general population. There were also some indications of sexual dysfunction and social maladjustment in the sample but these results are less interpretable. Link and Darling (1986) report notable percentages of infertile individuals (43 couples and 17 women) above clinically significant cutoffs on scales measuring depression, marital satisfaction, and sexual satisfaction, but norms are not provided for interpretation. In the final study of the eleven, Wiehe (1976) does not present sample means for 22 couples applying for adoption on the Adjective Check List which was used to assess defensiveness, self-confidence, lability, personal adjustment, and intraception.

In summary, the large majority of studies of this type do not find abnormally high levels of emotional distress or problems in esteem, marital, or sexual function among infertile individuals. Studies which do report variations from normative levels on standard measures tend to involve smaller samples and less established measures. As in the previous section, there are indications in this group of studies that women experience more distress than men (McEwan *et al.*, 1987), and that infertility can improve marital or family functioning (Daniluk, 1988; Hearn *et al.*, 1987). Furthermore, several studies indicate wide variability in psychological functioning; many individuals are described as experiencing some degree of distress, even if the sample as a whole is not above clinically derived cutoffs (e.g., Daniluk, 1988).

Studies with Control Groups But No Standard Measures

The five studies of this type are outlined in Table 4. Two of the five report no differences between infertile groups and control groups, and one reports clear differences. The other two report a few differences, but predominantly find none. For example, Mai, Munday, and Rump (1972) conducted psychiatric interviews with matched groups of 50 infertile and 50 fertile couples. The infertile men and women did not exhibit significantly more neuroticism, psychoticism, or sexual difficulties, and the marital relationship was rated as good or very good for about 80% of both groups. However, infertile wives exhibited significantly more hysterical and aggressive personality disorders than the fertile wives, and showed some evidence of ambivalence and difficulties concerning sexual relationships.

Nesbitt, Hollender, Fisher, and Osofsky (1968) studied 18 infertile women and 18 fertile control women through psychiatric interview and projective tests. The authors report that infertile women displayed somewhat more anxiety about sibling rivalry and more guilt than control women, and less anxiety about oral eroticism. Also, control subjects perceived nurturant tachistoscope pictures more rapidly than did infertile patients. No differences on other dimensions including anxiety about heterosexual relations were observed.

McGrade and Tolor (1981) conducted a retrospective study of 126 couples who had been in infertility treatment, 82 of whom had become pregnant and 44 of whom had not. A 30-item original questionnaire was used to assess the impact of infertility on husbands and wives. No significant differences between the two groups were found in self-worth, self-image, sexuality, sexual function, marital or emotional impact, although there were differences by gender in both the successful and unsuccessful groups. For example, women in both groups reported more emotional distress, self-image damage, and questions about their sexuality than their husbands.

Lalos, Lalos, Jacobsson, and von Schoultz (1985b) interviewed 30

Table 4. Designs with Control Groups But No Standard Measures

Authors	Sample/control groups	Method and measures	Results
Mai et al. (1972)	50 infertile couples 50 fertile couples	Psychiatric interview	No differences between groups in neuroticism, psychoticism, or sexual difficulties. Infertile wives exhibited significantly more hysterical and aggressive personality disorders than fertile wives and showed some evidence of ambivalence in sexual relationships.
McGrade & Tolor (1981)	126 couples previously in infertility treatment (82 now pregnant and 44 still infertile)	30 item mailed questionnaire	No significant differences between groups in self-worth, self-image, sexuality, sexual function, marital impact, or emotional impact.
Nesbitt et al. (1968)	18 infertile women 18 fertile control women	Psychiatric interview & projective tests	Infertile women displayed somewhat more guilt and anxiety about sibling rivalry than control women, and less anxiety about oral eroticism. Control women perceived nurturant tachistoscope pictures more rapidly. No differences on other dimensions including anxiety about heterosexual relations observed.
Lalos et al. (1985b)	30 women undergoing tubal microsurgery 30 pregnant women 101 pregnant women 459 women planning abortion	Interviewed before and two years after surgery. Report is about one open-ended item on reasons for wish to have child.	No differences between groups observed in motivations for childbearing.
Eisner (1963)	20 infertile women in treatment in private practice 20 fertile women	Rorschach	Infertile women were significantly more distressed.

women just before and two years after they underwent microsurgery for tubal infertility. These women were compared to two samples of pregnant women ($n = 30, n = 101$) and to 459 women planning an abortion in their answers to an open-ended question about reasons for wanting to have a child. In general, the motives of infertile women did not differ from those of women in the control groups.

Eisner (1963) administered the Rorschach to 20 infertile women under treatment in a private practice and to 20 fertile women under treatment in private obstetrics and gynecology practices. Blind ratings of the protocols by five experts showed infertility patients to be significantly more emotionally disturbed than matched controls.

In sum, the majority of results across the five studies indicate no difference between infertile groups and fertile control groups. Where there are indications of difference, they tend to reflect the focus of studies on psychodynamic or psychopathologic theoretical premises (e.g., anxiety about sibling rivalry, hysterical personality tendencies). One problem with these results is the lack of information about the reliability of the data. That is, it is not often apparent whether more than one judge independently rated interview material. Lack of reliable coding of data limits the usefulness of some results in drawing conclusions about the effects of infertility.

Studies without Control Groups or Standard Measures

Both of the studies that use neither control groups nor standard measures document adverse sexual effects of infertility (Berger, 1980; Keye, 1980). Keye (1980) interviewed 91 infertile women about the effects of infertility on their sexual functioning. Subjects also completed questionnaires. Rates of sexual dysfunction were about the same as for fertile women in the population. However, 58% reported altered self-image, emotional distress, physical problems related to infertility, or decreased enjoyment of sex as a result of the need for scheduled coitus. Berger (1980), who conducted unstructured interviews with 16 couples in which the husband had been diagnosed as infertile, reports that nearly three-quarters of the men experienced impotency. Also, 14 of 16 wives were angry with their husbands or experienced psychiatric symptoms or conflicted dreams.

Some of the studies reviewed earlier included results with nonstandard measures that are consistent with the results of these two studies (Lalos et al., 1985a). For example, Freeman et al. (1983) found women in treatment for anovulation reported more inhibited sexual attitudes than comparison women. The authors suggest that this finding can be attributed to the effects of infertility treatment on sexual attitudes.

In general, the studies in this group suggest that sexual difficulties may be common in infertile couples, although it is difficult to draw conclusions, given the lack of standard measures and control groups in research designs. Existing standard measures of sexual functioning have been used very rarely in infertility research to date, with the exception of Fagan *et al.* (1986) who found normal sexual functioning in couples in IVF treatment. This area is one deserving further methodologically rigorous investigation.

Conclusions from the Empirical Research

In summary, the empirical evidence does not clearly indicate that negative effects accompany infertility, although there is some evidence of adverse effects in a few studies. If the investigations are weighted according to quality, as reflected in sample size and measures, the picture focuses much more clearly. Empirical evidence from scientifically rigorous research on the psychological effects of infertility does not support contentions that specific reactions are common. On the contrary, it appears that there are few or no well-established divergences from normal levels among infertile people who have been studied thus far. Although individual studies find abnormally high levels of depression (McEwan *et al.*, 1987) or low levels of self-esteem (Freeman *et al.*, 1983), several others have failed to replicate these findings. Thus, it is difficult to conclude that these reactions are common among people experiencing infertility. With further research, it is possible that the picture would change, but currently available, methodologically rigorous research suggests that the majority of people with infertility do not experience clinically significant emotional reactions, loss of self-esteem, or adverse marital and sexual consequences. If anything, the effects of infertility on the marriage appear to be positive as often as negative, as measured by self-report. On the other hand, there are indications that infertility affects views of one's self as potent and also, the discrepancy between present and ideal selves (Freeman *et al.*, 1983; Platt *et al.*, 1973). Finally, effects on sexual functioning appear to be prevalent and are worthy of further attention (Seibel & Taymor, 1982).

INTEGRATING THE DESCRIPTIVE AND EMPIRICAL RESEARCH

The conclusions of the anecdotal-descriptive work on infertility and the empirical research literature on infertility are somewhat discrepant. The former concludes that a variety of psychological reactions are common in infertile individuals. The latter reports little or no consistent, strong evidence of these effects of infertility. What are some explanations for this discrepancy? One possibility is that the empirical research to date has not adequately tested the issues. Another possibility is that the descriptive literature exaggerates or misrepresents the experience of infertile people. Both of these are discussed below.

Regarding the research literature, either samples or measures could be the cause of underreporting psychologically significant effects of infertility. The samples studied to date have usually been individuals in treatment, often in IVF treatment, and typically just beginning treatment. This is a time of hope and possibly of more adaptive coping for many couples who are infertile; couples may not be as distressed at this time, or as likely to express problems. Would couples who are not in treatment show the same effects, such as couples seeking adoption, for example? Similarly, would couples at the end of treatments, such as *in vitro* fertilization, exhibit low levels of clinically significant dysfunction? These questions have also been raised in a review paper by Edelmann and Connolly (1986). One study that examined the psychological state of 44 couples who had not become pregnant after treatment found no differences compared to couples who became pregnant after treatment on many variables such as self-esteem, sexual function, and emotions (McGrade & Tolor, 1981). However, this study should be replicated with a larger sample and standard measures before concluding that couples with different infertility experiences are similar in their psychological responses.

Regarding assessment, one possibility is that most standard measures are too global and not sufficiently sensitive to the distress and personal changes that accompany infertility. Infertile individuals may not be clinically depressed or anxious, but they seem to be experiencing high levels of stress that are subjectively worse than anything they have previously experienced. The one exception is the use of the Semantic Differential to assess infertility effects; two studies using this procedure found effects of infertility on self-views (Freeman *et al.*, 1983; Platt *et al.*, 1973). It should be noted, however, that these are not necessarily clinically significant effects.

Another concern with assessment is that self-report measures may be susceptible to social desirability bias. It is understandable that infertile couples would want to present their emotional state in a positive light, especially if they are beginning treatment. Being accepted for treatment is often difficult, and the cheerful, well-adjusted couple may be seen as a better candidate emotionally, especially for highly selective treatments such as IVF. In this regard, Spencer's (1987) comments may be typical of some practitioners' beliefs:

> Only after they have worked through their feelings of anger, guilt, and depression and have successfully isolated their sense of themselves and their sexuality from their infertility can couples tackle the new challenge of pursuing alternatives to infertility (i.e., artificial insemination, adoption, in vitro fertilization, child-free living). (p. 226)

Such remarks demonstrate the pressures on infertile couples to present themselves as well adjusted. In addition, a method of coping with infertility and its treatment may involve perceiving the situation more favorably than it objectively warrants. Maintaining hope and an optimistic view may enable the couple to persevere in the quest for a child, and many people believe that a positive attitude will improve the chances of conception.

There are some indications that men in couples experiencing infertility are higher in socially desirable response bias than fertile men (O'Moore et al., 1983). This may help explain why women appear more distressed by infertility than men in many of the studies. On the other hand, gender differences in distress may be due to the fact that women are often more involved in treatment. Or, women and men may cope with infertility in different ways resulting in different levels of distress. Finally, true differences in the extent of emotional response to infertility may exist between men and women. Problems of self-report assessment methods and of confounded variables must be addressed for us to draw firm conclusions about the effects of infertility, and about gender differences in these effects.

Although there are flaws in the research literature, such as those just noted, we must also entertain seriously that the descriptive literature exaggerates the plight of the infertile individual. The mental health professionals who write these articles typically observe a select subset of the infertile population, the individuals who are having the most difficulty adjusting. Individuals who adjust quickly and successfully are not likely to be observed in clinical settings, particularly if they do not persist in seeking treatment. Thus, the descriptive literature may exaggerate the negative effects of infertility.

The most likely explanation for the discrepancy between the descriptive and research literatures, in our view, is that there is enormous variability in reactions to infertility. Variability in psychological responses has also been noted in other populations experiencing undesirable life events. A careful review by Silver and Wortman (1980) suggests that responses to loss of a loved one, diagnosis of illness, sexual assault, and other negative life events are characterized by large individual differences in the extent to which particular emotions such as depression, anger, and anxiety are experienced. Some individuals experience these responses and others never do. This point appears to be applicable to infertility, as well. Infertility is many different medical conditions, as described in an earlier chapter (Davajan & Israel). Thus, it is likely to be a different psychological experience for individuals with different circumstances and the experience may change over time. From this perspective, it is not surprising that the empirical research on infertility finds few or no normative negative reactions.

Another discrepancy between the descriptive and empirical work on infertility concerns the sequencing of emotional reactions or stages. Several of the descriptive reports assume that stages of emotional response exist, although the empirical research has not addressed this issue yet. Appropriate longitudinal studies have not been conducted and are necessary to test stage theories. Silver and Wortman's (1980) review on reactions to undesirable life events indicate that, in general, people do not experience similar reactions at the same point in time or in the same sequence in response to loss (see also Wortman & Silver, 1987). For example, some individuals experience anger early on whereas others do not experience anger until months or years later, or not at all. An individual may also vacillate between emotional states, experiencing anger or depression repeatedly rather than in stages. These facts about emotional responses to loss and life events may help further to account for the absence of clear patterns of adverse reactions across empirical studies.

It appears that generalizing about the psychological consequences for all infertile people may be misleading. If generalizations are necessary, better population-based studies are needed that randomly sample a large number of men and women in the community and administer a large set of standard psychological measures tailored to infertility. Such studies would need to control for the large variability existing in diagnosis and treatment variables. Ideally, future studies would be longitudinal and would be based in past research on similar types of loss and stress.

In conclusion, on the basis of what is known at present, it appears that the average infertile individual does not experience severe or clinically significant distress, marital problems, sexual problems, or other psychological difficulties, nor is there evidence for a set sequence of emotional reactions. Thus, the overall approach to the study of infertility that underlies the descriptive literature appears to be inaccurate as a general model. However, a minority of infertile people seems to experience these effects, and many individuals experience stress. A more appropriate approach to the study of psychological responses to infertility, in our view, is the stress and coping perspective adopted in this book.

INFERTILITY AS LIFE STRESS

As stated at the outset of this chapter, infertility is not a single event, but a stressful process. The process initially involves threat, and for many couples, this threat is transformed over time into circumstances of loss. The extended nature of infertility, the fact that it is a threat that gradually becomes a loss for many, and the constant ambiguity regarding the ultimate outcome are important features of this form of life stress that influence psychological reactions and have implications for adjustment.

Virtually all individuals who desire to have children will experience infertility as stressful, although the degree of stress may vary greatly from mild to severe. One of the greatest sources of stress identified in the literature is medical treatments (Cook, 1987; Domar & Seibel, 1990; Seibel & Taymor, 1982). Furthermore, emotional distress may increase as time passes without success in treatment (Edelmann & Connolly, 1986). Although stress may be experienced by the vast majority of infertile individuals, variations as a function of time, treatments, prognosis, gender, and other factors are to be expected (Edelmann & Connolly, 1986).

PLAN FOR THE NEXT SECTION OF THE BOOK

If we conclude that there is considerable variation in reactions to infertility, the next steps are to identify who is at greatest risk for adverse reactions, and to learn how we can target individuals at risk. One contribution of the chapters in the next section is that they provide information about these issues. Each chapter applies a set of theoretical constructs from the stress and coping literature to the study of infertility. The first chapter concerns social relationships and social support (Abbey, Andrews, & Halman). The second chapter is on coping and cognitive appraisal (Stanton). The third chapter focuses on causal explanations or attributions (Tennen, Affleck, & Mendola). The next is on perceptions of control (Campbell, Dunkel-Schetter, & Peplau), and the last is on cognitive processes following stress and loss (Clark, Henry, & Taylor). Most of these chapters contain results from new studies of infertile individuals. Altogether, the following chapters offer theoretically and empirically based knowledge about adjustment to the stress of infertility and ideas for future research.

REFERENCES

Adler, J. D., & Boxley, R. L. (1985). The psychological reactions to infertility: Sex roles and coping styles. *Sex Roles, 12,* 271–279.

Bell, J. S. (1981). Psychological problems among patients attending an infertility clinic. *Journal of Psychosomatic Research, 25,* 1–3.

Berger, D. M. (1980). Couples' reactions to male infertility and donor insemination. *American Journal of Psychiatry, 137,* 1047–1049.

Brand, H. J. (1982). Psychological stress and infertility. Part 2: Psychometric test data. *British Journal of Medical Psychology, 55,* 385–388.

Callan, V. J. (1987). The personal and marital adjustment of mothers and of voluntarily and involuntarily childless wives. *Journal of Marriage and the Family, 49,* 847–856.

Callan, V. J., & Hennessey, J. F. (1988). The psychological adjustment of women experiencing infertility. *British Journal of Medical Psychology, 61*, 137–140.

Clapp, D. (1985). Emotional responses to infertility. *Journal of Obstetric, Gynecologic, and Neonatal Nursing* (Supplement), 32s–35s.

Cook, E. P. (1987). Characteristics of the biopsychosocial crisis of infertility. *Journal of Counseling and Development, 65*, 465–470.

Daniels, K. R., Gunby, J., Legge, M., Williams, T. H., & Wynn-Williams, D. B. (1984). Issues and problems for the infertile couple. *New Zealand Medical Journal, 97*, 185–187.

Daniluk, J. C. (1988). Infertility: Intrapersonal and interpersonal impact. *Fertility and Sterility, 49*, 982–990.

Dennerstein, L., & Morse, C. (1985). Psychological issues in IVF. *Clinics in Obstetrics and Gynaecology, 12*, 835–846.

Domar, A. D., & Seibel, M. (1990). The emotional aspects of infertility. In M. Seibel (Ed.), *Infertility: A comprehensive test* (pp. 23–35). Appleton-Lange.

Edelmann, R. J., & Connolly, K. J. (1986). Psychological aspects of infertility. *British Journal of Medical Psychology, 59*, 209–219.

Eisner, B. G. (1963). Some psychological differences between fertile and infertile women. *Journal of Clinical Psychology, 19*, 391–395.

Elstein, M. (1975). Effect of infertility on psychosexual function. *British Medical Journal*, August 2, 296–299.

Fagan, P. J., Schmidt, C. W., Jr., Rock, J. A., Damewood, M. D., Halle, E., & Wise, T. (1986). Sexual functioning and psychologic evaluation of in vitro fertilization couples. *Fertility and Sterility, 46*, 668–672.

Fleming, J., & Burry, K. (1988). Coping with infertility. In D. Valentine (Ed.), *Infertility and adoption: A guide for social work practice* (pp. 37–41). New York: Haworth.

Freeman, E. W., Boxer, A. S., Rickels, K., Tureck, R., & Mastroianni, L., Jr. (1985). Psychological evaluation and support in a program of in vitro fertilization and embryo transfer. *Fertility and Sterility, 43*, 48–53.

Freeman, E. W., Garcia, C. R., & Rickels, K. (1983). Behavioral and emotional factors: Comparisons of anovulatory infertile women with fertile and other infertile women. *Fertility and Sterility, 40*, 195–201.

Garcia, C.-R., Freeman, E. W., Rickels, K., Wu, C., Scholl, G., Galle, P. C., & Boxer, A. S. (1985). Behavioral and emotional factors and treatment responses in a study of anovulatory infertile women. *Fertility and Sterility, 44*, 478–483.

Griffin, M. E. (1983). Resolving infertility: An emotional crisis. *AORN Journal, 38*, 597–601.

Hearn, M. T., Yuzpe, A. A., Brown, S. E., & Casper, R. F. (1987). Psychological characteristics of in vitro fertilization participants. *American Journal of Obstetrics and Gynecology, 156*, 269–274.

Honea-Fleming, P. (1986). Psychosocial components in obstetric/gynecologic conditions with a special consideration of infertility. *Alabama Journal of Medical Sciences, 23*, 27–30.

James, B., & Hughes, P. F. (1982). Psychological well-being as an outcome variable in the treatment of infertility by Clomiphene. *British Journal of Medical Psychology, 55*, 375–377.

Kaufman, S. A. (1969). Impact of infertility on the marital and sexual relationship. *Fertility and Sterility, 20(3)*, 380–383.

Keye, W. R. (1980). The impact of infertility on psychosexual function. *Fertility and Sterility, 34*, 308–309.

Kraft, A. D., Palombo, J., Mitchell, D., Dean, C., Meyers, S., & Schmidt, A. W. (1980). The psychological dimensions of infertility. *American Journal of Orthopsychiatry, 50*, 618–627.

Lalos, A., Lalos, O., Jacobsson, L., & von Schoultz, B. (1985a). The psychosocial impact of infertility two years after completed surgical treatment. *Acta of Obstetrics and Gynecology in Scandinavia, 64*, 599–604.

Lalos, A., Lalos, O., Jacobsson, L., & von Schoultz, B. (1985b). The wish to have a child: A pilot-study of infertile couples. *Acta of Psychiatry in Scandinavia, 72*, 476–481.

Lasker, J. N., & Borg, S. (1987). *In search of parenthood*. Boston: Beacon Press.

Lazarus, R. S. (1966). *Psychological stress and the coping process*. New York: McGraw-Hill.

Lazarus, R. S., & Folkman, S. (1984). *Stress, appraisal, and coping*. New York: Springer.

Lazarus, R. S. & Launier, R. (1978). Stress-related transactions between person and environment. In L. A. Pervin & M. Lewis (Eds.), *Perspectives in interactional psychology* (pp. 287–327). New York: Plenum.

Link, P. W., & Darling, C. A. (1986). Couples undergoing treatment for infertility: Dimensions of life satisfaction. *Journal of Sex and Marital Therapy, 12*, 46–59.

McCormick, T. M. (1980). Out of control: One aspect of infertility. *Journal of Obstetric, Gynecologic, and Neonatal Nursing, 9*, 205–206.

McEwan, K. L., Costello, C. G., & Taylor, P. J. (1987). Adjustment to infertility. *Journal of Abnormal Psychology, 96*, 108–116.

McGrade, J. L., & Tolor, A. (1981). The reaction to infertility and the infertility investigation: A comparison of the responses of men and women. *Infertility, 4*, 7–27.

Mahlstedt, P. P. (1985). The psychological component of infertility. *Fertility and Sterility, 43*, 335–346.

Mai, F. M., Munday, R. N., & Rump, E. E. (1972). Psychiatric interview comparisons between infertile and fertile couples. *Psychosomatic Medicine, 34*, 431–440.

Matthews, R., & Matthews, A. M. (1986a). Beyond the mechanics of infertility: Perspectives on the social psychology of infertility and involuntary childlessness. *Family Relations, 35*, 470–487.

Matthews, R., & Matthews, A. M. (1986b). Infertility and involuntary childlessness: The transition to nonparenthood. *Journal of Marriage and the Family, 48*, 641–649.

Mazor, M. D. (1978). The problem of infertility. In M. T. Notman & C. C. Nadelson (Eds.), *The woman patient* (pp. 137–160). New York: Plenum.

Mazor, M. D. (1984). Emotional reactions to infertility. In M. D. Mazor & H. F. Simons (Eds.), *Infertility: Medical, emotional, and social considerations*. New York: Human Sciences Press.

Menning, B. E. (1980). The emotional needs of infertile couples. *Fertility and Sterility, 34*, 313–319.

Miall, C. E. (1985). Perceptions of informal sanctioning and the stigma of involuntary childlessness. *Deviant Behavior, 6*, 383–403.

Nesbitt, R. E., Hollender, M., Fisher, S., & Osofsky, H. J. (1968). Psychologic correlates of the polycystic ovary syndrome and organic infertility. *Fertility and Sterility, 19*, 778–786.

O'Moore, A. M., O'Moore, R. R., Harrison, R. F., Murphy, G., & Carruthers, M. E. (1983). Psychosomatic aspects in idiopathic infertility: Effects of treatment with autogenic training. *Journal of Psychosomatic Research, 27*, 145–151.

Pantesco, V. (1986). Nonorganic infertility: Some research and treatment problems. *Psychological Reports, 58*, 731–737.

Paulson, J. D., Haarmann, B. S., Salerno, R. L., & Asmar, P. (1988). An investigation of the relationship between emotional maladjustment and infertility. *Fertility and Sterility, 49*, 258–262.

Platt, J. J., Ficher, I., & Silver, M. J. (1973). Infertile couples: Personality traits and self-ideal concept discrepancies. *Fertility and Sterility, 24*, 927–976.

Rosenfeld, D. L., & Mitchell, E. (1979). Treating the emotional aspects of infertility: Counseling services in an infertility clinic. *American Journal of Obstetrics and Gynecology, 135*, 177–180.

Sandelowski, M. (1987). The color gray: Ambiguity and infertility. *Image: Journal of Nursing Scholarship, 19*, 70–74.

Sawatzky, M. (1981, March–April). Tasks of infertile couples. *Journal of Obstetric, Gynecologic, and Neonatal Nursing*, 132–133.

Seibel, M. M., & Taymor, M. L. (1982). Emotional aspects of infertility. *Fertility and Sterility, 37*(2), 137–145.

Silver, R., & Wortman, C. B. (1980). Coping with undesirable life events. In J. Garber & M. E. P. Seligman (Eds.), *Human helplessness* (pp. 279–375). New York: Academic Press.

Slade, P. (1981). Sexual attitudes and social role orientations in infertile women. *Journal of Psychosomatic Research, 25*(3), 183–186.

Spencer, L. (1987). Male infertility: Psychological correlates. *Postgraduate Medicine, 81*, 223–228.

Taylor, S. E., & Lobel, M. (1989). Social comparison activity under threat: Downward evaluation and upward contacts. *Psychological Review, 96*, 569–575.

Valentine, D. P. (1986). Psychological impact of infertility: Identifying issues and needs. *Social Work in Health Care*, 11, 61–69.

Walker, H. E. (1978). Psychiatric aspects of infertility. *Urologic Clinics of North America, 5*, 481–488.

West, S. (1983). Infertility—Couples in crisis. *The Australian Nurses Journal, 13*, 40–41.

Wiehe, V. R. (1976). Psychological reaction to infertility. *Psychological Reports, 38*, 863–866.

Williams, L. S., & Power, P. W. (1977). The emotional impact of infertility in single women: Some implications for counseling. *Journal of the American Medical Women's Association, 32*, 327–333.

Wilson, E. A. (1979). Sequence of emotional responses induced by infertility. *Journal of the Kentucky Medical Association, 77*, 229–233.

Woollett, A. (1985). Childlessness: Strategies for coping with infertility. *International Journal of Behavioral Development, 8*, 473–482.

Wortman, C., & Silver, R. (1987). Coping with irrevocable loss. In G. R. VandenBos & B. K. Bryant (Eds.), *Cataclysms, Crises, and Catastrophes: Psychology in Action*. Washington, DC: American Psychological Association.

II

Application of Conceptual Models and Constructs in Psychology to the Study of the Infertility Process

4

The Importance of Social Relationships for Infertile Couples' Well-Being

ANTONIA ABBEY, FRANK M. ANDREWS,
and L. JILL HALMAN

REVIEW OF RELEVANT LITERATURE

Social relationships capacity for mitigating the negative impact of stress on physical and psychological well-being has been well documented. Hundreds of studies have examined the influence of social relationships on the way in which people cope with chronic and acute stressors such as bereavement, malignant disease, unemployment, rape, physical disability, pregnancy, and work overload (see Broadhead, Kaplan, James, Wagner, Schoenbach, Grimson, Heyden, Tibblin, & Gehlbach, 1983; Gottlieb, 1983; House, Landis, & Umberson, 1988; Kessler, Price, & Wortman, 1985; and Wallston, Alagna, DeVellis, & DeVellis, 1983, for reviews of this literature).

ANTONIA ABBEY • Wayne State University and the Institute for Social Research, University of Michigan, Ann Arbor, Michigan 48106.   FRANK M. ANDREWS and L. JILL HALMAN • Institute for Social Research, University of Michigan, Ann Arbor, Michigan 48106.

Social Support

At least three different positive aspects of social relationships have been examined: the presence of social ties, structural characteristics of social networks, and functions which provide social support. The preponderance of research in the social relationships field has focused on social support. The term "social support" has been conceptualized in many ways but most definitions focus on individuals' perceptions of various functional aspects of their social relationships. As many authors have noted, the mere existence of social ties or certain structural characteristics does not insure that social support will be provided (Cohen & Wills, 1985; Kessler *et al.*, 1985; Schaefer, Coyne, & Lazarus, 1981). Thus, what occurs within relationships must be examined, not simply their presence or structure.

Although many functions of social support have been described, most researchers focus on three: esteem, affirmation, and material aid. Esteem or emotional support involves the communication of love, care, and respect (Kahn & Antonucci, 1980; Schaefer *et al.*, 1981; Wills, 1985). This is typically viewed as the central component of social support. Many negative life events involve a sense of failure and threaten individuals' self-esteem and sense of mastery. The knowledge that one is loved and valued can mitigate the sense of loss (Wills, 1985).

Information or affirmation support involves providing individuals with information that helps them evaluate their situation or themselves (Kahn & Antonucci, 1980; Schaefer *et al*, 1981; Wills, 1985). This often entails affirming that their thoughts and feelings are normal, given the circumstances, as well as providing concrete information about the problem. Informational support is thought to be particularly helpful for stressed individuals who are unaware of how people experiencing such an event typically feel (Walker, MacBride, & Vachon, 1977).

Material or instrumental support involves providing concrete aid such as financial or housekeeping assistance. Of the three functions discussed here, instrumental support typically has the weakest links to well-being, perhaps because as Cohen and Wills (1985) suggested, the instrumental support provided must precisely match the recipients' needs to *be* supportive. (See Cobb [1979], Wills [1985], and Wortman & Dunkel-Schetter [1979] for descriptions of other socially supportive functions of social relationships.)

Major Methodological Issues in the Social Support Literature

Despite the large number of empirical studies and theoretical reviews of social support, many conceptual ambiguities exist. A thorough review of these issues is not attempted here, but a brief description of the issues most relevant to this chapter is presented (see the articles cited in this section for more information).

There is consensus among social support researchers that it is appropriate to measure *perceived* support; words or actions are not socially supportive unless the target individual perceives them as such. Researchers differ, however, as to the frame of reference considered. Some researchers have focused on how much social support individuals feel is *available* to them (Cohen & Hoberman, 1983; Henderson, 1981; Pearlin, Menaghan, Lieberman, & Mullan, 1981). Other researchers have measured the actual amount of social support *received* during a specified time frame (Abbey, Abramis, & Caplan, 1985; Barrera, 1981; Procidano & Heller, 1983). People may be overly optimistic about how much support is available to them, thus indicators of received support may be more accurate. While it seems reasonable that social support must be received to be useful, Cohen and Wills (1985), in their extensive review of the literature, concluded that measures of perceived availability more consistently relate to well-being than received support measures. This may partially be due to confounding; availability measures of social support may be tapping personality traits such as optimism as well as social support. Having a positive outlook has been shown to relate to overall happiness (Costa & McCrae, 1980; Vinokur, Schul, & Caplan, 1987). Also, as Cohen and Wills (1985) observed, received social support must match what the individual needs in order to be beneficial. Receiving general positive regard, when what one wants and needs is concrete assistance, may not promote enhanced well-being.

A methodological issue which has received tremendous attention in the social support literature concerns whether social support should be expected to have main or moderating effects on outcome measures such as life quality, affect, performance, and physical health. A main-effects model implies that increased social support is beneficial to all recipients, regardless of the level of stress they are experiencing. Kaplan, Cassel, and Gore (1977) argued that social support fills people's ongoing need for affiliation, belonging, respect, social recognition, affection, and nurturance. As Thoits (1985) argued, "day-to-day" social support is obtained from ongoing role relationships which are emotionally supportive because they provide meaning and purpose in life. Network members may also provide information or opportunities which help individuals avoid negative life events (Cohen & Wills, 1985). All of these functions should enhance well-being.

A moderating or buffering effects model suggests that social support is only (or most) beneficial to individuals experiencing stress. During times of stress, individuals may experience diminished self-esteem, reduced perceived control, and they may feel uncertainty about how to cope with what they are experiencing. Esteem and affirmation support should mitigate these effects, thus increasing psychological well-being.

Evidence for both main and buffering effects have been found (see Cohen & Wills [1985] and Kessler & McLeod [1985] for reviews of this literature). Cohen and Wills (1985) argued that buffering effects are most likely to be found when the type of support provided matches what the individual needs, while main effects are most likely to be found when structural aspects of the network are measured. Based on their data, Abbey and Rovine (1985) suggested that buffering effects are most likely to be found when individuals experience acute stress, while main effects are most likely to be found when individuals experience chronic stress (cf. Kessler & McLeod, 1985). It is difficult for networks to remain mobilized to provide specific support functions when a stressor lasts for years, as many chronic stressors do. Thus, over time, support providers may become less responsive to signs that support is required.

Negative Aspects of Social Relationships

Social support researchers have only recently acknowledged that significant others can act in ways which produce negative as well as positive effects (Abbey et al., 1985; Barrera, 1981; Rook, 1984; Shinn, Lehmann, & Wong, 1984; Suls, 1982). Interpersonal conflict occurs in close relationships for several reasons. First, significant others can attempt to be supportive but say or do things which are perceived as unhelpful by the recipient. As several researchers have emphasized (Abbey, Holland, & Wortman, 1980; Coates & Wortman, 1980; Coyne, Aldwin, & Lazarus, 1981; Suls, 1982; Wortman & Dunkel-Schetter, 1979), friends' and family members' ideas about what may help individuals through crises may not be accurate. If significant others misunderstand their loved ones' needs, then they are unlikely to behave in ways which are perceived as supportive. For example, friends may try to distract the distressed individual from the problem, when what he or she would most like to do is talk about it. Or family members may give advice that is perceived as coercive rather than supportive.

A second way in which interpersonal conflict can arise in relationships is when these relationships place excessive demands on individuals' time and energies. Individuals who feel overwhelmed by the amount of support others require of them are likely to feel frustrated, taken advantage of, and deficient. These feelings are likely to cause them to act in ways which are not perceived as supportive by the people soliciting their assistance.

Some researchers have argued that women more often than men play caregiving roles that can place excessive demands on their ability to provide support (Belle, 1982; Kessler, McLeod, & Wethington, 1985). Women also appear to receive more social support than men do (Burda, Vaux, & Schill, 1984; Sarason, Sarason, Hacker, & Basham, 1985; Stokes & Wilson, 1984), a finding that is generally interpreted as advantageous to women's physical and mental health (Verbrugge, 1985). Thus, women may give and receive more social support and interpersonal conflict than men do because of the expressive role they frequently play in relationships.

A third way in which interpersonal conflict can occur in close relationships is when a high level of social support is required for a prolonged period of time. As Silver and Wortman (1980) noted, most people underestimate how long it takes to adjust to a serious life crisis. Friends and family initially rally around a person in crisis, but as months or years pass and this individual is still depressed, preoccupied, and not back to normal, friends and family begin to feel resentful, burnt out, and helpless (Coates & Wortman, 1980; Coyne, Aldwin, & Lazarus, 1981). Support givers become frustrated when their well-intentioned efforts to be supportive appear to have no effect. With time, they begin to express their anger, frustration, and inability to understand why their loved one has not shown improvement, all of which makes the loved one feel even worse.

Close relationships almost inevitably involve conflict. People argue, fight, disagree, and compete with their spouses, friends, family, and coworkers. Negative affect and behavior are likely to be reciprocated, thus escalating the level of conflict (Gottman, Markman, & Notarius, 1977; Wills, Weiss, & Patterson, 1974). Some relationships involve more conflict than others, but all close relationships involve some conflict (Brickman, Dunkel-Schetter, & Abbey, 1987). Argyle and Furnham (1983), in a study of married couples, found that one's spouse was the greatest source of both satisfaction and conflict. Thus while members of infertile couples are likely to provide each other with social support, they are also likely to treat each other in unsupportive and conflictual ways.

Relevance of the Social Relationships Literature to Infertility

The discussion thus far in this chapter has focused on the general literature on social relationships. The stress and coping theoretical framework (Goldberger & Breznitz, 1982), which suggests that provisions of caring, affirmation, and aid can help people adjust to stressful life circumstances, applies to infertility as well as the stressors described above. The research which suggests that crises are exacerbated by unwanted advice, expressions of negative affect, and the inability of significant others to understand what one is going through is perhaps even more applicable to infertility. The infertility literature is full of anecdotes which vividly convey the insensitivity of some network members to the anguish which most infertile individuals experience. As one infertile woman interviewed by Miall (1985) stated:

> You get it all. My favorite is, "It's all in your head; go take a vacation and it will be fine." I think the other phrase I got that really drove me crazy was, "Well, you know, I had this friend who couldn't and then adopted a child and do you know what? Seven months later she was pregnant." (p. 392)

Most of the empirical evidence regarding the impact of infertility on individuals' well-being is methodologically weak. Many articles present anecdotal accounts based on a small number of infertile individuals, often only women. While these studies are rich sources of hypotheses, they fail to provide definitive evidence about the infertility experience. In the following sections of this chapter, the implications of social relationships theory for the study of infertility are examined. Brief descriptions of relevant infertility research are also included, but an exhaustive review is not attempted.

Research on Social Relationships and Infertility

Three aspects of social relationships have been examined with some frequency in the infertility literature: the unhelpful responses of friends and family members, the importance of social support from one's partner, and the value of self-help groups. Each of these are described in the following sections.

Negative Responses from Others. Unlike the general social support literature which emphasizes the benefits of social relationships, the infertility literature tends to emphasize the costs of social relationships. There are several reasons for this emphasis on the negative. Infertility can be kept secret from others and often is. Many couples are unwilling to discuss their infertility problem with others out of embarrassment or discomfort about discussing sexual issues (Menning, 1977; 1980). The ability to procreate is viewed as an essential part of individuals' masculinity or femininity, and it is difficult to discuss feeling "not a whole man or woman" with others (Seibel & Taymor, 1982). This secrecy, while understandable, makes it likely that infertile couples will be the target of painful comments. Because of their lack of knowledge, friends and family members often ask questions which are extremely painful to hear and answer, such as, "Won't I ever be a grandparent?" or "Are you too selfish to have children?" Miall (1985), who interviewed 71 infertile women drawn from various community sources, found that 52% had been asked extremely uncomfortable questions by friends and family members who were unaware of their situation.

As the social relationships literature suggests, even when friends and family members are told of the couples' infertility problem, they still may unwittingly make unhelpful remarks or suggestions. They may ask each month if the woman is pregnant yet, suggest folk remedies, alternative coital positions, or that the couple "just relax" (L. Andrews, 1984). It is extremely frustrating to receive advice which is inappropriate (Dunkel-Schetter, 1984). It seems rude to tell people who were trying to be helpful that their responses were insensitive, yet if honest feedback is not provided, then it is unlikely that the quality of the interaction will improve. Miall (1985) found that 38% of the women she interviewed found the initial responses of others unsupportive. Lalos, Lalos, Jacobsson, and von Schoultz (1985), who interviewed 29 couples who were receiving infertility treatment, indicated that 87% of the women and 86% of the men felt they received no genuine emotional support from friends or family members. Mahlstedt (1985), a psychologist who has provided treatment for many infertile clients, stated "well intentioned but insensitive remarks by others . . . leave the infertile person feeling unacceptable, misunderstood, unloved, or ashamed" (p. 337).

There are many anecdotal comments in the literature about infertile couples skipping christenings, baby showers, and other events which focus on young children because of the pain they experience with these vivid reminders of their childless status (Menning, 1977). Mahlstedt (1985) noted that friends and family sometimes avoid inviting infertile couples to these events because they feel awkward about exposing them to their children. Thus as Wortman and her colleagues (Coates & Wortman, 1980; Wortman & Dunkel-Schetter, 1979) have suggested, a vicious cycle is established. Members of infertile couples feel uncomfortable sharing information about their problem. Significant others unintentionally say and do things which upset the individual in need of support, who in turn withdraws. This response causes potential supporters to feel unappreciated and unwanted, so they too withdraw. Thus the infertile individual becomes even more isolated.

Spouse Support. Partly for the reasons described above, members of infertile couples tend to rely on each other for esteem, affirmation, and tangible support. McEwan, Costello, and Taylor (1987) found that perceiving one's husband as a confidant was related to enhanced emotional and social adjustment for infertile women. Having someone other than one's spouse as a confidant was not related to adjustment, perhaps as the authors suggested, because of the privacy of the problem or perhaps because other confidants could not fully understand how the infertile individual felt. McGrade and Tolor (1981) interviewed 82 infertile couples who eventually had children and 44 who did not. About 38% of both groups of couples agreed that the advice they received from friends was helpful. In contrast, approximately 75% of the members of couples who had children and 85% of the members of couples who did not have children agreed that they could talk to their spouse openly and meaningfully about the problem.

While relying on each other for support can make an infertile couple's relationship stronger, it also can place an enormous burden on it. Because each member of the couple is in crisis, it may be difficult to meet each other's needs. Also, if they are at different points of adjustment (e.g., one is willing to consider adoption while the other is not) or if they have different coping styles (e.g., distraction versus problem-solving), then what is helpful to one partner may be harmful to the other. As Mahlstedt (1985) commented, "because both the man and the woman are hurt, tired, and under great pressure, they may become less able to fulfill each other's needs" (p. 337).

A number of authors have described differences in men's and women's responses to infertility which can make it difficult for partners to fully understand and support each other. While parenting is a central component of society's expectations for both sexes, motherhood is traditionally perceived as the central role for women and paid employment is traditionally the central role for men. Many women cannot imagine a life without children (Mahlstedt, 1985). Miall (1985) vividly described how childlessness disqualifies women from being part of the "ingroup of mothers" (p. 391). They are frequently treated by women with children as second-class citizens who cannot contribute to conversations about child-rearing regardless of how much experience they have had with children. Thus women may feel more isolated and in need of emotional support than their partners if their childless status makes it more difficult for them to relate to same-sex friends.

Several investigators have found that women more often than men take the initiative to obtain treatment when pregnancy is not achieved and make the majority of the decisions about which treatments to pursue (Greil, Leitko, & Porter, 1988; McGrade & Tolor, 1981). Twenty-seven percent of the 22 women interviewed by Greil et al. (1988) were annoyed that their husbands were not more actively involved in their treatment, while some of the husbands thought their wives were overreacting. About 30% of the infertile couples interviewed by McGrade and Tolor (1981) found themselves arguing about their fertility problem.

Mahlstedt (1985) found that her male infertile clients were not willing to express their fears as openly as were the female infertile clients. This left the wives upset because they felt their husbands were not adequately concerned. She quotes one man who said, "My wife . . . feels like a failure . . . I hate going through all of this too, but I am most upset about what it is doing to her . . . And she believes I am not upset. I'm playing a game and we are both losing" (p. 343). The general literature on gender differences suggests that women may be more expressive than men (Spence, Deaux, & Helmreich, 1985); thus these findings for infertile couples reflect general gender differences in the ways in which men and women have been socialized to cope with negative affect.

Mutual Support Groups. Self-help groups are often described as being the solution to the problem infertile couples have in obtaining adequate social support from each other, friends, and family members (Batterman, 1985; Goodman & Rothman, 1984; Mahlstedt, 1988; Porter & Christopher, 1984). By sharing their experiences and concerns with other infertile individuals, both members of the couple should receive needed affirmation that their feelings are normal, information about treatment options, and emotional sustenance. The fact that self-help groups have sprung up throughout the country for victims of a variety of diseases and negative life events including cancer, alcoholism, divorce, and widowhood documents the natural appeal of discussing one's problems with others who have undergone a similar experience. RESOLVE is a national self-help group for infertile individuals and the Endometriosis Association, which has a self-help component, also includes many infertile individuals. Of course, infertile individuals can also talk one-on-one with others who have had similar experiences without being members of a formal group, and derive the same benefits.

While talking with other infertile individuals has many potential advantages, there is also the possibility of negative effects. For example, consider a couple which has recently discovered that they have a fertility problem due to the husband's low sperm count. They may be very hopeful about achieving a pregnancy through artificial insemination. How will they feel after talking with other infertile couples for whom such artificial insemination attempts have been unsuccessful? They have gained useful information but they may also lose hope and become anxious and depressed. Miall's (1985) study participants observed that new members of self-help groups were sometimes frightened by the stories told by others who had received extensive treatment.

Thus, as for all the other aspects of social relationships described in this chapter, social comparison with similar others, either through self-help groups or other means, has the potential to enhance or diminish well-being. The impact of sharing one's experiences with other infertile

individuals will vary, depending on a variety of factors, including willingness to engage in self-disclosure, ability to handle jealousy constructively,
the usefulness of the information shared about physicians and treatments,
and the amount of caring and respect exhibited toward one another.

THE STUDY

Overview of Purpose and Design

The data presented in this section are from a large, longitudinal study
of how couples cope with infertility. Infertility is conceptualized as a major
life stress which has an impact on a variety of mental and physical health
outcomes, including life quality, affect, self-esteem, sexuality, performance, physical health, and fertility-related behavior. A number of psychological and social factors, such as perceived control, coping strategies, and
social support are hypothesized to influence the relationship between infertility and well-being.

The results reported in this chapter focus on the interrelationships
between infertility, social support, interpersonal conflict, and well-being.
Because only one wave of data is available at this point, the actual causal
direction between these variables cannot be determined. As many other
authors have observed, the relationships between these concepts must be
examined over time to observe their causal influences on each other.

Procedures

Infertile couples were recruited from six infertility specialists in
Southeastern Michigan, which includes the Detroit Metropolitan area. All
but one of the major infertility practices in the area agreed to participate
in this study. Volunteers from RESOLVE, the Endometriosis Association,
newspaper advertisements, and referrals from study participants were also
included. Study participants were required to be married, white, to have
a high school education, a family income in the approximate range of
$20,000 to $100,000 a year, have no previous children by either member
of the couple, and to have not tried IVF or GIFT. The study population
was restricted to white, middle-class couples because these are the people
most likely to seek treatment (Henshaw & Orr, 1987); having a relatively
homogeneous group of respondents allows more sophisticated analyses to
be completed with a relatively small number of cases. Only couples with
primary infertility were accepted because it was our expectation that the
stresses associated with infertility would differ for those couples who had

children and those who did not. Because we wanted couples still relatively early in the process of dealing with infertility and because IVF and GIFT are often viewed as "last-resort" treatments, we did not want couples who had already tried these strategies.

New patients who fit these criteria were asked by their physician if they were willing to consider participating in a university study of how couples cope with fertility problems. Self-help group members were recruited through an article printed in their organizations' monthly newsletter. An advertisement was also placed in several local newspapers, and midway through the study respondents were sent a letter asking them if they knew of any eligible couples who would be interested in participating.

Couples who agreed to be contacted were first sent a letter and brochure describing the study and then they were called by an interviewer to set up an appointment for an interview. Separate one-hour, in-person interviews were scheduled with each member of the couple. Interviews were conducted with 157 infertile couples.[1] One hundred forty-four couples were recruited from infertility specialists, nine from self-help groups, three from newspaper advertisements, and one from study participants. Seventy-nine percent of the couples referred to the study by physicians were successfully interviewed.

Measures

Three sets of social relationship variables were assessed in the interview. A four-item short form of Sarason, Levine, Basham, and Sarason's (1983) satisfaction with social support measure (SSQ) was used to assess study participants' overall satisfaction with their support network. Sarason *et al.* (1983) argued that because individuals differ in the amount of support they desire, it is more appropriate to measure their satisfaction with what they have than the absolute level of social support. Respondents rated how satisfied they were with how much they could count on others to accept, care, console, and relax them, using 5-point Likert-type scales with response options which ranged from "very satisfied" to "very dissatisfied." This measure had a Cronbach alpha of .83.

The amount of social support and interpersonal conflict received from and provided to one's spouse in the last four weeks was also measured. We decided to focus on spouse support and conflict because of the importance of this relationship and this study's focus on the couple as a

[1] In this chapter, infertility is defined as both members of the couple reporting trying to have a child for 12 months or more. The larger study also included 118 couples recruited from similar sources who did not have a fertility problem or who did not meet this criteria. Their data will not be described in this chapter.

unit. By measuring both how much one has received and given, comparisons can be made between the amount of support one partner tried to give and the recipient's perception of how much was received.

The 15 social support and interpersonal conflict items were intermixed and presented in a series. First, study participants responded in terms of how their husband or wife had acted toward them (received), and then the items were repeated in terms of how participants had acted toward their husband or wife (provided). Two aspects of social support were assessed: esteem (e.g., show appreciation, love; Cronbach alpha = .78, .77 for received and provided, respectively) and affirmation (e.g., understand, let you know your feelings were normal; Cronbach alpha = .80, .78 for received and provided, respectively). In parallel fashion, two interpersonal conflict functions were assessed: negative affect (e.g., act cold, show dislike; Cronbach alpha = .79, .81 for received and provided, respectively) and disapproval (e.g., judge, make you feel you overreacted; Cronbach alpha = .68, .70 for received and provided, respectively). Ratings were made on 5-point Likert-type scales with response options which ranged from "not at all" to "a great deal."

Study participants were also asked if they talked about their fertility problem with (1) Friends or family members; and (2) other infertile people. If so, they were asked to rate how these interactions made them feel, using a 5-point Likert-type scale with response options that ranged from "much worse" to "much better." Then they were asked to explain their response in an open-ended item.

Other measures which will be discussed in this chapter include self-esteem, sexual dissatisfaction, marital life quality, and fertility problem stress. A six-item version of Rosenberg's (1965) self-esteem scale was used which had a Cronbach alpha of .76. Six items developed by the research team formed a sexual dissatisfaction index (e.g., "I feel inadequate sexually; I am dissatisfied with my sexual performance; I am seldom in the mood for sex"). This index had a Cronbach alpha of .83. Both self-esteem and sexual dissatisfaction were rated on 5-point Likert-type scales with response options which ranged from "strongly agree" to "strongly disagree." Marital life quality was measured using five items (e.g., satisfaction with marriage, spouse) based on Andrews and Withey (1974), which had a Cronbach alpha of .84. Responses were made on 5-point Likert-type scales with response options which ranged from "very satisfied" to "very dissatisfied."

Fertility problem stress was a 12-item index developed by the research team. It assessed the extent to which individuals found various aspects of their fertility problem stressful (e.g., tests and procedures, keeping track of ovulation) and how much their fertility problem had disrupted various domains of their lives (e.g., finances, sex, relationship with people with children). It is noteworthy that during pilot testing we discovered that study participants resisted the use of the term "infertility" because it sounded final. Thus, throughout the interview we used the term "fertility problem." Answers were made on 5-point scales with response options which ranged from "not at all" to "a great deal." The Cronbach alpha for this index was .88.

Results

First, a descriptive profile of the respondents is provided. Both their sociodemographic characteristics and information about their fertility problem are presented. Then the relationships between social support, interpersonal conflict, and several indicators of well-being are described. Gender differences are also presented.

Infertile women interviewed for this study ranged in age from 22 to 42; the average age was 32. Infertile men interviewed for this study ranged in age from 23 to 44; the average age was 33. These couples had been married an average of six years. The majority of study participants had some college education. The average total household income for 1987 was between $40,000 and $50,000. Ninety-nine percent of the male respondents and 92% of the female respondents were active members of the labor force.

These couples had been trying to have baby for one to eight years. The average length of time trying to conceive was 34 months. All but one of these couples had seen an infertility specialist. Based on their self-reports, 46% of the couples' fertility problem was due to female factors, 10% was due to male factors, 30% was due to a combination of male and female factors, and 14% was unexplained. This is a somewhat lower rate of male factors than appears to exist in the general infertile population (Benson, 1983).

Table 1 displays the most frequently mentioned causes of these couples' fertility problems. It also includes the most frequently received tests and treatments.

Ninety-five percent of the women and 94% of the men had received at least one test or treatment. Anecdotal evidence from our study participants, as well as those from other studies, indicates that many of these tests are perceived as stressful (Mazor, 1984; McGrade & Tolor, 1981; Seibel & Taymor, 1982). Most men report that providing a specimen for semen analysis is extremely embarrassing (Lalos et al., 1985; Menning, 1977). Twenty-two percent of the men in this study had received a semen analysis five or more times. Twenty-two percent of the women had their cervical

**Table 1. Descriptive Information on Study Participants'
Fertility Problem, Tests, and Treatments**

	Percentage (%)
Commonly mentioned causes of fertility problem	
Female factors	
Cyclical abnormalities	32
Endometriosis	25
Tubal problems	18
Male factors	
Low sperm count	30
Sperm deficiencies	13
Varicocele	12
Commonly received tests	
Females	
Hysterosalpingogram	72
Cervical-mucus	71
Serum progesterone levels	67
Sperm-mucus interaction	65
Laparoscopy	61
D & C	24
Ultrasound	21
Males	
Semen analysis	91
Serum testosterone	46
Commonly received treatments	
Females	
Ovulatory stimulating drugs	61
Progesterone supplements	
(to prevent miscarriage)	25
Surgery for endometriosis	20
Drugs for endometriosis	15
Tubal surgery	9
Males	
Varicocele removal	11
Both	
Artificial insemination with husband's sperm	23
Artificial insemination with donor's sperm	9
Artificial insemination with husband's	
and donor's sperm combined	1

Note. Multiple mentions allowed.

mucus checked five or more times and 11% had the sperm-mucus interaction test five or more times. The sperm-mucus interaction test is particularly stressful to couples because they are required to have sexual intercourse within several hours of the exam; being obligated to have sex at a
particular time causes performance difficulties in some couples (Freeman,
Garcia, & Rickels, 1983; Mazor, 1984; McGrade & Tolor, 1981; Menning,
1977; Seibel & Taymor, 1982).

Only 22% of these couples had insurance which had covered all the
costs of their treatment. Forty-eight percent had spent less than $500 of
their own money thus far for treatment. Another 20% had spent $500 to
$999; 20% had spent $1000 to $2499; and the remaining 12% had spent
more than $2500 thus far for infertility treatments. Twenty-three percent
of these couples were currently considering adoption and 6% were considering *in vitro* fertilization, neither of which is covered by medical insurance in Michigan.

Marital Social Support and Interpersonal Conflict. As expected, the two
measures of received social support, esteem and affirmation, were fairly
highly correlated ($r = .68$). Similarly, the two measures of interpersonal
conflict, negative affect and disapproval, were correlated .66. The four
social support and interpersonal conflict scales were moderately negatively
correlated (see Table 2; r's ranged from $-.42$ to $-.58$). Support and
conflict have been less strongly correlated in our own previous research
(Abbey *et al.*, 1985; Abbey & Andrews, 1985); however, these past studies

**Table 2. Interrelationships between Fertility Problem Stress,
Social Relationships Indicators, and Well-Being Indicators**

	A	B	C	D	E	F	G	H	I
A. Fertility problem stress	1.0								
B. Self-esteem	−.44	1.0							
C. Esteem social support	−.21	.28	1.0						
D. Affirmation social support	−.22	.25	.68	1.0					
E. Negative affect interpersonal conflict	.20	−.20	−.58	−.51	1.0				
F. Disapproval interpersonal conflict	.18	−.27	−.42	−.48	.66	1.0			
G. Social support satisfaction	−.14	.32	.37	.34	−.34	−.27	1.0		
H. Marital life quality	−.28	.22	.56	.46	−.56	−.46	.43	1.0	
I. Sexual dissatisfaction	.44	−.49	−.31	−.28	.25	.24	−.22	−.41	1.0

Note: For r's $\geq .20$, $p < .05$.

assessed the amount of social support and interpersonal conflict received from all network members. It is not surprising that the positive and negative responses received from one person are more strongly related than the positive and negative responses received from a number of individuals.

Respondents' assessments of the amount of support and conflict they provided to their spouses were quite highly related to the amount of support and conflict they reported receiving from their spouses. For example, received and provided esteem support correlated .68, while received and provided disapproval correlated .66. This suggests that there is a fair amount of reciprocity in these couples; those individuals who provided a great deal of support and/or conflict also received a great deal of support and/or conflict.

Gender Differences in Perceived Social Support and Interpersonal Conflict. Paired t tests were used to examine gender differences in husbands' and wives' perceived support and conflict levels. As can be seen in Table 3, women were significantly more satisfied than men were with the overall amount of social support that was available to them from their social network. It was noted earlier that women have frequently been found to receive more social support than men.

Women and men both reported receiving equally high levels of esteem and affirmation social support from each other. In contrast, women reported providing significantly more esteem and affirmation support to their spouses than men did.

Table 3. Mean Differences in Husbands' and Wives' Perceived Social Support and Interpersonal Conflict

	Women	Men	t value
Social support			
Satisfaction	3.29	2.96	4.05*
Esteem received	4.26	4.22	0.68
Affirmation received	3.78	3.73	0.60
Esteem provided	4.18	4.00	2.59*
Affirmation provided	3.83	3.68	2.05*
Interpersonal conflict			
Negative affect received	1.70	1.87	2.55*
Disapproval received	1.91	2.10	2.54*
Negative affect provided	1.94	1.97	0.38
Disapproval provided	1.93	2.13	2.54*

df=151; *p<.01.

Men reported receiving significantly more negative affect and disapproval than women did from their spouses. Men also reported providing significantly more disapproval than women did to their spouses.

In summary, both sexes reported *receiving* an equal amount of social support from each other but women reported that they *provided* more than men did. Men reported both providing and receiving more interpersonal conflict than women did. This suggests that women may become frustrated with their husbands because the women feel that they are giving more than they are receiving. In turn, men may become upset with their wives because the men are experiencing more interpersonal conflict in the relationship than women are. Men are apparently expressing their discontent since they report providing more disapproval as well as receiving it. When the Time 2 data are available, it will be important to determine if couples that differed in their perceptions of how much support and conflict they gave each other experienced a reduction in their marital life quality.

The Effects of Talking with Friends and Family. Ninety-six percent of the women and 88% of the men had discussed their fertility situation with a friend or family member in the past 12 months (McNemar's test of differences between proportions [1962] (1) = 3.31, $p < .001$). Both women and men reported feeling somewhat better after talking with friends and family ($M = 3.66$). When asked to explain their response, wives were significantly more likely than husbands to mention both positive and negative effects of talking with friends and family (e.g., provided emotional support, said something which made them feel worse). In contrast, husbands were more likely than wives to say that they just were not that influenced by what other people had to say (McNemar's test (1) = 3.53, $p < .001$).

In summary, more women than men had spoken with their friends and family about their problem. Women described more benefits and costs to these interactions than men did, while men described more reasons to be indifferent to the responses of others than women did.

The Effects of Talking with Similar Others. Seventy-three percent of the women and 53% of the men had talked to someone with a fertility problem in the previous 12 months (McNemar's test (1) = 4.18, $p < .001$). Among those study participants who had spoken with similar others, women found these discussions marginally more helpful ($M = 4.07$) than men did ($M = 3.87$, t (71) = 4.06, $p < .09$).

In a follow-up open-ended question, wives were significantly more likely than husbands to describe positive aspects of talking with similar others (e.g., made them feel hopeful, less alone). In contrast, husbands were more likely than wives to state that they were not particularly influenced by what others said (McNemar's test (1) = 2.45, $p < .02$).

In summary, women spoke with similar others more than men did and found these interactions more helpful. Women focused more on the positive aspects of interactions with similar others, while men expressed more indifference.

The Relationship between Social Interactions and Well-Being. Based on previous research, it was hypothesized that received social support would enhance these infertile couples' well-being, while received interpersonal conflict would diminish it. As described earlier in this chapter, some researchers have found main effects of social relationships on well-being while others have found moderating effects. In order to examine both possibilities, a series of regression analyses were conducted with two different well-being measures: marital life quality and sexual dissatisfaction. For each outcome measure, one regression analysis was conducted in which fertility problem stress, self-esteem, and an indicator of social relationships were included as predictor variables. In a second analysis, the same predictors were included, plus a product term representing the interaction of fertility problem stress and social relationships. If the product term adds a significant additional amount of explained variance, then buffering effects exist (Thoits, 1982).

The results of these analyses showed that, for these individuals, social relationships had main effects but no moderating effects on well-being. A stress-buffering model implies that social support is most beneficial to those individuals experiencing the highest levels of stress. Even though some individuals experienced more stress due to their fertility problem than others, it appears that either everyone experienced enough stress to benefit from social support or buffering does not occur in this context.

The results of the main effect analyses are presented in Table 4 separately for women and men. The predictors of marital life quality were comparable for women and men. The greater the amount of fertility-problem stress experienced, the lower the marital life quality. All five social relationship variables related to marital life quality (when entered in separate regression equations). Social support satisfaction and received esteem and affirmation social support related positively to marital life quality, while received negative affect and disapproval interpersonal conflict related negatively to marital life quality. Self-esteem was not a significant predictor of marital life quality.

The pattern of results was somewhat different for sexual dissatisfaction. For both men and women, social support satisfaction was not a significant predictor. While social support from others appears to posi-

Table 4. Multiple Regression Results: Self-Esteem, Received Social Support, and Received Interpersonal Conflict as Predictors of Marital Life Quality and Sexual Dissatisfaction

Predictors	Marital life quality		Sexual dissatisfaction	
	Women	Men	Women	Men
Fertility problem stress	$-.19^{**}$	$-.26^{**}$	$.31^{***}$	$.17^{**}$
Self-esteem	n.s.	n.s.	$-.33^{***}$	$-.39^{***}$
Social support satisfaction	$.38^{***}$	$.39^{**}$	n.s.	n.s.
R^2	.20	.28	.35	.24
Fertility problem stress	$-.21^{**}$	$-.16^{**}$	$.32^{***}$	.11
Self-esteem	n.s.	n.s.	$-.34^{***}$	$-.33^{***}$
Esteem support	$.49^{***}$	$.54^{***}$	$-.12^{*}$	$-.27^{***}$
R^2	.30	.40	.36	.30
Fertility problem stress	$-.20^{**}$	$-.17^{**}$	$.31^{***}$	$.14^{*}$
Self-esteem	n.s.	n.s.	$-.34^{***}$	$-.36^{***}$
Affirmation support	$.34^{***}$	$.48^{***}$	$-.15^{**}$	$-.13^{*}$
R^2	.20	.34	.36	.26
Fertility problem stress	$-.13^{*}$	$-.18^{**}$	$.30^{***}$	$.15^{*}$
Self-esteem	n.s.	n.s.	$-.35^{***}$	$-.38^{***}$
Negative affect conflict	$-.54^{***}$	$-.48^{***}$	$.15^{**}$	.11
R^2	.35	.35	.36	.25
Fertility problem stress	$-.18^{**}$	$-.22^{**}$	$.30^{***}$	$.16^{**}$
Self -esteem	n.s.	n.s.	$-.33^{***}$	$-.38^{***}$
Disapproval conflict	$-.44^{***}$	$-.37^{***}$	$.16^{**}$	.03
R^2	.26	.26	.37	.24

$^*p < .09.$ $^{**}p < .05.$ $^{***}p < .01.$

tively impact on overall marital life quality, sexual issues appear to be more personal and were only influenced by spouse support.

Fertility problem stress related positively to sexual dissatisfaction for both sexes, but the relationships were consistently stronger for women than for men. Women also reported experiencing more fertility problem stress than men did (M's = 2.68 vs. 2.15, t (151) = 7.69, $p < .01$). Similarly, received negative affect and disapproval interpersonal conflict were significantly positively related to sexual dissatisfaction for women, but not for men. In contrast, received esteem and affirmation social support negatively related to sexual dissatisfaction for both men and women.

Although self-esteem was not related to marital life quality, it consistently negatively related to sexual dissatisfaction for both men and women. It seems reasonable that high self-esteem was associated with positive feelings about sexual performance.

In summary, the results of multiple regression analyses indicated that received social support and conflict had main effects on well-being. For both women and men, spouse social support related positively to well-being and spouse interpersonal conflict related negatively to well-being. The relationships of well-being to social support from others and to self-esteem depended on the well-being indicator.

IMPLICATIONS

Several caveats are necessary before the implications of this study's results are described. First, the infertile couples interviewed for this study were not randomly sampled; instead, they were primarily white, middle-class, married couples seeking treatment from an infertility specialist. Descriptive information was provided about study participants in order to document the types of people to whom these results might generalize. However, because these couples were heterogeneous with regard to the levels of stress and life quality they reported, and with regard to the factors expected to moderate the effects of stress on life quality, these couples' responses provide good information about the relationships between psychosocial factors and infertility among couples seeking medical treatment.

Secondly, only cross-sectional results have been reported. No statements about causal direction can be made based on these data. When additional waves of data are available, it will be possible to determine the effects of social support and interpersonal conflict on well-being over time. For example, are couples with high levels of interpersonal conflict more likely to separate or divorce? Will individuals highly satisfied with their network support exhibit better adjustment if still childless at Wave 2 than couples dissatisfied with their network support? Will the types of support and conflict husbands and wives provide each other differ for couples that become parents as opposed to those who do not? These are the types of questions which can be addressed with longitudinal data.

This study's results indicate that social support from one's spouse, friends, family, and similar others enhanced infertile couples' well-being. In contrast, receiving negative affect and disapproval from one's partner reduced infertile couples' well-being. It is important to note that, overall, levels of received spouse support were high and levels of received spouse conflict were low. Thus, most couples were benefiting from their interactions with each other. Some conflict is inevitable in all relationships, particularly under times of stress. Those couples in which negativity predominated, however, experienced diminished marital and sexual satisfaction, and may benefit from marital therapy.

The infertility literature emphasizes the negative responses received from friends and family members. Overall, these couples were moderately satisfied with the availability of social support from their network and indicated that, on balance, conversations with friends and family members about their fertility problem made them feel somewhat better. Thus, in this study, social relationships seemed to provide more social support than what has been reported in previous research. This study included a larger number of couples and more reliable indicators of social relationships than much of the previous research. The media attention which infertility has received in the last few years (e.g., episodes of *L.A. Law, 48 Hours*) may be increasing general awareness of the stresses associated with infertility, thus making people more sympathetic and understanding of infertile couples' experiences.

Study participants were not specifically asked about self-help group membership, but they were asked if they had discussed their problems with other people who had fertility problems. The social comparison processes which occur in self-help groups can occur in a variety of settings. Respondents reported having discussions with similar others at work, at cocktail parties, and over dinner, as well as at group meetings. While people were less likely to have talked with similar others than friends and family members about their fertility problems, exchanges with similar others were viewed as more helpful. Although some negative effects were mentioned (e.g., depressing, cannot solve your problems for you), the vast majority of responses were positive. Thus for most people, talking with other infertile individuals enhanced well-being.

Women were consistently more likely than men to view social interactions positively. Men were much more likely than women to comment that they were not particularly influenced by their interactions with other people. Research suggests that many men only openly express their feelings and concerns with their wives, while women have a number of confidants, including their husbands (Cleary & Mechanic, 1983; Kahn & Antonucci, 1980). These couples show a similar pattern and this suggests that infertile women experience an extra burden because of their need to provide virtually all of their husbands' social support. As described earlier in this chapter, when women's caregiving roles become excessive, they may be unable to provide all that is required of them (Belle, 1982; Kessler, McLeod, & Wethington, 1985). This may explain why women in this study reported providing more social support to their spouses then men did and why men reported receiving and providing more interpersonal conflict to their spouses than women did. Women apparently tried to provide additional social support to their husbands, but perhaps out of exhaustion or frustration, they provided conflict as well.

In addition, women in this study experienced more fertility problem stress then men did and this stress had a larger positive impact on women's sexual dissatisfaction than on men's. Similarly, Freeman, Boxer, Rickels, Tureck, and Mastroianni (1985) found that more female patients than male patients perceived infertility as the most unsettling experience in their lives and stated that it had made their sex lives less pleasurable.

Women may perceive infertility as more stressful than men do for physical, psychological, and social reasons. Regardless of which member of the couple has physical problems producing the infertility, the majority of the tests and treatments focus on the woman's body. She is the one who must take her temperature each morning before rising and attend to her cyclical changes each month, including the depression evidence of failure associated with menstruation. As one woman interviewed by Menning (1977) stated about her husband:

> He's not the one the doctor is examining under a microscope. His life hasn't really changed . . . Because he's not the one going through all the tests he can't be faulted for not understanding when I dissolve each time my period comes. I blame myself for not being able to make him understand my pain. And then I feel angry. What *can't* he understand? (p. 106)

As described earlier in this paper, many women are socialized to view motherhood as their central adult role, so infertile women frequently feel personally inadequate and unfulfilled. Other people typically assume that infertility is the woman's fault (L. Andrews, 1984) and this adds to the social stigma associated with her childless status. Some infertile women may benefit from either individual or group counseling which focuses on helping them acknowledge the psychological and social burdens associated with their physical condition. Their husbands may benefit from counseling that focuses on helping them understand their partners' feelings and expressing their own feelings. Efforts to help infertile men find additional sources of social support, so that the emotional burden placed on their wives is reduced, may also improve the quality of infertile couples' marital and sexual relationships.

Despite the important gender differences described above, these results suggest, overall, that both infertile women and men benefit from social relationships, particularly from the support they receive from their spouse. Negative comments, unwanted advice, and rejection did occur, but not to as great an extent as previous research suggested. While these results are encouraging, future interviews with these couples will determine if those who are still childless are able to maintain a positive marital life quality in the face of further stress and disillusionment.

ACKNOWLEDGMENTS

This study was supported by grant #R01-HD21240 from the National Institute of Child Health and Human Development. We would like to thank Laurie Silver for computing assistance. Special thanks go to the couples who volunteered to share their experiences with us.

REFERENCES

Abbey, A., Abramis, D. J., & Caplan, R. D. (1985). Effects of different sources of social support and social conflict on emotional well-being. *Basic and Applied Social Psychology, 6*, 111–129.

Abbey, A., & Andrews, F. M. (1985). Modeling the psychological determinants of life quality. *Social Indicators Research, 16* 1–34.

Abbey, A., Holland, A. E., & Wortman, C. B. (1980). The misguided helper: An analysis of people's responses to their loved one's crises. In D. G. McGuigan (Ed.) *Women's lives: New theory, research, and policy* (pp. 257–266). Ann Arbor, MI.: University of Michigan Press.

Abbey, A., & Rovine, M. (1985, August). *An examination of the effects of positive and negative aspects of social relations on well-being.* Paper presented at the Annual Meeting of the American Psychological Association, Los Angeles.

Andrews, F. M., & Withey, S. B. (1974). Developing measures of perceived life quality: Results from seven national surveys. *Social Indicators Research, 1*, 1–26.

Andrews, L. B. (1984). *New conceptions.* New York: St. Martin's Press.

Argyle, M., & Furnham, A. (1983). Sources of satisfaction and conflict in long-term relationships. *Journal of Marriage and the Family, 45*, 481–493.

Barrera, N., Jr. (1981). Social support in the adjustment of pregnant adolescents: Assessment issues. In B. H. Gottlieb (Ed.), *Social networks and social support* (pp. 69–96). Beverly Hills, CA: Sage.

Batterman, R. (1985). A comprehensive approach to treating infertility. *Health and Social Work, 10*, 46–54.

Belle, D. (1982). The stress of caring: Women as providers of social support. In L. Goldberger & S. Breznitz (Eds.) *Handbook of stress: Theoretical and clinical aspects* (pp. 495–505). New York: Free Press.

Benson, R. C. (1983). *Handbook of obstetrics and gynecology.* Los Altos, CA: Lange Medical Publishers.

Brickman, P., Dunkel-Schetter, C., & Abbey, A. (1987). The development of commitments. In P. Brickman (Ed.), *Commitment, conflict, and caring* (pp. 145–221). Englewood Cliffs, NJ: Prentice-Hall.

Broadhead, W. E., Kaplan, B. H., James, S. A., Wagner, E. H., Schoenbach, V. J., Grimson, R., Heyden, S., Tibblin, G., & Gehlbach, S. H. (1983). The epidemiologic evidence for a relationship between social support and health. *American Journal of Epidemiology, 117*, 521–537.

Burda, P. C., Jr., Vaux, A., Schill, T. (1984). Social support resources: Variation across sex and sex role. *Personality and Social Psychology Bulletin, 10*, 119–126.

Cleary, P. D., & Mechanic, D. (1983). Sex differences in psychological distress among married people. *Journal of Health and Social Behavior, 24*, 111–121.

Coates, D., & Wortman, C. B. (1980). Depression maintenance and interpersonal control. In A. Baum & J. Singer (Eds.), *Advances in environmental psychology: Applications of personal control* (Vol. 11, pp. 149–182). Hillsdale, NJ: Lawrence Erlbaum.

Cobb, S. (1979). Social support and health through the life course. In M. R. White (Ed.), *Aging from birth death: Interdisciplinary perspectives* (pp. 93–106). Boulder, Colorado: Westview Press.

Cohen, S. & Hoberman, H. (1983). Positive events and social supports as buffers to life change stress. *Journal of Applied Social Psychology, 13,* 99–125.

Cohen, S., & Wills, T. A. (1985). Stress, social support, and the buffering hypotheses. *Psychological Bulletin, 98,* 310–357.

Costa, P. T., Jr., & McCrae, R. R. (1980). Influence of extroversion and neuroticism on subjective well-being: Happy and unhappy people. *Journal of Personality and Social Psychology, 38,* 668–678.

Coyne, J. C., Aldwin, C., & Lazarus, R. R. (1981). Depression and coping in stressful episodes. *Journal of Abnormal Psychology, 90,* 439–447.

Dunkel-Schetter, C. (1984). Social support and cancer: Findings based on patient interviews and their implications. *Journal of Social Issues, 40,* 77–98.

Freeman, E. W., Boxer, A. S., Rickels, K., Tureck, R., & Mastroianni, L., Jr. (1985). Psychological evaluation and support in a program of in vitro fertilization and embryo transfer. *Fertility and Sterility, 43,* 48–53.

Freeman, E. W., Garcia, C. R., & Rickels, K. (1983). Behavioral and emotional factors: Comparisons of anovulatory infertile women with fertile and other infertile women. *Fertility and Sterility, 40,* 195–201.

Goodman, K., & Rothman, B. (1984). Group work in infertility treatment. *Social Work with Groups, 7,* 79–97.

Goldberger, L., & Breznitz, S. (1982). *Handbook of stress.* New York: Free Press.

Gottlieb, B. H. (1983). Social support as a focus for integrative research in psychology. *American Psychologist, 38,* 278–287.

Gottman, J., Markman, H., & Notarius, C. (1977). The topography of marital conflict. *Journal of Marriage and the Family, 39,* 461–477.

Greil, A. L., Leitko, T. A., & Porter, K. L. (1988). Infertility: His and hers. *Gender and Society, 2,* 172–199.

Henderson, S. (1981). Social relationships, adversity, and neurosis: An analysis of prospective observations. *British Journal of Psychiatry, 138,* 391–398.

Henshaw, S. K., & Orr, M. T. (1987). The need and unmet need for infertility services in the United States. *Family Planning Perspectives, 19,* 180–186.

House, J. S., Landis, K. R., & Umberson, D. (1988). Social relationships and health. *Science, 241,* 540–545.

Kahn, R. L., & Antonucci, T. C. (1980). Convoys over the life course: Attachment, roles, and social support. In P. B. Bales and O. Brim (Eds.), *Life span development and behavior* (Vol. 3, pp. 253–286). Boston, MA: Lexington Press.

Kaplan, B. H., Cassel, J. C., & Gore, S. (1977). Social support and health. *Medical Care, 15,* 47–58.

Kessler, R. C. & McLeod, J. (1985). Social support and mental health in community samples. In S. Cohen & S. L. Syme (Eds.), *Social support and health* (pp. 219–240). New York: Academic Press.

Kessler, R. C., McLeod, J. D., & Wethington, E. (1985). The costs of caring. In I. A. Sarason & B. R. Sarason (Eds.), *Social support: Theory, research, and applications* (pp. 491–506). The Hague, The Netherlands: Martinus Nijhoff.

Kessler, R. C., Price, R. H., & Wortman, C. B., (1985). Social factors in pathology: stress, social support, and coping processes. *Annual Review of Psychology, 36,* 531–572.

Lalos, A., Lalos, O., Jacobsson, L., & von Schoultz, B. (1985). Psychological reactions to the medical investigation and surgical treatment of infertility. *Gynecologic and Obstetric Investigation, 20,* 209–217.

Mahlstedt, P. P. (1985). The psychological component of infertility. *Fertility and Sterility, 43*, 335–346.

Mazor, M. D. (1984). Emotional reactions to infertility. In M. D. Mazor & H. F. Simons (Eds.), *Infertility: Medical, emotional, and social considerations* (pp. 23–35). New York: Human Sciences Press.

McEwan, K. L., Costello, C. B., & Taylor, P. J. (1987). Adjustment to infertility. *Journal of Abnormal Psychology, 96*, 108–116.

McGrade, J. J., & Tolor, A. (1981). The reaction to infertility and the infertility investigation: A comparison of the responses of men and women. *Infertility, 4*, 7–27.

McNemar, Q. (1962). *Psychological statistics* (3rd ed.). New York: John Wiley & Sons.

Menning, B. E. (1977). *Infertility: A guide for the childless couple*. Englewood Cliffs, NJ: Prentice-Hall.

Menning, B. E. (1980). The emotional needs of infertile couples, *Fertility and Sterility, 34*, 313–319.

Miall, C. E., (1985). Perceptions of informal sanctioning and the stigma of involuntary childlessness. *Deviant Behavior, 6*, 383–403.

Pearlin, L. I., Menaghan, E. B., Lieberman, M. A., & Mullan, J. T. (1981). The stress process. *Journal of Health and Social Behavior, 22*, 337–356.

Porter, N. L. & Christopher, F. S. (1984). Infertility: Towards an awareness of a need among family life practitioners. *Family Relations, 33*, 309–315.

Procidano, M. E., & Heller, K. (1983). Measures of perceived social support from friends and from family: Three validation studies. *American Journal of Community Psychology, 11*, 1–24.

Rook, K. S. (1984). The negative side of social interaction: Impact on psychological well-being. *Journal of Personality and Social Psychology, 46*, 1097–1108.

Rosenberg, M. (1965). *Society and the adolescent self-image*. Princeton, NJ: Princeton University Press.

Sarason, I. B., Levine, H. M., Basham, R. B., & Sarason, B. R. (1983). Assessing social support: The social support questionnaire. *Journal of Personality and Social Psychology, 14*, 127–139.

Sarason, B. R., Sarason, I. B., Hacker, T. A., & Basham, R. B. (1985). Concomitants of social support: Social skills, physical attractiveness, and gender. *Journal of Personality and Social Psychology, 49*, 469–480.

Schaefer, C., Coyne, J. C., & Lazarus, R. S. (1981). The health-related functions of social support. *Journal of Behavioral Medicine, 4*, 381–406.

Seibel, M. M., & Taymor, M. L. (1982). Emotional aspects of infertility. *Fertility and Sterility, 37*, 137–145.

Shinn, M., Lehmann, S., & Wong, N. W. (1984). Social interaction and social support. *Journal of Social Issues, 40*, 55–76.

Silver, R. L., &Wortman, C. B. (1980). Coping with undesirable life events. In J. Barber & M. E. P. Seligman (Eds.), *Human helplessness* (pp. 279–340). New York: Academic Press.

Spence, J. T., Deaux, K., & Helmreich, R. L. (1985). Sex roles in contemporary American society. In G. Lindzey and E. Aronson (Eds.), *Handbook of social psychology*, Vol. 2 (3rd ed., pp. 149–178). New York: Random House.

Stokes, J. P., & Wilson, D. G. (1984). The inventory of socially supportive behaviors: Dimensionality, prediction, and gender differences. *American Journal of Community Psychology, 12*, 53–69.

Suls, J. (1982). Social support, interpersonal relations and health: Benefits and liabilities. In G. S. Sanders & J. Suls (Eds.), *Social psychology of health and illness* (pp. 255–277). Hillsdale, NJ: Lawrence Erlbaum.

Thoits, P. A. (1982). Life stress, social support, and psychological vulnerability: Epidemiological considerations. *Journal of Community Psychology, 10*, 341–362.

Thoits, P. A. (1985). Social support and psychological well-being: Theoretical possibilities. In I. B. Sarason & B. R. Sarason (Eds.), *Social support: Theory, research, and applications* (pp. 51–72). Boston, MA: Martinus Nijhoff Publishers.

Verbrugge, L. M. (1985). Gender and health: An update on hypotheses and evidence. *Journal of Health and Social Behavior, 26*, 156–182.

Vinokur, A., Schul, Y., & Caplan, R. D. (1987). Determinants of perceived social support: Interpersonal transactions, personal outlook, and transient affective states. *Journal of Personality and Social Psychology, 53*, 1137–1145.

Walker, K., MacBride, A., & Vachon, M. (1977). Social support networks and the crisis of bereavement. *Social Science and Medicine, 11*, 35–41.

Wallston, B. S., Alagna, S. W., DeVellis, B. M., & DeVellis, R. F. (1983). Social support and physical health. *Health Psychology, 2*, 367–391.

Wills, T. A. (1985). Supportive functions of interpersonal relationships. In S. Cohen and S. L. Syme (Eds.), *Social support and health* (pp. 61–82). New York: Academic Press.

Wills, T. A., Weiss, R. L., & Patterson, G. R. (1974). A behavioral analysis of determinants of marital satisfaction. *Journal of Consulting and Clinical Psychology, 42*, 802–811.

Wortman, C. B., & Dunkel-Schetter, C. (1979). Interpersonal relationships and cancer: A theoretical analysis. *Journal of Social Issues, 35*, 120–155.

5

Cognitive Appraisals, Coping Processes, and Adjustment to Infertility

ANNETTE L. STANTON

How does one cope with the demands of infertility? This chapter centers on a study of coping in infertile couples. Personal accounts of study participants and quantitative data are used to provide a rich portrait of the issues involved. Participants' responses reveal the remarkable diversity of coping methods initiated by those who carry this diagnosis:

> When the pregnancy test comes back negative, I laugh it off. I eat more pizza, do more work, and refuse to look at babies.

> I try to keep my emotions under control and instead just take it one day at a time. Right now we're waiting to see if this new medication works. Then we'll talk about the next step.

> I shout and cry and try to get my emotions out. I hit walls and pillows. I talk and talk and talk. If I don't express it, I'll go crazy.

As these examples illustrate, coping strategies range from restraint to expression, from active avoidance to active problem-solving. Are some of these coping skills more effective than others in managing the emotional, behavioral, and cognitive hurdles of infertility? Drawing primarily from their personal experience of infertility or work with infertile couples, writers have suggested a variety of methods to help couples coping with

ANNETTE L. STANTON • Department of Psychology, University of Kansas, Lawrence, Kansas 66045-2160.

infertility. Such recommendations include heightening feelings of control (Cook, 1987; Shapiro, 1988; Stephenson, 1987), working through the grief process (Mahlstedt, 1985; Menning, 1980), and maintaining supportive relationships (Domar & Seibel, 1990; Valentine, 1986). Although much has been written to aid infertile couples, researchers have directed very little systematic study toward understanding what couples actually do to cope with infertility and whether these strategies serve to enhance or impede emotional adjustment. By examining these coping processes, as is the goal of this chapter, we may contribute to the empirical base for clinical intervention with infertile couples. In turn, such study may enrich the knowledge base regarding coping with stressful encounters in general.

A THEORETICAL FRAMEWORK FOR STUDYING COPING PROCESSES IN INFERTILITY

Although the process of coping with infertility has received little systematic investigation, a rich theoretical and empirical base from the stress and coping literature is available to guide such inquiry. Perhaps the theoretical framework of Lazarus and Folkman (1984; Lazarus, 1966) has received the greatest attention in recent years. Their cognitive-phenomenological theory of stress, which underlies the work discussed in this chapter, has generated a substantial body of research on individuals coping with such diverse experiences as college examinations (Folkman & Lazarus, 1985), dual-earner life-styles (Alpert & Culbertson, 1987), and chronic illnesses (Felton, Revenson, & Hinrichsen, 1984). In this framework, infertility might be conceptualized as a stressful experience, a "relationship between the person and the environment that is appraised by the person as taxing or exceeding his or her resources and endangering his or her well-being" (Lazarus & Folkman, 1984, p. 19). This definition of stress, in which one's appraisal of an experience is central, applies particularly well to the experience of infertility. If parenthood is not an important goal, then infertility might carry few negative consequences and thus not be perceived as particularly stressful (see Clark et al., this volume). However, if one feels that a major life objective will be thwarted by the incapacity to bear children and sees no ready solution, then infertility may be quite stressful. It is these infertile individuals who may be at risk for negative emotional outcomes.

The Process of Cognitive Appraisal

According to Lazarus and Folkman (1984), negative consequences of stressful encounters in realms such as morale, interpersonal functioning, and physical health may be predicted by two central processes: cognitive appraisal and coping. When confronting a stressful situation, individuals initiate two component cognitive appraisal processes, which allow them to assess the situation with respect to its significance for well-being. Primary appraisal addresses the question, "What is at stake in this encounter?" Thus, the infertile person would be expected to evaluate the nature and magnitude of threats and challenges that accompany infertility. For example, to what extent does infertility threaten an important life goal, self-esteem, or financial security? Further, does infertility provide the opportunity for personal growth or for strengthening the marital bond? Infertile individuals in our research commented on the threats and challenges associated with infertility:

> Infertility is a threat to just about all of my beliefs. I used to believe that if you worked hard, good things would happen. I used to think that I had my life under control. I thought that life was fair. Now I'm up in the air about all that.

> I think some good things will come of all this. I'm starting to learn how strong our marriage is. Whatever happens, we'll be able to say that we got through it together.

Those who appraise infertility as carrying a high potential for harm or little potential for benefit might be particularly likely to experience distress.

In secondary appraisal, the individual poses the question "What, if anything, can I do about it?". The psychological literature reveals consistently that appraising a threatening encounter as unchangeable or uncontrollable impedes adjustment (Folkman, Lazarus, Dunkel-Schetter, DeLongis, & Gruen, 1986a; Taylor, Lichtman, & Wood, 1984). In infertility, the couple experiences a loss of control in an arena typically assumed to be controllable (i.e., the ability to bear children). Many writers (e.g., Cook, 1987; Mahlstedt, 1985) suggest that distress is a likely result. Thus, the conclusions the infertile individual reaches during the appraisal process would be expected to contribute to his or her psychological adjustment.

The Process of Coping

Coping processes comprise a second set of factors that may promote or hinder positive adjustment to infertility. Lazarus and Folkman (1984) defined coping as one's "constantly changing cognitive and behavioral efforts to manage specific external and/or internal demands that are appraised as taxing or exceeding the person's resources" (p. 141). Arguing that coping is multidimensional and at least in part situation-specific, they developed the Ways of Coping Questionnaire (Folkman & Lazarus, 1980; Folkman et al., 1986a; Lazarus & Folkman, 1984) to assess both problem-focused and emotion-focused coping efforts. Problem-focused coping efforts reflect attempts to change the problem itself. As one research participant commented:

> We take it step by step and talk about every possibility. We keep on with the next test, the next treatment. Knowing that we're doing everything we can is reassuring.

On the other hand, strategies such as avoidance and positive reappraisal represent attempts to regulate emotion. Infertile individuals also made use of these coping strategies:

> The hardest time for me to cope is going to the doctor's and seeing so many pregnant women. I literally bite my tongue, close my eyes, and wait to hear my name called. I just want to block it all out.

> I focus on something wonderful that I can do outside of parenting—traveling, going back to school, fulfilling myself in some other way.

Are particular coping strategies linked to better adjustment in stressful situations? Lazarus and Folkman argue that coping strategies are neither inherently adaptive nor maladaptive (Folkman & Lazarus, 1988; Lazarus & Folkman, 1984). For example, planful problem-solving, which often has been deemed an effective coping strategy, may in fact be counterproductive when used in situations that provide little opportunity for control. Similarly, avoidance strategies may be effective when one is confronting a short-term, uncontrollable stressor, whereas approach strategies may be more productive in stressful situations that are chronic or controllable (Roth & Cohen, 1986; Suls & Fletcher, 1985).

The match, then, between specific coping strategies and particular situational parameters may be important in determining adjustment during a negative encounter. An alternative possibility is that particular coping strategies may be maladaptive, regardless of the nature of the experience. Carver, Scheier, and Weintraub (1989) suggest that some coping strategies, such as venting emotion and behavioral disengagement, may be ineffective in modulating distress in a variety of situations.

Which of these possibilities is more likely for coping and adjustment in infertility? Infertility is often both chronic and uncontrollable, in that couples may for many years attempt to have a child and the desired outcome—parenthood—is not completely under couples' control, even if they pursue all available options. Both problem-solving and emotion-focused coping may be effective in managing such an experience. Problem-solving coping may aid the couple as they pursue an often lengthy course of diagnostic and treatment procedures, while emotion-focused coping may palliate the resultant distress and perceived lack of control. A primary goal of the research reported here is to explore the associations between coping strategies and psychological adjustment in infertile individuals.

The Interpersonal Context of Appraisal, Coping, and Adjustment

The involvement of intimate partners in the infertility experience provides the opportunity to extend the study of coping and adjustment to couples. Do infertile partners differ in their cognitive appraisals, coping processes, or psychological adjustment? Many who work clinically with infertile couples suggest that males and females use different coping strategies. For example, Mahlstedt (1985) observed:

> Men, for example, often cope with their pain by keeping it to themselves and focusing on their wives. Women often cope by talking continually about their pain with their husbands, who, feeling powerless to take away the pain, sometimes stop listening. In order to get him involved, she escalates her complaints and he, in response, retreats even further and may even cease participating in the treatment process. In these cases, the woman feels abandoned when she needs her husband most, and he feels overwhelmed because she needs him so much. (p. 337)

As this example illustrates, differences between partners in coping strategies or in reactions to infertility may carry implications for the well-being of and clinical intervention with infertile couples. In addition to actual differences in coping, partners' percepts of one another may be important in determining their interactions. This raises the question of whether infertile individuals think that males and females cope differently. By fostering a belief that one's partner would not understand one's own experience of infertility, the perception that few commonalities exist between males and females in coping with infertility may impair partners' communication.

Only by understanding both the intrapersonal and interpersonal contexts of appraising and coping with infertility can we effectively aid the infertile couple who is negotiating this process. Moreover, in-depth study of coping with infertility may further our understanding of coping with chronic, uncontrollable stressors in general. The study reported here provides a first step toward those goals.

AN INVESTIGATION OF COGNITIVE APPRAISALS, COPING PROCESSES, AND ADJUSTMENT IN INFERTILE COUPLES

The Research Context

This study of cognitive appraisal, coping processes, and adjustment to infertility began with the recruitment of 52 men and 61 women, including 52 married couples and 9 females whose partners chose not to participate. All were recruited through a five-physician obstetrics and gynecology practice located in a Southeastern university community. Couples who met study criteria of being age 20 to 45, being childless, and attempting pregnancy for at least 12 months without conception were identified through a medical record search and were sent a brief description of the study by their physicians. Interested individuals responded by mail (response rate = 65%) and were contacted to schedule participation. Subjects completed mailed questionnaires and returned them at the time of the structured interview. Different trained interviewers conducted separate interviews lasting approximately 90 minutes with each partner.

On the average, participants had been married for seven years and had been attempting pregnancy for four years (range = 1–10 years). Average age was 31 years for females and 33 for males. Ninety percent of the sample was Caucasian and 10% was black. The majority had some college education, and average yearly family income was $39,000. As gathered from medical records, diagnosed causes for infertility were: 13% male factor, 43% female factor, 20% combined male-female causation, and 24% undiagnosed cause. This represents a somewhat lower proportion of male factor infertility than appears to exist in the general infertile population (Benson, 1983) and may reflect recruitment from a gynecology practice. Preliminary analyses were conducted to determine whether appraisal, coping, or distress varied as a function of locus of diagnosed cause of infertility or of years attempting conception. This was not found to be the case, and thus subsequent analyses did not include these factors.

Measures fell into three domains: cognitive appraisal, coping processes, and psychological adjustment. The measures, along with sample items, are listed in Table 1. Two scales regarding primary cognitive appraisal were developed, assessing Threat and Challenge appraisals. Participants rated Threat appraisals on 5-point scales, indicating the extent to which their infertility had the potential for harm to such areas as important life goals and health (Cronbach α = .82). Items measuring Challenge asked subjects to what extent their infertility provided the potential for personal growth, a personal challenge, or the strengthening of a relationship (α = .76). Secondary cognitive appraisal was assessed with items measuring the perception of personal control over the course of and alternatives to infertility (α = .64).

Coping was assessed with the revised 66-item Ways of Coping Questionnaire (WOC; Folkman et al., 1986a; Lazarus & Folkman, 1984), which describes strategies that people may use to manage the demands of a stressful encounter. Respondents referred to their experience with infertility in completing the questionnaire. Eight subscales were derived, reflecting those found by Folkman et al. (1986a) in factor analyses of the questionnaire as completed by a sample of married couples: confrontive

Table 1. Questionnaires and Sample Items for Cognitive Appraisal, Coping Processes, and Adjustment

Construct and measure	Number of items	Sample items
Cognitive appraisal		
Threat	7	To what extent do you think your difficulty conceiving could threaten your financial security?
Challenge	3	To what extent do you think your difficulty conceiving could provide the potential for strengthening a relationship?
Perceived control	4	How much control do you feel you have over the course of your infertility?
Coping—Ways of coping		
Confrontive coping	6	Stood my ground and fought for what I wanted.
Distancing	6	Went on as if nothing had happened.
Self-controlling	7	I tried to keep my feelings to myself.
Seek social support	6	Talked to someone about how I was feeling.
Accept responsibility	4	Realized I brought the problem on myself.
Escape-avoidance	8	Hoped a miracle would happen.
Planful problem-solving	6	I made a plan of action and followed it.
Positive reappraisal	7	Changed or grew as a person in a good way.
Distress		
POMS total	65	Tense, angry, unhappy, blue, anxious
SCLGSI	90	Feeling lonely, trouble concentrating
Infertility distress	29	Empty, punished, disappointed, guilty
Well-being		
Index of well-being	9	Boring-interesting; Useless-worthwhile
Infertility well-being	27	Hopeful, calm, competent, confident

coping, distancing, self-control, seeking social support, accepting responsibility, escape-avoidance, planful problem-solving, and positive reappraisal. Several other interview questions regarded coping processes, and these are described in the pertinent sections that follow.

Measures of both distress and well-being were used to indicate psychological adjustment. Aldwin and Revenson (1987) pointed to the need for more research on positive adjustment to stress and found that positive and negative affect were linked to different forms of cognitive appraisal and coping in chronically ill adults (Felton *et al.*, 1984). In addition, both global and infertility-specific adjustment were assessed. Global distress was assessed with summary scales of two standardized measures of demonstrated reliability and validity: the Global Severity Index (GSI; i.e., an average of the summed 90 items) of the revised Symptom Checklist-90 (SCL-90-R; Derogatis, 1977) and the total score (weighting the Vigor subscale negatively) of the Profile of Mood States (POMS; McNair, Lorr, & Droppleman, 1971). On an author-constructed Infertility-Specific Distress scale, subjects indicated on 5-point scales how descriptive each item was of their feelings about infertility (α = .94). Global well-being was assessed with the Campbell, Converse, and Rodgers' (1976) Index of Well-Being, consisting of semantic differential items on which subjects are asked to describe their "present life." The Infertility-Specific Well-Being scale (α = .93) was comprised of 5-point scales regarding positive feelings about infertility. Items for the Infertility-Specific Distress and Well-Being scales were gleaned from pilot work in which infertile individuals provided positive and negative descriptors of their experience with infertility.

Correlations computed separately for males and females among the three distress measures ranged from .40 to .86 and between the two well-being scales from .21 to .25. All five scales were used for descriptive analyses. However, preliminary analyses conducted to examine the relations of appraisal and coping with adjustment indicated that findings were similar across the sets of distress and of well-being indices. For ease of explication in those analyses, scores in each of the two sets were standardized and summed to create one distress and one well-being index.

What Is the Interpersonal Context of Coping with Infertility?

Many researchers have suggested that infertility is more involving and distressing for women than for men (e.g., Greil, Leitko, & Porter, 1988; McEwan, Costello, & Taylor, 1987). If so, we might expect that, relative to their husbands, women would perceive infertility as more threatening, less challenging, and less controllable. Do infertile male and female partners differ on these cognitive appraisals? Descriptive statistics and multivariate and univariate comparisons for the sample of 52 couples are presented in Table 2. For these and all other results, a finding was considered statistically significant if p < .05.

Husbands and wives in this study did not differ in their perceptions of challenge, threat, and control connected with their infertility. Rather, women and men appraised infertility as potentially yielding both harm and benefit, a finding that also emerges in the general literature on appraisal of stressful experiences (Folkman & Lazarus, 1985). In general, participants felt relatively little control over their fertility problem, as indicated by average scores that fell below the midpoint on each control item. This result is consistent with the suggestion of clinical writers that couples often appraise their infertility as uncontrollable (Cook, 1987; Mahlstedt, 1985).

How did partners cope with their infertility? Consistent with research on coping with other stressful encounters (Folkman & Lazarus, 1980; Folkman & Lazarus, 1985), participants coped in many ways, with 83% of males and 93% of females using at least seven of the eight coping strategies. Couples differed in their use of coping strategies, with wives using more avoidance and social support than did their husbands. These results are consistent with the findings of others. Draye, Woods, and Mitchell (1988) found that women used more avoidance than men in coping with infertility. Further, Affleck, Tennen, and Rowe (1990) found that wives engaged in greater avoidance and sought more social support than hus-

Table 2. Descriptive Statistics and Tests of Differences between Partners on Cognitive Appraisals, Coping Processes, and Adjustment

Construct and measure	Males		Females		Dependent t
	M	SD	M	SD	
Cognitive appraisal—Hotelling's $T^2(3,43) = 1.46$					
Threat	2.12	1.22	2.54	1.31	1.67
Challenge	4.18	1.72	4.51	1.72	1.58
Perceived control	0.00	2.63	0.00	2.81	−0.09
Coping process–Hotelling's $T^2(8,42) = 4.97^{***}$					
Confrontive coping	0.66	0.46	0.68	0.49	0.14
Distancing	0.88	0.43	0.95	0.56	−0.11
Self-controlling	1.12	0.59	1.09	0.56	−0.55
Seek social support	0.95	0.75	1.27	0.73	2.24*
Accepting responsibility	0.58	0.53	0.49	0.60	−0.32
Escape-avoidance	0.62	0.40	0.82	0.42	2.27*
Planful problem-solving	1.25	0.66	1.05	0.58	−1.87
Positive reappraisal	1.06	0.68	1.19	0.63	1.15
Distress—Hotelling's $T^2(3,46) = 6.09^{**}$					
POMS total	62.33	32.67	63.20	36.28	0.11
SCLGSI	0.50	0.48	0.55	0.40	0.68
Infertility distress	1.59	0.57	2.07	0.78	3.57**
Well-being—Hotelling's $T^2(2,46) = 2.20$					
Index of well-being	11.06	2.02	10.93	2.10	−0.04
Infertility well-being	2.53	0.78	2.31	0.89	−2.10*

*$p < .05$. **$p < .005$. ***$p < .0005$.

bands in coping with a child's hospital intensive care experience, and Belle (1987) concluded in her review regarding gender and social support that "Throughout the life cycle, females show a greater propensity to mobilize social supports in times of stress" (p. 261).

Both actual and perceived gender differences in coping might influence partners' negotiation of the infertility process. What are participants' *perceptions* of how coping processes differ for females and males? When asked whether they thought males and females cope with infertility about the same or a little, somewhat, or much differently, 81% of men and 95% of women believed that the sexes cope differently. Only 19% of males and 5% of females believed that the sexes cope in about the same way. Compared with their spouses, females were more likely to perceive gender differences in coping, $t(45) = 3.09, p < .005$. These perceptions did not vary as a function of diagnosed cause of infertility. When subjects who cited a difference were asked how males and females might differ, open-ended responses fell into two major categories. Participants believed that men and women differ in either their emotional experience of or in their expression of distress regarding infertility. Thus, 63% of men and 40% of women reported that infertility is more distressing for women than for men and that coping consequently is a more difficult task for them. Twenty-one percent of men and 43% of women thought that although infertility is equally distressing for men and women, women are more likely to cope through emotional expression.

Are women actually more distressed about their infertility than husbands, as many participants suggested? Infertility-specific distress was greater for wives than husbands, and well-being surrounding infertility was lower. That females may be more engaged in the experience also is supported by the finding that females reported thinking about infertility six days a week and males four days, on the average, $t(46) = 3.09, p < .005$. Further, females were more likely than their partners to feel that infertility dominated their lives, $t(44) = 6.35, p < .0001$.

Infertile partners did not differ on global distress and well-being, however. In general, global distress was higher for this sample than for normative adult comparison groups. Compared to a nonpatient norm group (Derogatis, 1977), 35% of the males and 39% of the females obtained scores that were greater than one standard deviation above the mean (T > 60) on the GSI of the SCL-90-R. Assuming that these scores are normally distributed, only 16% would exceed this same value in the norm group. Infertile subjects' means on the POMS also were substantially higher than a group of male ($M = 41$) and female ($M = 45$) college students (McNair *et al.*, 1971). Scores on the Index of Well-Being were slightly but not remarkably lower than the mean of 11.77 found by Campbell *et al.* (1976) in a national adult sample.

In sum, partners did not differ in their appraisals of infertility. However, some differences emerged in partners' mechanisms for coping with the problem, and most participants were of the opinion that substantial gender differences exist in coping with infertility. Participants evidenced more global distress than would be expected in a general adult sample, although general well-being was comparable. Women acknowledged more distress specific to infertility than did their partners. However, greater distress surrounding infertility did not translate into greater general emotional distress for women than for men.

Are Cognitive Appraisals and Coping Processes Related to Adjustment?

Clearly, some infertile participants were quite distressed. Which cognitive appraisal and coping processes might help or hinder adjustment for those experiencing infertility? Because partners' data were not statistically independent, correlations among appraisal, coping, and adjustment variables were computed separately for the full samples of males and females, and these are displayed in Table 3. It was predicted that those who perceived infertility as highly threatening, as carrying little potential benefit, and as relatively uncontrollable would evidence more distress and lower well-being. Findings for primary appraisal revealed that when infertility was perceived as a greater threat, females reported more distress and males lower well-being. When greater potential benefits were thought to result from the infertility experience, females reported greater well-being and males less distress. Significant associations between secondary appraisal and adjustment also emerged. Both females and males who felt greater control over the course of their fertility problem evidenced higher well-being, and women also reported less distress. Thus, predictions regarding the associations of appraisal and adjustment received support, although the obtained results were somewhat inconsistent across different adjustment measures.

No previous literature served as a guide for postulating adaptive coping mechanisms for the specific experience of infertility. Consequently, no hypotheses were advanced concerning the associations between particular coping strategies and adjustment. Table 3 reveals that, in general, coping mechanisms were related differentially to distress and well-being. Both females and males who coped through avoidance evidenced more distress. In addition, males who used confrontive and self-controlling coping were more distressed, as were females who accepted responsibility for their fertility problem. Both females and males who used positive reappraisal reported greater well-being. Additionally, self-controlling coping was associated negatively with well-being for males, and planful problem-

Table 3. Correlations of Cognitive Appraisals, Coping Processes,
and Psychological Adjustment for Infertile Males and Females

Construct and measure	Distress index		Well-being index	
	Males	Females	Males	Females
Cognitive appraisal				
Threat	−.04	.34*	−.33*	−.12
Challenge	−.30*	−.10	.25	.34*
Perceived control	−.09	−.31*	.38*	.30*
Coping process				
Confrontive coping	.52***	.09	−.19	.07
Distancing	.18	−.13	.18	.14
Self-controlling	.41**	−.03	−.31*	.24
Seek social support	.09	−.20	.19	.38**
Accept responsibility	.23	.53***	−.09	−.15
Escape /avoidance	.28*	.34*	−.22	−.12
Planful problem-solving	.23	−.12	.01	.40**
Positive reappraisal	−.02	−.20	.38*	.47***

$^*p < .05.$ $^{**}p < .005.$ $^{***}p < .0005.$

solving and seeking social support were positively related to well-being for females.

Which appraisal and coping variables are the strongest predictors of adjustment? When the three appraisal variables and the set of four coping variables that were correlated significantly with distress were entered as predictors in multiple regression equations, they accounted for 45% of the variance in distress for males and 52% for females. When the other predictors in these equations were controlled statistically (i.e., semi-partial correlations were computed), it was found that confrontive coping was the most powerful predictor of distress for males, whereas low appraisal of control and coping through accepting responsibility were the unique predictors of distress for females. Analogous analyses conducted on the well-being index revealed that the appraisal and coping variables accounted for 47% of the variance in well-being for males and 36% for females. Well-being was best predicted by low perceived threat from infertility for males and coping through positive reappraisal for females.

Did the appraisal, coping, or adjustment of one partner predict the other's adjustment? Correlations computed for husband-wife pairs revealed that the only variable of one spouse found to be related to the other's adjustment was coping through seeking social support. As wives sought more social support, their husbands reported less distress ($r = −.30$).

IMPLICATIONS OF THE PRESENT FINDINGS

Implications for Theory and Research

Commonalities in Appraisal, Coping, and Adjustment Processes across Stressful Encounters. A first theoretical implication arising from this study is that commonalities exist between the process of coping with infertility and with other experiences. In general, those who encounter stressful circumstances see the potential for both harm and benefit and initiate a variety of coping methods in attempting to manage the encounter, and the experience of infertility provides no exception. Further, commonalities emerge in the findings regarding relations of cognitive appraisal, coping processes, and distress. With regard to results that emerged for both males and females, avoidance coping was found to be related to distress. This finding is common to other studies of coping with chronic illness (Felton, *et al.*, 1984; for the wish-fulfilling fantasy component of avoidance) and recent stressful life events (Cronkite & Moos, 1984; Folkman, Lazarus, Gruen, & DeLongis, 1986b). Cronkite and Moos (1984) found in a longitudinal study that avoidance coping strengthened the relation between stress and subsequent illness. This finding provides particularly strong evidence for the deleterious consequences of avoidance coping over the long run.

Why is avoidance coping problematic for infertile individuals? Perhaps avoidance impedes the grief process, an experience that some suggest is necessary for successful adjustment to infertility (Menning, 1980). Another possibility is that the individual avoids thoughts of infertility by engaging in such behaviors as binge-eating or drinking alcohol, thus creating additional difficulties. Further, the individual is likely to confront constant reminders of infertility through medical treatment and contact with others. Attempts to avoid these reminders might engender increasingly greater restriction of activity, thereby limiting opportunities for rewarding experiences. These and other mechanisms by which avoidance may engender distress deserve continued study.

Fewer studies have examined the relations of appraisal and coping with well-being. However, evidence from this and other studies reveals that greater perceived control over a stressor (or seeing the stressor as changeable) is associated with encounter outcomes that are perceived as more satisfactory (Folkman *et al.*, 1986a) and with better adjustment (Taylor *et al.*, 1984). In addition, this and other studies (Felton *et al.*, 1984; Folkman & Lazarus, 1988) have shown that those who cope through positive reappraisal or related methods experience greater well-being.

Clearly, this study and the evidence to date suggest that positive and negative affect comprise independent dimensions (Diener & Emmons, 1984; Watson & Tellegen, 1985) and that these are related to different coping mechanisms (Felton *et al.*, 1984). Most often, studies of adjustment to stressful experiences focus on distress. As many theorists have suggested, we may learn little about effective coping from such investigation. This study provides an empirical illustration of this point, because the coping mechanisms that related to well-being would have been neglected had distress been the only variable to be assessed. For example, seeking social support, planful problem-solving, and positive reappraisal were related to women's well-being but were not related significantly to distress. By contrast, accepting responsibility and avoidance were related to women's distress, but not to their well-being. These data suggest that more active and engaged strategies, whether behavioral or cognitive, might facilitate well-being, whereas passive or disengaged approaches might engender distress. However, the relation between the active strategy of confrontive coping and distress for males provides an exception to this suggestion. Certainly, if the goal is to understand both the mechanisms that ameliorate distress and facilitate well-being, these data and those of others (Campbell *et al.*, this volume) suggest that both must be studied.

Implications of Studying the Experience of Marital Partners. Few studies have examined couples who are coping with the same stressful encounter. Rather, most of the studies that have sampled married couples (e.g., Cronkite & Moos, 1984; Folkman & Lazarus, 1988) have not requested that their respondents refer to the same stressful experience (see Affleck *et al.*, 1990, for an exception). The shared nature of the infertility experience allows extension of stress and coping frameworks to the marital dyad. First, it was found that infertility engendered similar appraisals of threat, challenge, and control in partners. However, coping processes differed somewhat, with women more likely to cope through avoidance and seeking social support than their partners. As with the commonalities cited above, these obtained differences are not specific to coping with infertility (Affleck *et al.*, 1990; Belle, 1987; Billings & Moos, 1981; Stone & Neale, 1984), but rather apply to gender differences in coping with other events as well. These findings have been obtained both when individuals are coping with the same and with different events, suggesting that they may reflect relatively stable gender differences in coping. The absolute magnitudes of these differences were not very great, however, and consequences of the differences for theories of coping require further study. Further, males were not more likely to use problem-solving (cf. Miller & Kirsch, 1987), and no significant differences emerged on the remaining six of eight coping scales. Thus, although some differences were obtained, gender similarities may be more the rule than gender differences in coping with infertility.[1]

The finding that women reported greater infertility-specific distress than men is consistent with qualitative observation (e.g., Greil *et al.*, 1988) and with some of the empirical research (e.g., McEwan *et al.*, 1987). Indeed, Greil *et al.* (1988) suggested that infertile females experienced infertility as a "cataclysmic role failure," whereas their husbands viewed infertility as "a disconcerting event but not as a tragedy" (p. 172). Why were women more likely to report distress regarding infertility? One plausible interpretation of this difference is that particular consequences of infertility may have more impact on women than men, on the average. Several writers have suggested that parenthood is a more central role for women (e.g., Greenglass, 1982), and hence the potential loss of this option may be more disruptive for them. Anecdotally, although no males mentioned changing their professions as a result of infertility, several women revealed that they originally had intended their primary career to be motherhood, but had changed occupational plans upon experiencing infertility. Infertility, then, may lead some women to reorganize their role structure (Matthews & Matthews, 1986), potentially resulting in distress. Further, if the "motherhood mandate," as coined by Russo (1976), remains intact, many women may believe that they are somehow inadequate as women if they cannot have children and hence may experience more negative emotions. In addition, women often carry the physical burdens of infertility, in that they are more likely to report initiating diagnostic and treatment procedures (Draye *et al.*, 1988; Greil *et al.*, 1988), to have a greater number of these procedures available to them, and to monitor their own bodies for signs of pregnancy.

Several other potential explanations arise for the obtained gender difference. First, the possibility that the finding resulted from the relatively high proportion of female-factor infertility patients in this sample was not supported empirically. Distress did not vary as a function of diagnosed cause of infertility, although this possibility deserves further exploration with a larger subject sample. Second, rather than reflecting an actual difference in experience, perhaps men are simply less willing to admit to negative emotions concerning infertility. However, they were not less willing to acknowledge *global* distress, suggesting that this was not a general

---

[1]We recently (Stanton, Tennen, Affleck, & Mendola, in press) have found that, when a relative scoring method is used rather than employing raw coping scores, husbands and wives differed on five of eight coping scales in a study combining two samples. In addition to wives engaging in more avoidance and seeking social support than husbands, husbands used more distancing, self-controlling coping, and planful problem-solving than their wives.

tendency for males in this study. To be plausible, this interpretation would require that specific characteristics of the infertility experience (e.g., threat to manhood) would create males' unwillingness to report distress. For example, infertility may be a more stigmatizing condition for men than women (Miall, 1986), rendering men more likely to conceal their status and reactions to it. An alternative, although not incompatible, interpretation is that this finding may reflect the tendency of women in general to appraise negative events as more stressful than do men (Kessler & McLeod, 1984; Miller & Kirsch, 1987). This issue might be addressed by assessing both infertility-specific distress and distress connected with an infertility-irrelevant event in infertile couples to test whether the difference emerges across events.

In sum, the most plausible explanation for the gender difference in infertility-specific distress may involve the greater centrality of parenthood to women's role structure, but further study of this and competing hypotheses is warranted. It is important to note that the difference in infertility-specific distress was not accompanied by greater global distress for wives. Both women and men evidenced higher levels of global distress than norm groups, but general life satisfaction was not markedly lower. These data suggest that many infertile couples maintain rewarding life-styles even in the face of a very emotionally distressing experience.

A final obtained difference is that adjustment was best predicted by different variables for men and women. Confrontive coping best predicted distress for men, whereas low perceived control over infertility and coping through accepting responsibility were unique predictors of distress for women. Well-being was best predicted by low perceived threat from infertility for males and coping through positive reappraisal for females. Confrontive coping has been found in other studies to predict distress (e.g., Folkman & Lazarus, 1988) and has been suggested to reflect unskillful forms of confrontation (Folkman et al., 1986a). Indeed, some of the items on that scale have an impulsive quality ("I did something which I didn't think would work, but at least I was doing something"), and others include a blaming component (e.g., "I expressed anger to the person(s) who caused the problem").

By contrast, the most distressed women coped through *assuming* the blame for infertility. McEwan et al. (1987) also obtained this finding, and several studies reveal that women are likely to attribute infertility to themselves even when the diagnosis is unknown (Draye et al., 1988; McEwan et al., 1987) or when there is male factor infertility (Greil et al., 1988; McEwan et al., 1987; Tennen et al., this volume). Perhaps as Tennen et al. suggest, this self-blame reflects a spouse-protecting function. Such caretaking responsibilities certainly may exact an emotional cost (Kessler & McLeod,

1984; Solomon & Rothblum, 1986). In addition, because women typically are expected to shoulder the reproductive responsibilities in intimate relationships (Greenglass, 1982), infertile women who strongly internalize this gender role expectation may cope through accepting responsibility and attempt to protect their partners from assuming it. Thus, strong conformity to social role expectations may lead one to select particular coping mechanisms, which in turn may produce distress. Interestingly, men who initiated confrontive coping also may have been responding to a culturally based expectation for masculine aggressiveness in managing problems. Whether coping mediates a relationship between gender role conformity and distress in infertility is a question for further study.

Study Limitations and Suggestions for Future Research. A first limitation of the present study regards generalizability of results. These infertile subjects were primarily from the middle socioeconomic class, had been attempting conception for four years, on the average, and had somewhat more female factor infertility than generally would be expected. Generalizability of these results to a broader range of infertile couples requires study. In addition, the traditional level of statistical significance ($p < .05$) was selected so that power would be sufficient to yield significance when moderate relationships ($r = .30$) were obtained. However, because some significant relations may have emerged by chance, replication with other samples also is essential. Second, this study design was neither longitudinal nor experimental. Thus, causal statements are not warranted. For example, avoidance-coping might produce distress. However, that greater distress stimulates attempts to avoid such distress also is plausible, and reciprocal causation is likely. Longitudinal studies conducted with couples who are just beginning to attempt conception, as well as carefully designed intervention studies that target coping processes in infertile couples, are necessary.

Third, as do the great majority of studies on coping with negative events, the present study relied on self-report measures. Although some respondents may have presented themselves in a favorable light, the observation that individuals often shared highly personal and painful information suggests that a social desirability motive was not strong. Nonetheless, although self-report is not necessarily more fallible than other assessment methods, the coping literature would benefit from the use of additional methods to assess the processes involved. For example, during a specific stressful encounter (e.g., *in vitro* fertilization), infertile couples might be requested to monitor their thoughts and behaviors each day, and these records could be coded by observers trained to classify appraisal, coping, and adjustment indicators. Physiological and behavioral indicants of distress also could be gathered during visits to the physician's office. However, given this study's results, one should note that observational methods may be biased by observers' strong beliefs regarding gender differences in coping.

A final suggestion is that continued study is warranted to identify the specific adaptive tasks associated with infertility. In this study, individuals reflected upon their infertility experience in general, but one cannot assume that infertility is a unitary stressor. Rather, for some, the primary adaptive task of infertility may be to make sense of an unexpected assault on their belief in the fairness of life, whereas others may struggle with interpersonal negotiations accompanying infertility. These challenges may require different sets of coping strategies for resolution. In addition, unique coping demands may arise during different points in the process. A problem-focused coping approach may be most adaptive when preparing to undertake a new treatment procedure, for example, but an emotion-focused strategy may be helpful when a negative pregnancy test result is received. The question, "With what must infertile individuals cope, and what coping strategies best address each task?" requires continued investigation.

Implications for Infertile Couples and Health Care Providers

This study provides a "snapshot" of coping from individuals who had been attempting conception for some time and who had sought treatment for their difficulty. Recommendations for the infertile couple and those who work with them must be tempered by an acknowledgment that the effectiveness of one's coping efforts may vary as a function of the problem's chronicity and of individual differences in the salience of various adaptive tasks posed by infertility. Thus, the couple and the health care provider must evaluate carefully the applicability of the present findings to the specific couple's situation.

One finding relevant to infertile couples is the demonstration that most participants believed that men and women cope in different ways with infertility. If this belief translates into an expectation for one's partner's coping and emotional expression, then partners may magnify differences between themselves and neglect similarities in their attempts to cope with the demands of infertility. The consequence may be an emotional gulf between partners when both actually are seeking intimacy.

Of course, real differences may occur between partners in their approaches to infertility. For example, compared with their husbands, women may express more distress about the fertility problem. How these differences are evaluated and managed has import for well-being. Consider a scenario in which Brian engages in self-controlling coping to manage his feelings about infertility, and Shelley copes through expressing her distress. Brian believes that Shelley is overreacting and feels helpless to palliate her distress, while Shelley feels that Brian's approach is insensitive and uncaring. Both members of this couple see their own approach as "right," and their partner's as "wrong," or, at least, as misguided. Perhaps if this couple could view variations in their coping strategies as differences rather than deficits, then they could go on to evaluate how best to meet each other's needs rather than remaining "stuck" in comparative evaluations.

Similarly, recommendations by professionals for particular "adaptive" coping strategies must be offered with care. The present findings might lead to the conclusion that professionals should enhance perceptions of control, discourage avoidance, and promote positive reappraisal of infertility. However, adaptive coping in a naturalistic encounter must be distinguished from therapeutic prescription of such coping. Thus, a self-generated focus on positive consequences of infertility may facilitate adjustment in infertile couples, whereas encouragement by clinicians or others to "look on the bright side" may have little effect or may even provoke anger. Empirical determination of the most effective therapeutic strategies with distressed infertile couples is essential.

Finally, just as researchers have focused on maladjustment, couples and clinicians may focus too often on distress, as well. Consideration of means by which to enhance well-being may be equally or more helpful. This is not to suggest that couples should attempt to deny that infertility is distressing, but rather that this should not preclude a search for positive identities and activities. The couples in the present study demonstrated that distress and well-being can co-occur, many commenting that infertility had brought them intimacy, humor, and strength, as well as pain. As one study participant commented:

> We walked into an infertility support group at the same time that all these pregnant people were carrying their pillows and babies into their Lamaze class. I laughed at the coincidence and felt like crying at the loss. Then I went into my group and bitched about it. And I came out more okay, stronger.

Such emotional balance may comprise an optimal goal of coping. As Stephenson (1987) summarized her experience of coping with infertility:

> Coping isn't asking us to be jump-up-and-down happy with our situation. Coping will probably not even alleviate all the pain and sadness. But what it will do is give us back our lives. And that's no small thing. There really is much that is ours to control. And if our coping attempts do nothing else but teach us that, it's worth the effort.

In turn, we believe that researchers and health care providers who attempt to understand and aid infertile couples in their coping attempts also will find their efforts worthwhile.

ACKNOWLEDGMENTS

I gratefully acknowledge the help of Dr. Joel Pittard, Lee Obstetrics and Gynecology, and the clinical interviewers, as well as the couples who so willingly shared their experiences. The study discussed in this chapter was funded in part by the Auburn University Faculty Grant Program.

REFERENCES

Affleck, G., Tennen, H., & Rowe, J. (1990). Mothers, fathers, and the crisis of newborn intensive care. *Infant Mental Health Journal, 11*, 12–20.

Aldwin, C. M., & Revenson, T. A. (1987). Does coping help? A reexamination of the relation between coping and mental health. *Journal of Personality and Social Psychology, 53*, 337–348.

Alpert, D., & Culbertson, A. (1987). Daily hassles and coping strategies of dual-earner and nondual-earner women. *Psychology of Women Quarterly, 11*, 359–366.

Belle, D. (1987). Gender differences in the social moderators of stress. In Barnett, R. C., Biener, L., & Baruch, G. K. (Eds.), *Gender and stress* (pp. 257–277). New York: Free Press.

Benson, R. C. (1983). *Handbook of obstetrics and gynecology.* Los Altos, CA: Lange Medical Publishers.

Billings, A. G., & Moos, R. H. (1981). The role of coping responses and social resources in attenuating the stress of life events. *Journal of Behavioral Medicine, 4*, 139–157.

Campbell, A., Converse, P. E., & Rodgers, W. L. (1976). *The quality of American life: Perceptions, evaluations, and satisfactions.* New York: Russell Sage Foundation.

Carver, C. S., Scheier, M. F., & Weintraub, J. K. (1989). Assessing coping strategies: A theoretically based approach. *Journal of Personality and Social Psychology, 56*, 267–283.

Cook, E. P. (1987). Characteristics of the biopsychosocial crisis of infertility. *Journal of Counseling and Development, 65*, 465–470.

Cronkite, R. C., & Moos, R. H. (1984). The role of predisposing and moderating factors in the stress-illness relationship. *Journal of Health and Social Behavior, 25*, 372–393.

Derogatis, L. R. (1977). *SCL-90-R: Administration, scoring and procedures manual—I.* Baltimore, MD: Clinical Psychometrics Research Unit.

Diener, E., & Emmons, R. A. (1984). The independence of positive and negative affect. *Journal of Personality and Social Psychology, 47*, 1105–1117.

Domar, A. D., & Seibel, M. (1990). The emotional aspects of infertility. In M. Seibel (Ed.), *Infertility: A comprehensive text* (pp. 23–35). Norwalk, CT: Appleton-Lange.

Draye, M. A., Woods, N. F., & Mitchell, E. (1988). Coping with infertility in couples: Gender differences. *Health Care for Women International, 9*, 163–175.

Felton, B. J., Revenson, T. A., & Hinrichsen, G. A. (1984). Stress and coping in the explanation of psychological adjustment among chronically ill adults. *Social Science and Medicine, 18*, 889–898.

Folkman, S., & Lazarus, R. S. (1980). An analysis of coping in a middle-aged community sample. *Journal of Health and Social Behavior, 21,* 219–239.

Folkman, S., & Lazarus, R. S. (1985). If it changes it must be a process: Study of emotion and coping during three stages of a college examination. *Journal of Personality and Social Psychology, 48,* 150–170.

Folkman, S., & Lazarus, R. S. (1988). Coping as a mediator of emotion. *Journal of Personality and Social Psychology, 54,* 466–475.

Folkman, S., Lazarus, R. S., Dunkel-Schetter, C., DeLongis, A., & Gruen, R. J. (1986a). Dynamics of a stressful encounter: Cognitive appraisal, coping and encounter outcomes. *Journal of Personality and Social Psychology, 50,* 992–1003.

Folkman, S., Lazarus, R. S., Gruen, R. J., & DeLongis, A. (1986b). Appraisal, coping, health status, and psychological symptoms. *Journal of Personality and Social Psychology, 50,* 571–579.

Greenglass, E. R. (1982). *A world of difference: Gender role in perspective.* Toronto, Canada: Wiley.

Greil, A. L., Leitko, T. A., & Porter, K. L. (1988). Infertility: His and hers. *Gender and Society, 2,* 172–199.

Kessler, R. C., & McLeod, J. D. (1984). Sex differences in vulnerability to undesirable life events. *American Sociological Review, 49,* 620-631.

Lazarus, R. S. (1966). *Psychological stress and the coping process.* New York: McGraw-Hill.

Lazarus, R. S., & Folkman, S. (1984). *Stress, appraisal, and coping.* New York: Springer.

Mahlstedt, P. P. (1985). The psychological component of infertility. *Fertility and Sterility, 43,* 335–346.

Matthews, R., & Matthews, A. M. (1986). Infertility and involuntary childlessness: The transition to nonparenthood. *Journal of Marriage and the Family, 48,* 641–649.

McEwan, K. L., Costello, C. G., & Taylor, P. J. (1987). Adjustment to infertility. *Journal of Abnormal Psychology, 96,* 108–116.

McNair, D. M., Lorr, M., & Droppleman, L. F. (1971). *EITS manual for the Profile of Mood States.* San Diego: Educational and Industrial Testing Service.

Menning, B. E. (1980). The emotional needs of infertile couples. *Fertility and Sterility, 34,* 313–319.

Miall, C. E. (1986). The stigma of involuntary childlessness. *Social Problems, 33,* 267–282.

Miller, S. M., & Kirsch, N. (1987). Sex differences in cognitive coping with stress. In R. C. Barnett, L. Biener, & G. K. Baruch (Eds.), *Gender and stress* (pp. 278–307). New York: Free Press.

Roth, S., & Cohen, L. J. (1986). Approach, avoidance, and coping with stress. *American Psychologist, 41,* 813–819.

Russo, N. F. (1976). The motherhood mandate. *Journal of Social Issues, 32,* 143–153.

Shapiro, C. H. (1988). *Infertility and pregnancy loss: A guide for helping professionals.* San Francisco: Jossey-Bass.

Solomon, L. J., & Rothblum, E. D. (1986). Stress, coping and social support in women. *Behavior Therapist, 9,* 199–204.

Stanton, A. L., Tennen, H., Affleck, G., & Mendola, R. (in press). Coping and adjustment to infertility. *Journal of Social and Clinical Psychology.*

Stephenson, L. R. (1987). *Give us a child: Coping with the personal crisis of infertility.* San Francisco: Harper & Row.

Stone, A. A., & Neale, J. M. (1984). New measure of daily coping: Development and preliminary results. *Journal of Personality and Social Psychology, 46,* 892–906.

Suls, J., & Fletcher, B. (1985). The relative efficacy of avoidant and nonavoidant coping strategies: A meta-analysis. *Health Psychology, 4,* 249–288.

Taylor, S. E., Lichtman, R. R., & Wood, J. V. (1984). Attributions, beliefs about control, and adjustment to breast cancer. *Journal of Personality and Social Psychology, 46,* 489–502.

Valentine, D. P. (1986). Psychological impact of infertility: Identifying issues and needs. *Social Work in Health Care, 11,* 61–69.

Watson, D., & Tellegen, A. (1985). Toward a consensual structure of mood. *Psychological Bulletin, 98,* 219–235.

6

Causal Explanations for Infertility

Their Relation to Control Appraisals and Psychological Adjustment

HOWARD TENNEN, GLENN AFFLECK, and RICHARD MENDOLA

INFERTILITY AS A THREATENING EVENT

Infertility offers an ideal opportunity to examine people's cognitive adaptation in the face of threat. First, it is a major life event that is an impediment to a developmental milestone, the transition to parenthood (Belsky, Spanier, & Rovine, 1983; Hobbs & Cole, 1976). The magnitude of this threat is captured in the following spontaneous descriptions offered by our research participants:

> I think it's the worst experience of my life. The only other tragedy I can compare it to in my life was when my father died, out of the blue . . .

> Devastating, frustrating, painful, rageful. As many negative adjectives I could think of to describe it. It's not an experience I would wish on anyone.

Second, the cause of the problem is often ambiguous. Even when a medical cause is identified, the distal causes often remain enigmatic:

HOWARD TENNEN, GLENN AFFLECK, and RICHARD MENDOLA • Department of Psychiatry, University of Connecticut School of Medicine, Farmington, Connecticut 06032.

Why did this happen . . . what is the reason for it? . . . My husband . . . has the low
sperm count, but that's as far as we got. We don't know why it's low and that's a worry
in my mind.

Finally, infertility is usually unexpected. Couples who may have spent
their sexually active years trying to avoid pregnancy are surprised when
this does not occur easily:

You expect that the day you throw away your diaphragm you're going to be able to
get pregnant and your life is going to change . . . Then suddenly you realize . . . that
you might have a problem. It's shocking!

Thus, infertility is characterized by *threat, uncertainty,* and *unexpected-
ness.* These are the very circumstances that have been shown to lead to
stress (Lazarus & Folkman, 1984), the search for causes (Weiner, 1985) and
attempts to regain a sense of mastery and control (Seligman, 1975). In this
chapter we describe how individuals with impaired fertility search for
causes and attempt to regain a sense of mastery and meaning in their lives.
We present findings from a study of infertile individuals to demonstrate
both the emotional significance of people's causal explanations for their
infertility and how these explanations are related to their attempts to
regain control.

Causal Search and Explanations for Infertility:
The Quest for Mastery and Meaning

The search for explanations of a threatening event may serve two
related functions. The first is that knowing the cause may enhance one's
sense of control. Once a cause is identified, there is hope that it can be
rectified. Consider the following comments:

It seems that this problem should have an answer, and it seems that the answer should
be easily attainable and the problem resolved. I am baffled . . . as to why it has taken
this amount of time.

But finding a cause doesn't always mean that a solution will follow:

I asked my mother repeatedly if she had taken any medication. There were no
subsequent children, even though my parents wanted children. So that gives me the
feeling that there's something at work, but nothing anyone has any control over.

Finding an explanation can also help make sense out of what might
otherwise seem like meaningless victimization:

That's the way God wanted it to be. He didn't want me to have children. He wanted
me to go through this. Maybe it's to make me a stronger person. Maybe it's to make
me appreciate children more.

Causal explanations that enhance an individual's sense of mastery should be associated with better psychological functioning. According to Abramson, Seligman, and Teasdale (1978) three dimensions of causal explanation will determine if a perceived cause enhances or impairs psychological and social functioning. An *internal* explanation for a negative event places the cause within oneself. A *stable* explanation refers to a cause that is not likely to change. Finally, a *global* explanation suggests that the cause influences other areas of one's life. Internal, stable, and global explanations for bad outcomes are thought to produce the most devastating psychological consequences, because they undercut self-esteem, suggest that the future will be no different from the past, and imply that the cause will affect all areas of one's life (Abramson, Metalsky, & Alloy, 1989). "Characterological self-blame" (Janoff-Bulman, 1979) is an example of an internal-stable-global explanation, because one's character is internal and consistent over time and across situations.

Abramson *et al.*'s (1978) formulation suggests that a bad event attributed to one's own behavior (behavioral self-blame) may decrease self-esteem, but should otherwise lead to enhanced adaptation, because behavior, unlike character, is modifiable and situation-specific. But the literature examining causal explanations for threatening events has produced complex findings. Some investigators have found that explaining bad events as due to one's own behavior is associated with more psychological symptoms (Major, Mueller, & Hildebrandt, 1985; McEwan, Costello, & Taylor, 1987; Meyer & Taylor, 1986). Others, however, have found that behavioral explanations are associated with a sense of mastery and fewer psychological symptoms (Tennen, Affleck, & Gershman, 1986; Timko & Janoff-Bulman, 1985).

One aspect of the infertility experience complicates the role of causal explanations in adapting to this crisis. Specifically, infertility, unlike many other threatening events, represents the absence of a desired outcome. When someone has a seriously ill infant (Tennen *et al.*, 1986), breast cancer (Timko & Janoff-Bulman, 1985), or has had a heart attack (Affleck, Tennen, Croog, & Levine, 1987a), certain causal explanations, such as behavioral self-blame, may enhance adaptation by suggesting that a recurrence can be avoided. But recurrence is irrelevant to an individual with impaired fertility. Similarly, an external, unstable, and specific causal explanation (e.g., "It was a fluke") may be the least troublesome interpretation of most negative events, because it minimizes one's expectation of similar events in the future. But explaining one's impaired fertility as a fluke offers neither a sense of mastery nor a sense of meaning; and unlike other threatening circumstances, this explanation for infertility does not offer protection from future harm. For these reasons, we thought it was particularly important to study causal explanations for infertility and their relation to psychological functioning.

Another factor that may affect findings of relations between causal explanations and adjustment is measurement strategy. Causal explanations have been measured by one of two strategies: open-ended interview questions and rating scales. In open-ended inquiry, beliefs about causality are probed with a question such as, "Do you have any ideas or hunches about what might have caused this problem?" (Affleck, Allen, Tennen, McGrade, & Ratzan, 1985; Taylor, Lichtman, & Wood, 1984; Tennen, Allen, Affleck, McGrade, & Ratzan, 1984). These responses are then categorized by judges. In the second method, participants are presented a list of possible causal factors derived from prior research or theory and are asked to rate the causal influence of each factor on a scale (e.g., from 0 to 10) (Janoff-Bulman, 1979; Major *et al.*, 1985; Timko & Janoff-Bulman, 1985).

We have found only two published studies that employed both methods. In their investigation of coping with breast cancer, Taylor *et al.* (1984) reported only moderate concordance between these methods. Tennen *et al.* (1986) found that specifically asking about behavioral causes doubled their frequency compared with replies to an open-ended question. Evidence from the achievement literature (Whitley & Frieze, 1986) also suggests that these two measurement strategies may not yield equivalent attributions. It follows that different methods of measurement may contribute to the equivocal findings relating attributions for threatening events to psychological adjustment. The study we describe in this chapter attempts to address directly how variation in measurement may influence both an explanation's magnitude and its relation to adjustment.

Psychological Control and Adjustment

Perceptions of personal control figure prominently in most accounts of how people adapt to threatening events (Klinger, 1975; Kobasa, 1979; Langer & Rodin, 1976; Miller, 1980; Seligman, 1975; Suls & Mullen, 1981). There is now abundant evidence that individuals facing acute or modifiable stressors are well-served by the belief that they can control outcomes. But for a prolonged crisis like impaired fertility, personal control beliefs may be ineffective and even counterproductive. By trying to produce the desired outcome, an individual may miss the opportunity to accommodate to this threatening situation and prepare for alternative outcomes.

Primary control, which is the experience of personal influence over an aversive situation (Rothbaum, Weisz, & Snyder, 1982), may also come at a significant emotional cost (Averill, 1973; Burger, 1989; Folkman, 1984; Tennen & Affleck, 1987; Thompson, 1981). The diagnostic and treatment procedures for infertility are invasive and prolonged (Stangel, 1979), and the need to engage in sexual relations at specified times may produce sexual dysfunction and emotional distress (Mazor & Simons, 1984; Menning, 1977). These emotional costs were described well by our participants:

> It almost completely disrupts my life in terms of being able to hold a steady job because of the medical things. We never know what we're going to be trying next. It has interrupted my career, it's interrupting my husband's business life.

> For over a year, we have been doing everything faithfully . . . like remembering to take the medication, remembering to take the temperature every morning and write all that stuff down . . . It's a pain in the neck!

Secondary control appraisals involve attempts to redefine a situation so as to reduce its threat (Rothbaum *et al.*, 1982; Thompson, 1985). These appraisals include: *interpretive control,* which is accepting the situation by giving it meaning or purpose; *cognitive control,* which is thinking about a situation in a different way, such as construing benefits or gains; *predictive control,* which is an attempt to predict events so as to avoid disappointment; *vicarious control,* which involves ascribing control to an authoritative other; and *retrospective control,* in which the threat is seen as having been avoidable, thus buttressing one's confidence that future victimization can be averted.

Secondary control appears to enhance adjustment. In our investigations of individuals coping with the birth of a seriously ill infant (Affleck, Tennen, & Gershman, 1985), and those afflicted with rheumatoid arthritis (Affleck, Tennen, Pfeiffer, & Fifield, 1987b) we found that interpretive control was associated with fewer psychological symptoms. Similarly, cognitive control was a precursor of adjustment and long-term morbidity in our study of heart attack patients (Affleck *et al.*, 1987a), and was associated with better adjustment among mothers of ill newborns (Affleck *et al.*, 1985a).

Rothbaum *et al.* (1982) hypothesize a possible relation between primary and secondary control. They suggest that in the face of ongoing threat, individuals who are unable to reduce the threat by changing the situation (primary control) may reappraise the circumstance in a way that helps them accommodate (secondary control). Despite the intuitive appeal of this hypothesis, we know of only one published study that reported the relation between primary and secondary control appraisals. Affleck *et al.* (1985b) found no relation between these appraisals among mothers of diabetic children.

Causal explanations may themselves reflect secondary control strategies. For example, attributing an aversive event to one's own behavior may be a manifestation of retrospective control, as the individual assures himself/herself that he/she will behave differently in the future. To the extent that causal explanations bring meaning to misfortune, they may promote interpretive control. Explaining infertility as God's will is an example of how a causal explanation can bolster a sense of interpretive control. If explanations serve the same coping function as secondary control strategies, they should not account for variation in adjustment beyond that due to these control strategies.

Another possibility is that causal explanations influence different aspects of adaptation than do primary and secondary control strategies. Primary control may have its most important impact on an individual's sense of mastery; secondary control may have its greatest impact by imparting a sense of meaning to a threatening event like infertility; whereas certain causal explanations can bolster or diminish self-esteem (Abramson et al., 1978). Following this line of reasoning, primary control, secondary control, and causal explanations may play independent roles in adaptation. To evaluate these possibilities, we assessed both causal explanations and control strategies in a study of how these factors relate to one another and how each relates to psychological adaptation to infertility.

INVESTIGATION OF CAUSAL EXPLANATIONS, CONTROL APPRAISALS, AND ADAPTATION TO INFERTILITY

We have been conducting a study of how causal explanations and control appraisals are related to one another and to the psychological adjustment of women and men with impaired fertility. Sixty-five women and 35 men were recruited from three sources. Fifty-three came from the infertility clinic of a university hospital. Since these women and men were seeking treatment, they may not have well represented individuals with fertility problems. Therefore, participants were also recruited from two other sources: 23 responded to a request for volunteers at a meeting of the Greater Hartford Connecticut Chapter of RESOLVE, and 24 others responded to a newspaper advertisement. None of the men in our study participated without their wives, but nearly half the women participated without their husbands. Thirty-three of the 65 women had primary infertility, and 80% were actively pursuing medical treatment.

To be eligible for the study, a couple had to be trying to have a child for a year or more through regular sexual relations without contraception, a criterion endorsed by the American Fertility Society (Thompson, 1984). Among clinic patients, 62% of those approached for the study agreed to participate. Those who refused were not significantly different from participants with regard to age or socioeconomic status.

The mean age of participants was 31 years for women and 33 years for men. They were married an average of six years and had been trying to have a child for an average of three years. They were well-educated, with the average participant having obtained a college degree. Fourteen percent said that they had been told by doctors that their infertility was associated with a male factor, 46% that only a female factor was involved, 15% that both a male and female factor was implicated, and 25% that the causes of their impaired fertility were unknown. To determine the accuracy of these reports, we compared the responses of clinic patients with their doctors' opinions. There was perfect concordance.

A semi-structured interview was conducted that lasted about 90 minutes and focused on the psychological and social consequences of impaired fertility. The interview assessed causal explantions, control appraisals, and adjustment. Most of the interviews were conducted at the University of Connecticut School of Medicine. In some cases we conducted home or telephone interviews. Sudman and Bradburn (1974) and Groves and Kahn (1979) have established the comparability of responses to face-to-face and telephone interviews. All interviews were tape recorded and transcribed.

We employed the Symptom Checklist 90-Revised (SCL-90-R; Derogatis, 1977) as our major measure of psychological adjustment. The SCL-90-R is a 90-item self-report checklist that measures nine symptom clusters and also provides an index of global symptoms. Participants rated each symptom as it was experienced in the week prior to the interview. Each symptom was rated from 0 (not at all) to 4 (extremely). The SCL-90-R is a reliable and widely used self-report measure of distress (Tennen, Affleck, & Herzberger, 1985). Overall, participants' global symptom scores were somewhat higher than those of the normal standardization sample but remained in the normal range (Derogatis, 1977).

We set three goals in evaluating the inverview data. Specifically, we wanted to determine: (1) Whether men and women differed in their causal explanations; (2) if the manner in which we inquired about causal explanations influenced the explanations we received; and (3) whether causal explanations were related to adjustment after controlling for background factors, participants' appraisal of how threatening infertility was for them, and their control appraisals. As we mentioned earlier, if certain causal explanations enhance an individual's sense of control, and others help bring meaning to adversity, these explanations may serve the same adaptational functions as primary and secondary control appraisals. Therefore, it was important to determine if there was a *unique* association between causal explanations and adjustment. Similarly, those individuals who view infertility as more threatening should exhibit more psychological symptoms. Thus we needed to know if the relation between causal explanations and adjustment was independent of perceived threat. Finally, we reasoned that serious medical conditions other than infertility might influence both control appraisals and adjustment. Accordingly, in our analysis of the unique contribution of causal explanations to adjustment, we controlled for the presence of serious medical problems.

To address the issue of how variation in assessment method influences causal explanations, we used an open-ended question and specific rating scales. The open-ended question was: "People in your situation often wonder about things that might have caused their infertility. Today, what do you think contributed to your infertility?" Eleven-point rating scales also were used by participants to evaluate the causal influence of five factors: (a) something you did or didn't do; (b) something somebody else did or didn't do; (c) chance; (d) biological-medical causes; and (e) emotional factors. We selected these causal factors because they were the most common causes offered spontaneously in pilot interviews. To facilitate comparison of these two methods of measuring explanations, two judges independently rated responses to open-ended questions on the same five causal factors presented to participants. The judges showed good concordance, with a mean Kappa of .91.

MAJOR STUDY FINDINGS

Gender Differences in Causal Explanations for Infertility

To determine whether men and women had different causal explanations for their infertility, we compared the 31 men and 33 women in our sample who were not married to each other. Attributional discrepancies between marital partners are important both conceptually and clinically, but the clearest test of gender differences requires the comparison of unrelated individuals (Kenny, 1988). Means and standard deviations of participant-generated and judge-generated causal explanations are presented in Table 1.

We conducted a multivariate analysis of variance in which gender was the between-subjects factor, measurement method was the within-subjects factor, and causal explanations served as the dependent variable. The MANOVA revealed a significant effect for gender. There was no significant gender × method interaction. Univariate analyses revealed that

Table 1. Respondent- and Judge-Generated Causal Atrributions

		Males		Females	
	Variables	Mean	SD	Mean	SD
Respondent-	Self-blame	2.27	2.94	4.16	3.33
generated	Other-blame	3.48	3.78	3.97	3.98
	Chance	5.09	3.59	5.42	2.69
	Biomedical	7.18	2.59	7.48	2.86
	Emotional	3.03	2.70	2.94	3.11
Judge-	Self-blame	1.24	2.04	3.00	2.49
generated	Other-blame	2.11	2.44	1.69	2.48
	Chance	2.60	2.58	4.35	2.36
	Biomedical	7.81	1.62	6.42	2.20
	Emotional	0.76	1.80	1.00	2.25

Note. Ratings were made on 11-point scales ranging from 0 (not at all a factor) to 11 (an extremely strong factor).

women more than men believed that their own behavior caused their infertility. This finding may be interpreted in several ways. One interpretation is that women made more accurate appraisals of the situation. But we have no evidence that this was the case. Specifically, we found no relation between the causes as told by medical staff (male factors, female factors, or both) and attributions to personal behavior.

Another way of viewing this gender difference is from an interpersonal perspective. A woman may take on the responsibility for impaired fertility to protect her husband from having to acknowledge a potential deficit in procreative functioning. The literature on coping with threatening events has not incorporated findings on attributions in couples (Fincham, 1985), but nurses in our infertility clinic mentioned spontaneously that they have observed what appears to be a "spouse protecting" function of women's attributions, with women experiencing relief if they were the cause of the problem.

The Convergent Validity of Causal Explanations

To determine how well causal attributions transcend variations in how they are measured, we constructed a multi-trait multi-method matrix (Campbell & Fiske, 1959) in which we correlated each of the self-rated attributions with each of the judges' ratings. The correlations between methods for each of the five attributional categories provides an index of convergence. These correlations ranged from .14 to .62 with a mean of only .37, indicating that the two methods are not interchangeable.

Causal Explanations and Adjustment

To determine whether individuals' causal explanations for their infertility are associated with their psychological adjustment, we performed two multiple regression analyses with the total SCL-90-R score serving as the criterion variable. In one regression model, gender was entered as the first predictor, followed by participant-generated causal explanations entered as a block, and finally explanation × gender interactions. The second analysis replaced participant-generated explanations with judge-generated explanations. Gender accounted for less than 1% of the variation in symptom scores. Causal explanations accounted for a significant proportion of additional variance (19% for participant-generated and 17% for judge-generated), but which explanations contributed to the prediction depended on how they were measured. Among the self-reported explanations, greater *behavioral self-blame* (such as having taken birth control pills) and stronger attributions to *biomedical factors* (such as a structural abnormality) and *chance* were associated with more distress. But among the judge-rated explanations, only *emotional factors* (such as being too tense) emerged as a significant predictor. For neither respondent-generated nor judge-generated causal explanations did the gender × explanation interaction terms entered as a block or individually make a unique contribution to symptom scores.

The results of these two regression analyses indicate that respondent explanations and judge-generated explanations may relate differently to adaptation. To determine whether there were significant differences in the correlations between respondent explanations and adaptation and judge-generated explanations and adaptation, we computed tests for the difference between dependent correlations (Bruning & Kintz, 1968). These tests showed that the relation between respondent explanations to emotional factors and adaptation ($r = -.07$) was significantly different from the relation between judge-generated explanations to emotional factors and adaptation ($r = .30$).

It appears that previous findings relating causal explanations to adjustment must be interpreted with appropriate caution because findings may be measurement-specific. Moreover, each significant causal explanation related to symptoms in a way that stronger endorsement of the explanation was associated with more distress. Thus, causal search may be more important than specific explanations in the prediction of psychological adjustment. With these caveats in mind, we now examine the unique contribution of causal explanations to adjustment.

Causal Explanations, Primary Control, and Secondary Control: Their Relation to Psychological Adjustment

To determine whether causal explanations, primary control appraisals, and secondary control appraisals make separate contributions to adaptation, we examined the interview responses of the 65 women in our study. We coded serious medical problems (e.g., chronic pain, seizure disorders, inoperable aneurysm), which were exhibited by 24% of the women in our sample, as present or absent. We also asked these women to rate on an 11-point scale the seriousness of their infertility. We took this rating as a measure of threat appraisal. Primary control was assessed by a single question asking participants how much control they believed they had over the outcomes of their infertility. Responses were made on a scale anchored at 0% = no control and 100% = total control.

We measured three aspects of secondary control: interpretive control, vicarious control, and cognitive control. Interpretive control was assessed through the following interview question, derived from previous investigations (e.g., Bulman & Wortman, 1977; Kiecolt-Glaser & Williams, 1987): "Some people we've talked to have asked themselves "*Why me?* Why am I the one who is unable to conceive? Have you asked yourself "Why me?" If so, what conclusions have you reached?" *Vicarious control* was assessed through the question: "Is there anything your doctor can do to resolve your infertility?" Finally, *cognitive control* was measured by asking: "As difficult as this situation may be, do you believe that anything positive has come from this, some benefit or gain that has occurred that wouldn't have occurred if you were able to have a child?" These interview responses were coded independently by two judges who showed good agreement (Kappas ranged from .79 to .85). Descriptive statistics for primary and secondary control variables are presented in Table 2.

To determine whether control appraisals and causal explanations made unique contributions to psychological adjustment, we evaluated a multiple regression model in which psychological symptoms (as measured by the SCL-90-R) served as the dependent variable. Table 3 summarizes the results of this analysis.

The first predictor entered into the equation was the presence of medical problems unrelated to the infertility. As expected, medical problems explained a significant proportion of variation in psychological symptoms. Our measure of threat appraisal, entered next, also predicted varia-

Table 2. Descriptive Statistics for Threat and Control Appraisals

	Frequency (%)	Mean	SD
Threat appraisal			
Seriousness of problem(0–10)		6.30	2.86
Primary control			
Self-reported control (0–100)		40.32	31.98
Secondary control			
"Why me?"			
Had asked themselves this question	91.00		
No answer	25.90		
Fate	31.00		
Chance	24.10		
Personal behavior	10.00		
Vicarious			
Anything doctors can do	79.40		
Cognitive			
Benefits			
No benefit	25.00		
Strengthen marriage	48.40		
Personal growth	23.40		
Greater appreciation	17.20		

tion in symptoms beyond the effect of medical problems. Primary control appraisal, entered next, was not associated significantly with symptoms. But a secondary cognitive control appraisal did make a unique contribution to symptoms when entered into the equation after medical problems, threat appraisal, and primary control: Women who believed that their infertility had strengthened their marriage reported fewer symptoms.

Finally, we entered participants' self-rated causal explanations in a stepwise fashion, after medical problems, threat appraisal, and primary and secondary control appraisals were incorporated into the equation. The only secondary control variable that was retained at this step in the regression equation was the benefit of a strengthened marriage. This procedure was deemed appropriate for two reasons: First, secondary control measures were not correlated highly enough to be considered a single factor (rs ranged from $-.18$ to $.20$). Thus, it was not necessary to retain all measures of secondary control. More important, the inclusion of the entire set of secondary control factors would have resulted in an unacceptable ratio of independent variables to subjects for statistical inference. The resulting stepwise entry of attributions revealed that only ascriptions to biomedical factors significantly improved the prediction, accounting for an additional 6% of the variation in symptom scores. The beta weights for the final equation revealed that all of the variables except primary control made unique contributions to symptomatology.

Our findings support the conceptual distinction between causal explanations and control appraisals. As we anticipated, primary control, which has an empirically demonstrated relation with adjustment in other circumstances, was not associated with symptoms. This may be due to the emotional costs of maintaining control in this situation. The absence of a relation between primary control appraisals and adjustment may also reflect an important difference between infertility and many other stressful events that we mentioned earlier: namely, the salience of recurrence. Thus, a potentially important link between control appraisals and adjustment may be irrelevant to the person experiencing infertility.

It is also noteworthy that women who were more likely to attribute their impaired fertility to biomedical causes were encountering greater distress. Infertility specialists often emphasize the biomedical causes of the problem. To pursue the relation between biomedical explanations and adjustment, we compared what these women said they were told about the cause of the infertility with their own causal explanations. We found that they made stronger ascriptions to biomedical causes when they were told that their impaired fertility was related to something about their husband.

Table 3. Summary of Regression Analysis Predicting Global Symptoms

	Beta	Overall R^2	F-value for change in R^2	df
Step 1				
Presence of medical problems	.36	.11	7.28**	(1,59)
Step 2				
Perceived severity of problem	.33	.27	12.47**	(1,58)
Step 3				
Primary control	.15	.31	3.04*	(1.57)
Step 4				
Perceived benefit: Strengthened marriage	−.23	.36	4.46*	(1,56)
Step 5				
Attribution to bio-medical causes	.25	.42	5.30*	(1,55)

*$p < .05$. **$p < .01$.

Might this be another indication of the spouse protecting function of attributions? Might women who are told that the cause resides with their husband be more likely to explain it in biomedical terms in order to keep their spouse from being held responsible? This question deserves closer examination in future investigations.

In summary, we found that our strategy for measuring causal explanations influenced the magnitude of the explanations we obtained. We also found that men and women offer somewhat different explanations for their infertility and that these explanations appear to make a unique contribution to psychological adjustment. We now examine some of the implications of these findings for future research, for the infertile couple, and for treatment and counseling.

IMPLICATIONS FOR RESEARCH

Measurement Strategies

We found that whether a specific causal explanation correlates with psychological symptoms among infertile individuals depends on the method of measuring these explanations. Participant-rated explanations were more often associated with symptoms than were judge-rated explanations. Moreover, ascriptions to emotional factors, which was the only judge-generated explanation showing a significant correlation with symptoms, was not among the participant-rated explanations correlated with symptoms. That the association between causal explanations and adaptation is method-dependent should be cause for concern. For those interested in how people adapt to threatening events, our findings indicate that we cannot always compare results based on different measurement strategies. To appreciate more fully people's causal explanations, researchers may need to move to standardized assessment techniques including structured interviews.

The measurement of primary and secondary control has problems of its own. Most studies of coping with threatening events, including our own, have employed single-item measures of control whose reliability is unknown. Thus, we do not know if primary control is unrelated to adjustment to infertility because of something unique to the infertility experience or because our measure was unreliable. Since investigators have employed idiosyncratic assessment procedures, we cannot readily compare findings across studies. In response to this problem, we recently developed a multi-item scale to measure primary and secondary control appraisals, with items that can be adapted to a particular stressor. We are now using the scale in our studies of coping with chronic pain and in studies of coping with chronic fatigue and rheumatoid arthritis. We view this scale as a preliminary step in the reliable assessment of primary and secondary control appraisals.

Timing of Inquiry

Recruiting patients from infertility specialty clinics, support groups, and newspaper ads may have produced a skewed group of participants. These individuals had already tried to conceive for at least a year, visited their family physician, and defined themselves as having difficulty conceiving or bringing a pregnancy to term. The relations we obtained among control appraisals, causal explanations, and adjustment may reflect the duration of our participants' infertility. One could readily imagine an individual who is just beginning to experience impaired fertility, for whom a strong belief in personal control over pregnancy outcomes enhances adjustment. Yet we found that after several years of dealing with the problem, primary control appraisals are unrelated to emotional well-being. Similarly, it is unlikely that people who are just beginning to experience fertility problems believe that impaired fertility strengthens their marriage. But for our participants, nearly half believed that the experience strengthened their marriage. For these reasons we urge investigators to pursue samples who have only recently begun to have troubles conceiving or carrying to term.

We suspect, however, that it is difficult to find people who are just beginning to experience fertility problems. First, these people will be encouraged by professionals to wait at least a year before they view themselves as having a fertility problem. Most of them will not be seen by an infertility specialist until well into their second year of failed attempts to conceive. This may interfere with efforts to recruit participants early in the coping process. Nonetheless, information about individuals who are just beginning to experience the threat of impaired fertility is needed to reach a more complete understanding of how people adapt cognitively to this major life event.

Global Appraisals and Psychological Adjustment

We have described the relation between infertility-specific appraisals and psychological adjustment. There is increasing evidence, however, that *global* appraisals may serve as buffers in the face of a chronic stressor. One such global appraisal is *dispositional optimism*. Scheier and Carver (1985, 1987) define dispositional optimism as a generalized expectancy for favorable outcomes. They have developed the Life Orientation Test (LOT) to measure the expectation that positive outcomes will occur. Scheier and

Carver (1985) have demonstrated that dispositional optimism predicts physical health.

We believe that infertility presents a novel situation in which to test whether optimism enhances psychological adjustment. Will optimistic individuals experience less distress than their pessimistic counterparts when faced with impaired fertility? Tennen and Affleck (1987) speculate that optimists believe that they are uniquely invulnerable to adverse outcomes, and that this belief may help them get through temporary setbacks. When faced with an irreversible setback, however, the optimist's cherished assumption of invulnerability may be shattered and he/she may be even more distressed than less optimistic individuals. We would thus predict that optimism may be a temporary buffer, and for those who go on to have children of their own, the illustion of invulnerability is maintained, awaiting another test. Among women and men who permanently are unable to have a child, we suspect that optimism will be associated with *greater* distress because the optimist must deal with two losses: that of a desired child and that of a cherished assumption of invulnerability. Tests of these competing hypotheses will require longitudinal investigations and large samples. We believe that such studies are worth the effort. They will advance both our knowledge of how people adapt to infertility and our conceptualization of the benefits and costs of dispositional optimism.

In Vitro Fertilization: A Natural Experiment

In vitro fertilization (IVF) offers another area in which to apply the concepts of primary and secondary control appraisals and causal explanations. The vast majority of IVF participants are going to experience a negative outcome, and by assessing their control appraisals and causal explanations *before* the procedure, we can determine the influence of these appraisals on adjustment to failure. In collaboration with Mark Litt (Litt, 1989), we have begun to examine this issue.

We have thus far interviewed 32 women prior to IVF, and one to two weeks after they were informed of their pregnancy test. Thirty women failed to conceive as a result of IVF. Four of these women developed clinical depression. Also, women who reported a general loss of control over their lives as a result of infertility were more distressed following IVF, even after controlling for pre-IVF depression levels. Interestingly, women who showed better recovery following IVF failure were more likely to have explained their infertility as due to their own behavior. These findings are preliminary. Yet we believe that IVF represents a natural experiment in which we can examine longitudinally global appraisals, coping strategies, and causal explanations as potential buffers against the threat of IVF failure.

IMPLICATIONS FOR THE INFERTILE COUPLE

There may be implications of our findings for those experiencing impaired infertility. Any discussion of implications, however, must acknowledge significant caveats. First, the findings we report are cross-sectional and may not apply to the early stages of coping with infertility. Second, although we made an effort to sample broadly, most of our participants had sought treatment. Since seeking treatment may itself reflect control appraisals and causal explanations (e.g., biomedical explanations predominate the explanations of our participants), our findings may not apply to those who do not seek medical intervention. With these caveats in mind, we will describe potential implications for the infertile couple.

The most fundamental implication is that people ponder the causes of their infertility and entertain certain causes as more plausible than others. These causal explanations were more "distal" than the explanations offered by treating physicians, and some may appear unrealistic to a spouse. For example, the husband of a woman who believes that she caused their infertility may try to convince her that she couldn't possibly be the cause, and that it was just a biomedical problem. But by ascribing the cause to herself, she may have brought meaning to this threatening experience, or may be relieved that her spouse is not responsible. A biomedical explanation, on the other hand, may have deleterious emotional consequences. We believe that spouses should generally try to accept their partners' causal explanations, even though they appear incorrect. It is unlikely that a rational discussion of the causes of infertility will change an individual's causal beliefs. Such discussions, in fact, may have the untoward effect of one spouse feeling unsupported and misunderstood.

There are circumstances, however, in which causal explanations may actually influence the *outcome* of impaired fertility. Individuals who believe that their impaired fertility is due to stable and global (i.e., unmodifiable) causes may not only be distressed, but may also fail to examine options that could influence both the cause and the outcome of the infertility. Even in this situation, there is no reason to believe that a direct assault on a spouse's preferred explanations will lead to the desired examination of options. A less threatening approach might be to "test" a causal belief. For example, a husband who has concluded that his infertility is due to a low sperm count, and that nothing can be done about it, might be encouraged by his spouse to engage in procedures that would test his rationally derived conclusion.

We found that men and women offered different explanations for their infertility. Although we did not directly assess differences between marital partners, we suspect that husbands and wives often hold different causal explanations, particularly different distal explanations. It is tempting to hypothesize that spousal explanatory concordance is associated with better adjustment. But we suspect that the situation is complex and that spouses should not necessarily attempt to hold identical causal explanations. For example, a woman may believe that her infertility is due to her prior birth control methods. But when her well-meaning husband agrees, she may view this agreement as a moral assault. Moreover, a particular explanation may have different implications for each partner. To one, an explanation involving a behavioral cause engenders hope, because change in behavior may influence the outcome. To the other partner it may imply deservedness for prior moral transgressions. For these reasons, we believe that it is wise to respect rather than challenge or identify with a partner's causal explanations.

IMPLICATIONS FOR TREATMENT AND COUNSELING

Our findings may also have implications for how physicians, counselors, friends, and relatives might best respond to infertility. Here we address briefly the notion of "stages" in coping with infertility, the distinction between control appraisals that are self-generated and those that are imposed by others, and implications for the clinical interview and for our conception of maladaptation.

There is a rich, descriptive literature addressing the stages of coping with threatening events (Kübler-Ross, 1969; Shontz, 1975). It is within this tradition that Menning (1977, 1980) described infertility as a grief reaction in which couples pass through the stages of shock, denial, anger, isolation, and guilt. Despite its intellectual and clinical appeal, the stage concept has not received empirical support (Silver & Wortman, 1980). Our own cross-sectional findings can neither support nor disconfirm a stage model. Yet the burden of proof is on those who endorse a stage notion of adjustment to threatening experiences.

The major risk associated with a stage conceptualization of adjustment is that it may create *expectations* about appropriate ways to behave (Lazarus & Folkman, 1984). The same may be said about the adaptational benefits of certain control appraisals or causal explanations. We found that there may be emotional advantages associated with finding benefits in infertility. But this does not imply that clinicians should point out potential benefits to their patients. In our investigation of mothers of acutely ill newborns we found that optimistic appraisals and a philosophical perspective enhance well-being, but that similar appraisals, when offered as support gestures, are sometimes viewed as unhelpful (Affleck, Tennen, Rowe, Walker, & Higgins, in press).

For those involved in infertility treatment and counseling, our findings suggest that traditional interview techniques, which usually elicit responses to open-ended questions, may not capture fully patients' causal beliefs, nor the associations between explanations and adjustment. Recall that simply asking about causal beliefs did not produce the same findings as asking about *specific* causes. It is here that the advantages of an open-ended clinical interview may clash with the potential loss of important information.

Our findings also suggest that inquiring about perceived benefits may have diagnostic and prognostic value. We found that those individuals who believed that their infertility strengthened their marriage experienced less emotional distress. It may at first appear insensitive to inquire clinically about the benefits of infertility, but we have found that these benefits do not usually emerge in an open-ended interview and may require specific probes. None of the participants in our study appeared to be offended by our inquiry, and many seemed relieved. In fact, by asking about benefits, the clinician may be providing needed "permission" to examine the positive aspects of the infertility experience.

We also found that the benefit of a strengthened marriage (a cognitive control appraisal), but not an answer to "why me?" (an interpretive control appraisal) was associated with enhanced adjustment. The failure of interpretive control to predict adaptation may reflect some unique features of the threat of infertility and may also have implications for the health care professional.

One way in which impaired fertility differs from other threatening events is that it represents an ambiguous circumstance in which nothing specific has actually occurred. Our participants did not know if they were permanently infertile. They only know that they hadn't been able to conceive or bring a birth to term. This feature of infertility may help explain why having no answer to the "why me?" question was not linked with greater distress. We suspect that once an individual decides that he/she will never have a child of her/his own (i.e., when the threat of loss becomes an acknowledged loss), he/she is much more likely to search for answers to the question "why me?" But such answers do bring with them a sense of finality or completion that is incongruent when there remains hope of having a child of one's own. Thus, for our participants, having no answer did not signal disturbance. Two important clinical implications emerge from this interpretation of our findings. First, an answer to the question "why me?" may enhance adaptation, but only when the threatening event is an actual or acknowledged loss. Second, health care professionals should not be too quick to bring meaning to the plight of their patients, particularly when such meaning brings with it premature closure.

Finally, as clinicians and investigators, we must examine carefully our conceptions of psychological adjustment. In a recent review, Tennen and Affleck (1990) found that nearly every published study of causal attributions for threatening events assumed that emotional distress signalled maladaptation. There is, in fact, little empirical support for the assumption that a period of distress is required for subsequent adaptation (Wortman & Silver, 1987). Yet clinicians have argued cogently (Shur, 1953; Zetzel, 1965) that the capacity to tolerate distress in the face of chronic strain may be an emotionally mature response. The inability to experience depression following loss or threat of loss may signal a failure to accept that which cannot be controlled. Rather than something to be eliminated, depression—particularly in the normal range—may be something to be experienced.

We view our findings as preliminary. Future investigations should examine responses to impaired fertility early in the process of adjustment, as individuals begin to suspect that their expectations may be shattered. Studying how *couples* adjust to infertility (Daniluk, 1988; Daniluk, Leader, & Taylor, 1987; Edelmann & Connolly, 1986; Link & Darling, 1986; Stanton, this volume) will further advance our knowledge of the adjustment process by placing infertility into an interactional perspective. Finally, examining the burden placed on those providing support for infertile couples will help fill gaps in our understanding of the social context of infertility. Together with the cognitive appraisals examined in this chapter, these investigational approaches will enhance treatment and supportive services for those who must contend with infertility.

REFERENCES

Abramson, L. Y., Metalsky, G. I., & Alloy, L. B. (1989). Hopelessness depression: A theory based subtype of depression. *Psychological Review, 96,* 358–372.

Abramson, L. Y., Seligman, M. E. P., & Teasdale, J. D. (1978). Learned helplessness in humans: Critique and reformulation. *Journal of Abnormal Psychology, 87,* 49–74.

Affleck, G., Tennen, H., & Gershman, K. (1985a). Cognitive adaptations to high risk infants: The search for meaning, mastery, and protection from future harm. *American Journal of Mental Deficiency, 89,* 653–656.

Affleck, G., Allen, D. A., Tennen, H., McGrade, B. J., & Ratzan, S. (1985b). Causal and control cognitions in parent coping with a chronically ill child. *Journal of Social and Clinical Psychology, 3,* 369–379.

Affleck, G., Tennen, H., Croog, S., & Levine, S. (1987a). Causal attribution, perceived benefits, and morbidity after a heart attack: An 8-year study. *Journal of Consulting and Clinical Psychology, 55,* 29–35.

Affleck, G., Tennen, H., Pfeiffer, C., & Fifield, J. (1987b). Appraisals of control and predictability in adapting to a chronic disease. *Journal of Personality and Social Psychology, 53,* 273–279.

Affleck, G., Tennen, H., Rowe, D., Walker, L., & Higgins, P. (in press). Mother's interpersonal relationships and adaptation to hospital and home care of high risk infants. In R. Anatonak & J. Mulick (Eds.), *Transitions in Mental Retardation*, Vol. V. Norwood, NJ: Ablex Publishing.

Averill, J. (1973). Personal control over aversive stimuli and its relationship to stress. *Psychological Bulletin, 80,* 286–303.

Belsky, J., Spanier, G. B., & Rovine, M. (1983). Stability and change in marriage across the transition to parenthood. *Journal of Marriage and the Family, 45,* 567–576.

Bruning, J. L., & Kintz, B. L. (1968). *Computational handbook of statistics.* Glenview, IL: Scott, Foresman.

Bulman, R., & Wortman, C. (1977). Attributions of blame and coping in the "real world": Severe accident victims react to their lot. *Journal of Personality and Social Psychology, 35,* 351–363.

Burger, J. M. (1989). Negative reactions to increases in perceived personal control. *Journal of Personality and Social Psychology, 56,* 246–256.

Campbell, D. T., & Fiske, D. W. (1959). Convergent and discriminant validity by the multitrait-multimethod matrix. *Psychological Bulletin, 56,* 81–105.

Daniluk, J. C. (1988). Infertility: Intrapersonal and interpersonal impact. *Fertility and Sterility, 49,* 982–990.

Daniluk, J. C., Leader, A., & Taylor, P. J. (1987). Psychological and relationship changes of couples undergoing an infertility investigation: Some implications for counsellors. *British Journal of Guidance and Counselling, 15,* 29–36.

Derogatis, L. R. (1977). SCL-90: Administration, scoring and procedures manual for the revised version. Baltimore: Clinical Psychometric Research.

Edelmann, R. J., & Connolly, K. J. (1986). Psychological aspects of infertility. *British Journal of Medical Psychology, 59,* 209–219.

Fincham, F. D. (1985). Attribution process in distressed and non-distressed couples: 2. Responsibility for marital problems. *Journal of Abnormal Psychology, 94,* 183–190.

Folkman, S. (1984). Personal control and stress and coping processes: A theoretical analysis. *Journal of Personality and Social Psychology, 46,* 839–852.

Groves, R. M., & Kahn, R. (1979). *Comparing telephone and personal interview surveys.* New York: Academic Press.

Hobbs, D. F., & Cole, S. P. (1976). Transition to parenthood: A decade replication. *Journal of Marriage and the Family, 38,* 723–731.

Janoff-Bulman, R. (1979). Characterological versus behavioral self-blame: Inquires into depression and rape. *Journal of Personality and Social Psychology, 36,* 1798–1809.

Kenny, D. A. (1988). The analysis of data from two-person relationships. In S. Duck (Ed.), *Handbook of interpersonal relations* (pp. 51–62). London: Wiley.

Kiecolt-Glaser, J. K., & Williams, D. A. (1987). Self-blame, compliance, and distress among burn patients. *Journal of Personality and Social Psychology, 53,* 187–193.

Klinger, E. (1975). Consequences of, commitment to, and disengagement from incentives. *Psychological Review, 82,* 1–25.

Kobasa, S. C. (1979). Stressful life events, personality and health: An inquiry into hardiness. *Journal of Personality and Social Psychology, 37,* 1–11.

Kübler-Ross, E. (1969). *On death and dying.* New York: Macmillan.

Langer, E., & Rodin, J. (1976). The effect of choice and enhanced personal responsibility for the aged: A field experiment in an institutional setting. *Journal of Personality and Social Psychology, 34,* 191–198.

Lazarus, R. S., & Folkman, S. (1984). *Stress, appraisal, and coping.* New York: Springer.

Link, P. W., & Darling, C. A. (1986). Couples undergoing treatment for infertility: Dimensions of life satisfaction. *Journal of Sex and Marital Therapy, 12,* 46–59.

Litt, M. D. (March, 1989). Attributions of causality and control in adaptation in in-vitro fertilization. Presented at the tenth annual meeting of the Society of Behavioral Medicine, San Francisco.

Major, B., Mueller, P., & Hildebrandt, K. (1985). Attributions, expectations, and coping with abortion. *Journal of Personality and Social Psychology, 48*, 585–599.

Mazor, M. D., & Simons, H. F. (Eds.). (1984). *Infertility: Medical, emotional and social considerations.* New York: Human Sciences Press.

McEwan, K. L., Costello, C. G., & Taylor, P. J. (1987). Adjustment to infertility. *Journal of Abnormal Psychology, 96*, 108–116.

Menning, B. E. (1977). *Infertility: A guide for the childless couple.* Englewood Cliffs, NJ: Prentice-Hall.

Menning, B. E. (1980). The emotional needs of infertile couples. *Fertility and Sterility, 34*, 313–319.

Meyer, C. B., & Taylor, S. E. (1986). Adjustment to rape. *Journal of Personality and Social Psychology, 51*, 1226–1234.

Miller, S. (1980). Why having control reduces stress: If I can stop the roller coaster, I don't want to get off. In J. Garber & M. Seligman (Eds.), *Human helplessness: Theory and applications* (pp. 71–95). New York: Academic Press.

Rothbaum, F., Weisz, J. R., & Snyder, S. S. (1982). Changing the world and changing the self: A two-process model of perceived control. *Journal of Personality and Social Psychology, 42*, 5–37.

Scheier, M. F., & Carver, C. S. (1985). Optimism, coping, and health: Assessment and implications of generalized outcome expectancies. *Health Psychology, 4*, 219–247.

Scheier, M. F., & Carver, C. S. (1987). Dispositional optimism and physical well-being: The influence of generalized outcome expectancies on health. *Journal of Personality, 55*, 169–210.

Seligman, M. E. P. (1975). *Helplessness.* San Francisco: W. H. Freeman.

Shontz, F. C. (1975). *The psychological aspects of physical illness and disability.* New York: Macmillan.

Shur, M. (1953). The ego and anxiety. In R. M. Lowenstein (Ed.), *Drives, affects, and behavior* (pp. 279–375). New York: International Unversities Press.

Silver, R. L., & Wortman, C. B. (1980). Coping with undesirable life events. In J. Garber & M. E. P. Seligman (Eds.), *Human helplessness: Theory and applications* (pp. 279–375). New York: Academic Press.

Stangel, J. J. (1979). *Fertility and conception.* New York: Paddington Press.

Sudman, S., & Bradburn, N. M. (1974). *Response effects in surveys: A review and synthesis.* Chicago: Aldine.

Suls, J., & Mullen, B. (1981). Life events, perceived control and illness: The role of uncertainty. *Journal of Human Stress, 7*, 30–34.

Taylor, S. E., Lichtman, R. R., & Wood, J. V. (1984). Attributions, beliefs about control, and adjustment to breast cancer. *Journal of Personality and Social Psychology, 46*, 489–502.

Tennen, H., & Affleck, G. (1987). The costs and benefits of optimistic explanations and dispositional optimism. *Journal of Personality, 55*, 377–393.

Tennen, H., & Affleck, G. (1990). Blaming others for threatening events. *Psychological Bulletin, 108*, 209–232.

Tennen, H., Affleck, G., & Gershman, K. (1986). Self-blame among parents of infants with perinatal complication: The role of self-protective motives. *Journal of Personality and Social Psychology, 50*, 690–696.

Tennen, H., Affleck, G., & Herzberger, S. (1985). SCL-90-R. In D. J. Keyser & R. C. Sweetland (Eds.), *Test critiques* (Vol. 3, pp. 583–594). Kansas City, MO: Test Corporation of America.

Tennen, H., Allen, D. A., Affleck, G., McGrade, B. J., & Ratzan, S. (1984). Causal attributions and coping with insulin-dependent diabetes. *Basic and Applied Social Psychology, 5,* 131–142.

Thompson, I. E. (1984). The medical workup: Female and combined problems. In M. D. Mazor & H. F. Simons (Eds.), *Infertility: Medical, emotional, and social considerations* (pp. 3–12). New York: Human Sciences Press.

Thompson, S. C. (1981). Will it hurt less if I can control it? A complex answer to a simple question. *Psychological Bulletin, 90,* 89–101.

Thompson, S. C. (1985). Finding positive meaning in a stressful event and coping. *Basic and Applied Social Psychology, 6,* 279–295.

Timko, C., & Janoff-Bulman, R. (1985). Attributions, vulnerability, and psychological adjustment: The case of breast cancer. *Health Psychology, 4,* 521–544.

Weiner, B. (1985). "Spontaneous" causal thinking. *Psychological Bulletin, 97,* 74–84.

Whitley, B. E., & Frieze, I. H. (1986). Measuring causal attributions for success and failure: A meta-analysis of the effects of question-wording style. *Basic and Applied Social Psychology, 7,* 35–51.

Wortman, C. B., & Silver, R. C. (1987). Coping with irrevocable loss. In G. R. VandenBos & B. K. Bryant (Eds.), *Cataclysms, crises, and catastrophies: Psychology in action* (pp. 189–235). Washington, DC: American Psychological Association.

Zetzel, E. (1965). Depression and the capacity to bear it. In M. Shur (Ed.), *Drives, affects, and behavior* (Vol. 2, pp. 243–274). New York: International Universities Press.

7

Perceived Control and Adjustment to Infertility among Women Undergoing *In Vitro* Fertilization

SUSAN MILLER CAMPBELL,
CHRISTINE DUNKEL-SCHETTER, and
LETITIA ANNE PEPLAU

Infertility is, by definition, a loss of control over one's reproductive ability. Yet very little systematic empirical research has examined how the objective facts of infertility translate into subjective experiences of personal control. On the one hand, infertile individuals are poignantly aware of their inability to control reproduction, and this perceived lack of control might increase the psychological distress of infertility. On the other hand, infertile individuals may differ widely in how they interpret their unsuccessful efforts to conceive. Some may emphasize the available options for enhancing the probability of becoming pregnant, rather than focusing on their past failure to conceive. Particularly for those who persist in efforts to conceive, the belief that personal efforts make a difference may be essential.

SUSAN MILLER CAMPBELL, CHRISTINE DUNKEL-SCHETTER, and LETITIA ANNE PEPLAU • Department of Psychology, University of California, Los Angeles, California 90024-1563.

Anecdotal evidence has identified feelings of loss of control as common among involuntarily childless individuals (Mahlstedt, 1985; McCormick, 1980; Matthews & Matthews, 1986; Menning, 1977; Sandelowski & Jones, 1986; Seibel & Taymor, 1982). Valentine (1986), for example, interviewed infertile couples and found that one of the many losses they reported was loss of control over their bodies. Because adults of reproductive age are part of a generation that is unique in its ability to avoid unwanted pregnancy, the inability to control getting pregnant may be all the more distressing for today's infertile couples (McCormick, 1980; Valentine, 1986).

Platt, Ficher, and Silver (1973) also found that infertile individuals experience a loss of control. Infertile couples were compared to couples who had no difficulty conceiving, and the infertile people were more likely to perceive themselves as controlled by external forces, as assessed by Rotter's (1966) I-E Locus of Control Scale. The researchers suggested that experiences with the loss of control inherent in infertility may have altered these individuals' perceptions of the amount of control they have in their lives in general (see also Paulson, Haarmann, Salerno, & Asmar, 1988).

Treatments for infertility typically involve a significant loss of control. Diagnostic procedures and treatments for infertility are generally invasive, technically complicated, and difficult for even an educated layperson to understand. Details of a couple's sexual relationship are recorded and prescriptions for changes in the frequency and timing of intercourse are common. Such procedures can threaten the couple's sense of control over their sexual relationship and the privacy it is usually accorded (Matthews & Matthews, 1986). The stress of treatment can be compounded if the physician does not inform or involve the couple in decision-making. These are just a few of the ways in which medical treatments may substantially erode an infertile couple's sense of personal control.

In vitro fertilization (IVF) is a particularly stressful treatment that may further threaten perceptions of control (see Davajan & Israel, this volume, for procedures). IVF is expensive and invasive, and the probability of conception is low (Dennerstein & Morse, 1985). The chances of becoming parents through IVF appear to be about 16% in the U.S. (Medical Research International and American Fertility Society, 1989). For most couples, IVF is a "last chance" treatment, following years of unsuccessful attempts at conception. The inability to become pregnant through IVF usually means that women must acknowledge that they are permanently infertile (Dennerstein & Morse, 1985). Sophisticated IVF procedures require much expertise from medical personnel and little from the couple, perhaps further reducing the infertile individual's sense of control.

In this chapter, we explore the complex ways in which infertile women understand the issue of control and the impact that perceptions of control have on psychological adjustment. Relevant theory and findings from the psychology of control are presented along with the results of our study of women undergoing IVF treatment. First, we discuss theories and approaches, as well as data from our own study, highlighting the ways that infertile women perceive and experience control. Second, we review studies documenting the costs and benefits of control and, from our own data, examine the role of perceived control in predicting women's psychological adjustment to infertility. Finally, implications of our work for future research are considered.

THE PSYCHOLOGY OF CONTROL

In this section, we selectively highlight four perspectives on the study of control, as well as more recent distinctions among types of control, that are relevant to our study of involuntarily infertile women. This is not a comprehensive review of the psychological control literature; rather, we have attempted to organize previous and current thinking about control in a way relevant to the study of infertility. We also present data from our study of women in IVF treatment pertaining to these recent distinctions.

Approaches to the Study of Control

In psychology, one of the first research traditions to consider the importance of control investigated situations that deprive individuals of control over desired outcomes and thus lead to psychological reactance (Brehm, 1966) or learned helplessness (Seligman, 1975). These researchers explored the nature of individuals' reactions to an objective loss of control. Loss of control was viewed as aversive and likely to lead to depression and other negative effects (Wortman, 1976). The experience of infertility inherently involves such a loss of control, since all infertile individuals find themselves in a situation where they are unable to conceive. Based on control research in this tradition, one would expect infertile couples to experience considerable distress.

In a second early approach, Rotter (1966) emphasized individual differences in beliefs about control. He suggested that people tend to develop fairly stable beliefs about their ability to affect their personal outcomes. Whereas some people tend to believe that they have a high degree of personal control (an "internal" locus of control), others believe their outcomes are largely determined by factors outside their control (an "external" locus of control). Folkman (1984) addressed the same issue in terms of individuals' generalized beliefs that they have high or low control over events in their lives. As applied to infertility, this research tradition raises two important questions. Do individuals who believe they generally have much control over their lives react differently to infertility than individuals who believe they have little control? Do IVF patients who have a long history of infertility come to believe that they have little personal control over their lives in general?

A third research tradition has emphasized the importance of subjective perceptions of control. In this conceptualization, perceived control refers to the subjective belief that one has the capacity to influence outcomes in a specific set of circumstances, regardless of whether one actually has this capacity (Langer, 1983). One recent example of this approach would be Bandura's (1982, 1986) concept of self-efficacy, which is a judgment or perception of one's ability to "execute courses of action required to deal with prospective situations" (1982, p. 122). This tradition does not attempt to assess the accuracy of perceptions of control, but rather considers the adaptiveness of perceptions of control even when they are illusory (Taylor, 1983). In the case of infertility, the issue becomes the extent to which individuals perceive that they can affect their reproductive outcomes and the adaptiveness of such perceptions. Individuals seeking treatment for infertility are never certain whether they will eventually conceive, and this ambiguity allows for variation in perceptions of personal control. Whereas some infertile individuals may think that there is little they can do to change their situation, others may think that they can enhance their chances of pregnancy significantly by behaviors such as watching their diet, adhering carefully to medical regimens, maintaining a positive attitude, and so on. Research on perceived control also raises questions pertinent to infertility. Given the uncertainty of conception, to what extent and in what ways do infertile people perceive that they possess personal control over their situation? Are levels of perceived control adaptive with respect to the psychological adjustment of infertile women?

A fourth research tradition has emphasized behaviors that individuals may use to seek or exert control (Averill, 1973; Rothbaum, Weisz, & Snyder, 1982). Folkman (1984) has suggested that individuals use both problem-focused coping that seeks to change the situation, and emotion-focused coping that seeks to influence the individual's reactions to the situation. In the case of infertility, the questions are: What do individuals do to alter their chances of conception? How do they attempt to control or manage their emotional reactions to infertility and treatment?

The Research Context

Our study of IVF patients enabled us to consider many of these questions in detail. Participants were 38 women either waiting for or receiving IVF treatment in Southern California. IVF patients were selected because control seemed particularly relevant to their experiences. In addition, because most IVF patients have been seeking treatment for an extended period, it seemed possible that at least some of the women in our sample would exhibit high levels of distress.

Participants were recruited at two sites. All participants completed a self-administered questionnaire accompanied by an introductory letter explaining the nature and purpose of the research. Most (74%) of the final sample were contacted through the UCLA In Vitro Fertilization Program. A total of 70 questionnaires were distributed to UCLA patients, either by mail or in person, and 40% were returned by mail to the researchers. The actual response rate for this group may be somewhat higher, however. Some addresses on the mailing list were not current, so it is likely that some questionnaires were never received by the potential participants. The remaining 26% of participants received a questionnaire in person at the Hoag Fertility Services Center in Newport Beach, California. Of the 19 questionnaires distributed at Hoag, 53% were returned to the Program Coordinator at the clinic.

Participants from the two infertility programs did not differ significantly on any background or demographic characteristics. The average age of the respondents was 36 years, and the average family income was between $55,000 and $70,000. This income level is high relative to the general population but is not surprising, given the costs of IVF treatment. Those who seek IVF must either be able to pay for the treatment themselves or have jobs that provide health insurance that will reimburse costly infertility treatments. Most (76%) women in the study were white, and more than 70% were employed outside the home. They had been seeking treatment for infertility for one to more than 10 years, with a median of 4 years. Most (70%) were being treated for primary infertility; 30% had previously given birth and were being treated for secondary infertility.

General versus Situation-Specific Control

Folkman (1984) has explored aspects of control that have implications for the study of stressful life events and, in particular, infertility. She emphasized the importance of two conceptually distinct types of control: *generalized beliefs* about control and *situation-specific appraisals* of control.

Folkman proposed that a generalized sense of control has implications for appraisals of stressful situations, particularly when the situation is ambiguous or novel. In such a situation, those who believe that they have a high degree of general control are more likely to perceive opportunities for control; conversely, those individuals who generally believe they have little or no control will be likely to assess the situation as uncontrollable (Folkman, 1984; Rotter, 1966). On the other hand, perceived situational control involves an individual's perception of the control opportunities available in a particular situation. Folkman argued that this perception is developed by evaluating the extent to which personal control is possible, as well as the availability of coping strategies.

Consistent with Folkman's (1984) distinction between general and situation-specific control, our study assessed both general control and infertility control. The Pearlin Mastery Scale was used to measure general control beliefs (Pearlin, Menaghan, Lieberman, & Mullan, 1981). The scale consists of seven items, each rated on a 7-point scale from "agree" to "disagree." It includes such items as "I have little control over the things that happen to me" and "I can do just about anything I really set my mind to." A total score is computed as the average response to the 7 items. Internal consistency of the scale (Cronbach's alpha) for our sample was .78. We developed a second control measure (adapted from Skokan, 1987) to assess control specific to infertility. It appears in Figure 1. Participants rated the extent to which they felt they could control three specific domains of infertility: The probability that they would become pregnant (items 1 and 2); their medical treatment (item 3); and their emotional reactions to infertility (items 4 and 5). Ratings were made on 5-point scales ranging from 1, "not at all," to 5, "completely." The infertility control score was computed as the average of the five items. The internal consistency of this scale was .76.

Folkman (1984) argued that general and situation-specific control are conceptually distinct from one another. In our study, the question is: Are these measures of two types of control among IVF patients actually independent? A partial answer was provided by the low correlation between the two measures ($r = .25$, $p = .06$). Women who felt a great deal of control over their lives in general did not necessarily report a high degree of control over infertility. Consistent with Folkman's analysis, these constructs seem to have been fairly independent as measured, although the magnitude of the correlation may have been slightly attenuated due to low variance and high means on both variables.

On average, perceptions of general control were quite high in our sample. The mean score on the Mastery scale was 5.9 (S.D. = .97) com-

The Measure of Infertility Control

1. How much can you control the likelihood that you will get pregnant by the
    things you do or the actions you take (diet, exercise, reducing stress, etc.)?

1	2	3	4	5
Not at all	A little	Somewhat	Very much	Completely

2. How much can you control the likelihood that you will eventually get
    pregnant by your mental attitude and the way you look at your situation?

1	2	3	4	5
Not at all	A little	Somewhat	Very much	Completely

3. How much can you control the type of treatment and quality of medical
    services you receive by the things you do or the actions you take?

1	2	3	4	5
Not at all	A little	Somewhat	Very much	Completely

4. How much can you control the negative feelings you have about your
    infertility by the things you do and the actions you take?

1	2	3	4	5
Not at all	A little	Somewhat	Very much	Completely

5. How much can you control the negative feelings you have about your
    infertility by your mental attitude and the way you look at your situation?

1	2	3	4	5
Not at all	A little	Somewhat	Very much	Completely

Note: Items 1 and 2 assess control over pregnancy, item 3 assesses control over
medical treatment, and items 4 and 5 assess control over emotional responses to
infertility. In addition, items 1, 3 and 4 assess behavioral control over these aspects
of infertility, and items 2 and 5 assess cognitive control.

FIGURE 1

pared to means of 3.7 and 3.8 for two community samples of men and
women, aged 18 to 65 years (Pearlin *et al.*, 1981). Sixty percent of our
sample scored 6.0 or higher on the 7-point scale. Further, the women we
studied felt moderate control over their infertility. On our measure of
perceived infertility control, the mean score was 3.1 (S.D. = .76), with a
possible range of 1.0 to 5.0.

Behavioral versus Cognitive Control

A further distinction is also useful, namely, to differentiate behavioral
from cognitive control. Building upon previous conceptualizations of control (e.g., Averill, 1973; Miller, 1979), Thompson (1981) defined *behavioral
control* as the "belief that one has a behavioral response available that can
affect the aversiveness of an event" (p. 90). She defined *cognitive control* as
the "belief that one has a cognitive strategy available that can affect the
aversiveness of an event" (p. 90). We investigated whether the conceptual
distinction between behavioral and cognitive control is meaningful for
women undergoing IVF, and whether perceptions of behavioral and cognitive control are independent. The five items in our infertility control
measure (see Figure 1) were designed to distinguish between behavioral
and cognitive control. Items 1, 3, and 4 assessed behavioral control by
asking the extent to which control can be achieved "by the things you do
or the actions you take." Items 2 and 5 assessed cognitive control achieved
"by your mental attitude and the way you look at your situation."

Subscales were created by computing separate means for the two sets
of items. Indices of perceptions of behavioral and cognitive control were
highly correlated ($r = .75, p < .01$). Women who perceived a high degree
of behavioral control over their infertility also tended to perceive high
levels of cognitive control. This may suggest that the behavioral versus
cognitive distinction is not applicable in the infertility setting, or that the
two concepts were not operationalized in a way that was meaningful for
women in this sample.

Domains of Infertility Control

In reference to her analysis of situational control, Folkman (1984) also
asked the important question, "control over what?" She argued that in any
situation there is often more than one possibility for control. That is, "an
individual might be expected to control one aspect of a situation but not
another" (Folkman, 1984, p. 843). Based on this premise, we varied the
particular domain of control in our infertility control measure. Respondents assessed the degree of perceived control they felt over the probability
of their becoming pregnant (items 1 and 2), their medical treatment for

infertility (item 3), and their emotional reactions to infertility (items 4 and 5).

On the average, women felt a bit more than "a little" control over the likelihood that they would get pregnant. The mean rating for control over pregnancy was 2.41 on a 5-point scale. They felt between "somewhat" and "very much" control, however, over their medical treatment and their emotional reactions to infertility. The mean ratings.for control over medical treatment and emotions were 3.74 and 3.49, respectively.

To examine whether women experienced greater control over some aspects of infertility than others, we conducted paired t-tests for the differences among the three domain means, and found a significant difference between perceived control over pregnancy and control over the other two domains. Perceptions of pregnancy control were significantly lower than perceptions of control over medical treatment [$t(37) = 7.38, p < .01$] and significantly lower than perceptions of control over emotional responses [$t(36) = 5.56, p < .01$]. The medical treatment and emotional control scores were not significantly different from each other [$t(36) = 1.49, p = .15$].

The three domains were conceptualized to assess meaningfully distinct aspects of perceived control over infertility. Were perceptions of control over each of the three domains actually independent in our sample? Correlational analyses found small-to-moderate associations among the three domains of control. Perceptions of control over pregnancy and over medical treatment were weakly related ($r = .26, p = .06$). It would be possible to interpret "control over medical treatment" as meaning "control over treatment *as a means of becoming pregnant*," making control over treatment a subset of control over pregnancy. However, the small correlation between the two domains indicates that perceptions of control over treatment and of control over pregnancy items were largely distinct. The other domains were moderately related. Control over treatment shared about 16% variance with control over emotional reactions ($r = .42, p < .01$). The correlation between perceived control over pregnancy and perceived control over emotional reactions was similar in magnitude ($r = .36, p < .05$). Perceptions of control over different domains of infertility were therefore related in varying degrees. This may reflect underlying general beliefs about control over infertility, but the aspects were distinguishable in general.

Examples of Control among Women Undergoing IVF

In addition to providing ratings of five types of infertility control, participants were also asked to provide examples of the ways in which they exercise the five types of control. Answers illustrated the surprising variety of options for exercising control felt by women undergoing *in vitro* fertilization.

In response to the question about control of pregnancy by behaviors, most women reported engaging in health behaviors such as abstaining from cigarettes, drugs, and alcohol, attempting to maintain a healthy diet, beginning an exercise regimen, and reducing or managing stress. As one woman wrote, "I want to purify my body as much as possible." A few reported prayer as a means of exercising control in this domain.

When answering the item about cognitive control over pregnancy, women's views on the importance of their thoughts and attitudes for becoming pregnant ranged from wholehearted enthusiasm to skepticism, although they tended to be favorable more often than not. Many women tended to describe attempts to maintain a positive attitude and why they thought this was important. In particular, some believed that there was a link between their mental state and their body's functioning. One woman said, "Keeping positive and relaxed can help the body work to its best potential!" Not all women believed that optimism leads to pregnancy, however. Said one respondent, "I'd like to think that keeping a good attitude can only help our chances of getting pregnant, but I'm not sure it's true. We keep a good outlook anyway—it feels better." Another stated less equivocally, "I think I *have* a good mental attitude, and it hasn't gotten me pregnant."

When asked how they felt they could control their treatments through their actions, most women referred to their choice of physicians, treatment centers, and types of treatment. They also reported seeking information about treatment options and adhering to the treatment regimen. One woman wrote:

> I have received the best medical care possible . . . I know this without a doubt because all along the way I have been active in my infertility treatment. I have read books, articles, medical journals, attended information related meetings, etc. and always asked my doctor questions when something was unclear.

The topic of controlling negative feelings by behaviors elicited a variety of coping strategies. These included seeking information, seeking social support, and focusing on the goal of having a baby. One woman explained, "When I feel depressed . . . talking it out with my husband really works." Other behaviors mentioned were keeping busy, distraction, and avoiding the issues. Another said, "I bury myself in paperwork to forget."

With respect to controlling negative emotions through attitude, most respondents indicated that they tried to keep perspective or to change the way they thought about the situation. One woman wrote, "My husband

and I have been through a lot of trials, and yet I think we have controlled all negative feelings by keeping this in perspective and knowing that this is only a part of our lives." Another said, "Although I would like to have children, I do not need children to have a fulfilling life. I have a successful career." Other women mentioned that they try to "count their blessings." In general, these answers conveyed a strong desire to avoid dwelling on negative thoughts associated with infertility. Reframing the problem and keeping it in perspective seemed to be useful ways of coping for many women in our sample (see also, Stanton, this volume).

CONTROL AND ADJUSTMENT TO INFERTILITY

A further goal of this research was to explore the relationship between perceived control and psychological adjustment to infertility. As background, a brief review of previous research on the benefits and costs of continued perceptions of control is useful. Data from our own study are then presented.

Benefits and Costs of Control

Much research documents the benefits of perceived control on responses to stress (see Averill, 1973; Thompson, 1981, for reviews). Laboratory studies, using such stressors as electric shock, bursts of noise or ice-water immersion, have associated perceived control with increased tolerance of noxious or painful stimuli (Kanfer & Goldfoot, 1966; Kanfer & Seider, 1973; Staub, Tursky, & Schwartz, 1971), reduced physiological arousal (Geer, Davison, & Gatchel, 1970), decreased anxiety (Holmes & Houston, 1974; Houston, 1972), and reports of fewer physical symptoms (Pennebaker, Burnam, Schaeffer, & Harper, 1977).

Studies in field settings have also shown that greater control can reduce negative reactions to stress. For example, Langer and Rodin (1976) showed that residents of a nursing home who were experimentally provided with some degree of control over their environment reported feeling happier and more alert, and were more likely to participate in planned activities than residents for whom control opportunities were not emphasized. Hobfoll and Lerman (1988) studied a sample of Israeli mothers experiencing the stress of a child's illness. The women who perceived themselves as having a high degree of general control over their environment and their future experienced less distress and more satisfaction with their social support than did women who perceived less control.

Health psychologists have theorized about the role of control in adjustment to health problems (Michela & Wood, 1986; Wallston, Wallston, Smith, & Dobbins, 1987) and have conducted correlational studies linking perceived control over health-related outcomes to psychological adjustment. Taylor, Lichtman, and Wood (1984) found that breast cancer patients who believed they could control their cancer were better adjusted than patients reporting low personal control over the disease (Taylor, 1983; Taylor & Brown, 1988). Affleck, Tennen, Pfeiffer, and Fifield (1987) investigated appraisals of control among rheumatoid arthritis patients and found that perceived control over treatment was associated with better mood and psychosocial adjustment. These findings, taken with the laboratory and field studies reported above, support the contention that perceived control is adaptive.

However, some researchers have considered the possibility that perceived control may not always be beneficial. Wortman and Brehm (1975) argued that it may be maladaptive to perceive personal control in a situation where none exists. They suggested that the most adaptive response to a truly uncontrollable situation may be acceptance. Consistent with this view, Wortman (1976) argued that attempts to gain or restore control when none can be achieved may only postpone acceptance, coping, and recovery. Thus, although perceived control can sometimes be beneficial, it can also be detrimental to well-being.

Our study considered the benefits and costs of control for infertile women. Specifically, we studied how perceptions of control of various kinds were related to psychological adjustment among women undergoing IVF treatment.

Measures of Adjustment

Psychological adjustment is a multidimensional concept, including such components as emotion, morale, and self-esteem (see Stanton & Dunkel-Schetter, this volume). Two dimensions of adjustment that are conceptually distinct and appropriate to the problem of infertility were selected for this study. These were depression and perceived quality of life. In our study, higher levels of depression and lower quality of life ratings were considered to be indicators of poor psychological adjustment.

Depression has been well documented as a response to infertility (Bell, 1981; Eisner, 1963; McGrade & Tolor, 1981; Menning, 1977; Platt et al., 1973; Wilson, 1979). We used the Center for Epidemiologic Studies Depression Scale (CES-D) (Radloff, 1977). The 20-item scale asks respondents to rate the frequency of symptoms associated with depression. A rating of 0 indicates that a symptom was not experienced during the past week, and a score of 3 indicates that a symptom was experienced from five to seven days in the last week. Sample items are: "I felt that I could not shake off the blues even with help from my family and friends," and "I had crying spells." Scores for the CES-D are summed over the 20 items, and range from 0.0 (indicating that all depressive symptoms were experienced less than one day) to 60.0 (indicating that all symptoms were experienced from five to seven days in the last week).

For our sample, the mean depression score was 12.7 with a standard deviation of 10.85, and scores ranged from 1.0 to 37.0. The majority of our sample (76%) had a score of 15.0 or less. In previous research, mean scores on the CES-D for three community samples of white men and women ranged from 8.0 to 9.3, and the mean score for a sample of psychiatric patients was 24.4 (Radloff, 1977). Thus, women in our sample experienced depressive symptoms more frequently than community samples, but less frequently than the psychiatric sample.

The second adjustment measure, quality of life, was included to examine general feelings of life satisfaction. We used a 20-item version of the Quality of Life Index (QOL) (Andrews & Withey, 1974, 1976) to assess how a woman felt in the past week about various areas of her life, including her job, marriage, friends, and income. Variations of the QOL have been used in other infertility studies (Callan, 1987; Callan & Hennessey, 1988). Our version used a 7-point response scale, from 1, having felt "terrible," to 7, having felt "delighted." Scores for our sample ranged from 3.2 to 6.9, with a mean score of 5.2 and a standard deviation of .79. Women in our sample were "mostly satisfied" with their lives.

General versus Situation-Specific Control and Adjustment

How might situation-specific and general control affect psychological adjustment to infertility? Low control over fertility choices should have adverse consequences for adjustment, particularly if parenting is a highly valued goal. Generalized control beliefs may also be important. Despite a loss of infertility control, infertile women with a strong belief that they control their lives in general (i.e., who are high in mastery) may be better adjusted than infertile women with weaker generalized control beliefs. In other words, feeling effective in work, avocational activities, or interpersonal relationships might buffer an infertile woman from the adverse effects of loss of infertility control. It is possible, however, that a woman's level of adjustment also affects her perceptions of control. That is, well-adjusted women may find it less difficult to perceive control in adverse circumstances. In either case, both situation-specific and generalized control ratings should be significantly related to indices of adjustment.

To examine this issue in our sample, separate regression analyses were performed using the two control variables to predict depression and quality of life. Two additional issues were addressed in the regression models. First, income was also included in all analyses. Although women in our sample tended to be comfortable financially, family incomes ranged from less than $25,000 to more than $85,000; more than 70% of the sample had family incomes over $55,000. Given the high cost of IVF treatment and the general link between low income and stress, we expected that higher income would be associated with better psychological adjustment. Income was correlated with both depression ($r = -.24$, $p = .08$) and quality of life ($r = .41$, $p < .01$). Second, we explored the possibility of an interaction between the effects of situation-specific and generalized control to test the possibility that low perceived control of infertility is only detrimental to women high in general control. An interaction term was entered in all initial regression analyses. However, because the interaction term was not a significant predictor in any equation, it was dropped from further analyses.

Results of regression analyses for depression and quality of life are presented in Table 1. Opposite patterns emerged for depression and quality of life. Depression was significantly predicted by lower perceived infertility control and lower income, but not by general control. In contrast, quality of life was significantly predicted by general control and income, but not by infertility control. The data are consistent with the following conclusions. Infertility-specific perceptions of control are beneficial with respect to depression, but not with respect to life quality.

Table 1. Results of General/Infertility Control Multiple Regression Analyses with Depression and Quality of Life as Dependent Variables

Predictor	Standardized coefficient	Standard error	T	Total R squared	F value
Dependent variable = Depression				.32	6.27**
General control	-.12	(.10)	-1.23		
Infertility control	-.36	(.10)	-3.47**		
Income	-.10	(.05)	-2.17**		
Dependent variable = Quality of life				.34	6.82**
General control	.40	(.14)	2.77**		
Infertility control	.25	(.15)	1.66		
Income	.21	(.07)	3.03**		

*$p < .05$. **$p < .01$.

General beliefs about control, on the other hand, are beneficial with respect to life quality, but not with respect to depression. Thus, the more specific control measure is predictive of the more specific outcome, and the more general measure of control predicts the more global outcome. A "match" in the level of conceptualization may be important in understanding the relationship between various types of control and aspects of adjustment (Dunkel-Schetter, Folkman, & Lazarus, 1987). Reverse causality is also possible such that depression leads to lower perceptions of infertility control, and lower life satisfaction reduces general control beliefs. Longitudinal studies would be necessary to address these issues of causal inference adequately.

Domains of Infertility Control and Adjustment

As discussed earlier, the women in our sample perceived substantially less control over becoming pregnant than over their treatment or emotional reactions. Do assessments of these three facets of infertility control have differential effects on psychological adjustment? Our data suggest that they do. The results of multiple regression analyses, with depression and quality of life as the dependent variables, are presented in Table 2. Income and control over medical treatment were significant predictors of both depression and quality of life. Control over emotional reactions pre-

Table 2. Results of Domain of Infertility Control Multiple Regression Analyses with Depression and Quality of Life as Dependent Variables

Predictor	Standardized coefficient	Standard error	T	Total R squared	F value
Dependent variable = Depression					
				.37	5.74**
Pregnancy	−.82	(1.43)	−0.57		
Medical treatment	−3.73	(1.74)	−2.33*		
Emotional responses	−3.29	(1.43)	−2.30*		
Income	−2.12	(0.91)	−2.33*		
Dependent variable = Quality of life					
				.49	8.96**
Pregnancy	−.13	(.10)	−1.30		
Medical treatment	.53	(.13)	4.26**		
Emotional responses	.14	(.10)	1.39		
Income	.15	(.06)	2.33*		

*$p < .05.$ **$p < .01.$

dicted depression but not quality of life, and control over pregnancy did not significantly predict either measure of adjustment.

In summary, perceptions of control over "the type of treatment and quality of medical services" were very important in our sample. Women who felt they could make a difference in their treatment were less likely to be depressed and dissatisfied than women who felt relatively less control over their treatment. For women undergoing a complex, invasive, and costly form of medical intervention, this result makes sense.

We also found that perceived control over negative emotional reactions was predictive of depression, but not of life satisfaction. Women who felt they could effectively manage the negative feelings they had about their infertility were significantly less likely to report depressive symptoms, indicating that their perceptions of emotional control were not merely illusory. In contrast, women who experienced less control over their emotions were more depressed. The lack of association between perceived control of emotions and quality of life is consistent with the view that life satisfaction reflects a fairly stable assessment of several aspects of one's life that may be unaffected by negative experiences in one particular life domain.

IMPLICATIONS

The results of our study have implications both for understanding the nature of perceived control and for understanding reactions to infertility.

Types of Control

Our results provide strong support for Folkman's (1984) distinction between general and situation-specific control. General control and infertility control were for the most part unrelated to each other, and each predicted different aspects of psychological adjustment in our sample. Although generalized beliefs about control were related to quality of life, perceptions of control over infertility were related to depression.

Distinctions among the three specific domains of infertility control proved to be meaningful for the women in our sample. Women's ratings of perceived control over pregnancy were lower than perceived control over either medical treatment or emotional reactions, suggesting that individuals do distinguish between control over specific domains of infertility. For the women in our sample, becoming pregnant is truly uncontrollable, whereas treatment and emotions are at least somewhat amenable to control. In addition, these three domains were differentially predictive of psychological adjustment, providing further evidence for the usefulness of the distinction.

Our research also addressed the distinction between behavioral and cognitive control, but these results were less clear-cut. Perceptions of behavioral and cognitive control over infertility were highly intercorrelated, and the mean ratings of the two concepts were not significantly different. Quantitative data did not verify the differentiability of cognitive and behavioral control perceptions. In contrast, qualitative data suggested that the behavioral/cognitive distinction may be useful. For example, women reported maintaining a healthy diet, reading about treatment options, and increasing involvement with work as ways of asserting behavioral control, whereas they reported cognitive control strategies such as maintaining a positive attitude and keeping fertility problems in perspective.

Degree of Perceived Control

Despite the objective loss of control inherent in infertility and repeated anecdotal observations that infertile individuals feel a substantial loss of control (see review in Dunkel-Schetter & Lobel, this volume), participants in our study generally felt a great deal of control. Women felt at least moderate control over various aspects of their infertility, and their ratings of generalized life control were quite high relative to published norms. Thus, extended treatment for infertility was not associated with perceptions of low control. Although systematic studies have not been published to date on infertility-specific control, three studies on locus of control in infertile individuals do exist. Our results on general control are consistent with those of Dennerstein & Morse (1985) who found women awaiting IVF treatment to be toward the internal end of a locus of control measure. However, our results are inconsistent with the results of Paulson et al. (1988) and Platt et al. (1973), both of whom found that infertile women tended to be more external than control groups (although the difference between infertile and control women in the former and most rigorous study was not significant). A possible explanation for the divergence of findings involves the nature of the samples studied. Paulson et al. (1988) and Platt et al. (1973), who found greater external locus of control, studied general infertility patients and their spouses. On the other hand, both our study and that of Dennerstein & Morse (1985) sampled IVF patients and found more internal locus of control scores.

This suggests the possibility that women undergoing IVF are a select subset of infertile women who have higher perceptions of control. Women who pursue treatment for extended periods of time in general may be unusual in their ability to find opportunities for perceiving and exercising control. Because they are so adept at finding and exercising control, the treatment process may be less stressful, and they may therefore find it easier to continue treatment. Those who discontinue treatment early in the process or pursue other options, such as adoption or childlessness, may have much lower perceptions of control over infertility and their lives in general.

Individuals undergoing IVF may also be unique in their powerful desire for biological parenthood. IVF patients are likely to be a subset of infertile individuals whose motivation for parenthood is so strong that it overrides the financial and psychological costs of extended treatment (Callan, 1987; Callan & Hennessey, 1988). Their persistence in pursuing treatment is testimony to their willingness to go to great lengths to achieve their desired goal. Their substantial personal investments in infertility treatment and their strong desire for parenthood may motivate them to seek control in treatment situations that do little to encourage perceptions of control.

Our sample may also be atypical because of the income levels of women undergoing IVF treatment. On average, the participants in this research were financially quite secure. Over 70% of our sample had a family income greater than $55,000 per year. Perceptions of control may be enhanced by a comfortable income (see also Pearlin et al., 1981; Ross & Mirowsky, 1989). Income was not correlated with either infertility control or general control in our study, but our sample had a restricted range of family incomes, which may not have been adequate to demonstrate a relationship between income and control. Although it is not clear whether financial well-being plays a role in the elevated perceptions of control in our sample, future studies might usefully explore this issue.

Thus, there are a number of important ways in which couples who undergo IVF treatment may be different from other infertile individuals prior to treatment. On the other hand, strong perceptions of control may develop during the process of extended treatment for infertility. An enhanced sense of control over infertility specifically would be an adaptive method of coping with the chronic difficulties of this treatment. Taylor's (1983) cognitive adaptation theory argues that enhanced perceptions of control are adaptive in cancer patients and victims generally. Such perceptions enable them to maintain stability in the face of threat and loss experiences. The women in our sample who are in IVF treatment may have responded to infertility with this form of adaptive coping that enables them to persist in the face of what seem to others to be overwhelming challenges.

It is not clear, however, which of the foregoing explanations for the relatively high levels of control is most accurate. Are women in IVF treatment self-selected strong believers in control, or do they develop strong

feelings of control as a result of a strong desire for parenthood and prolonged infertility experiences? Future research with representative samples of IVF patients, non-IVF infertile patients at different stages of diagnosis and treatment, and fertile women is needed to clarify this result.

A different possibility is that the high degree of control reported by
the women in our sample could be a function of self presentational concerns, as with all self-report measures. This seems unlikely, however, given
that questionnaires were anonymous and were completed in the privacy of
participants' homes. In addition, participants provided many specific examples of the ways in which they exercise control over their infertility in
open-ended descriptions. Their responses illustrated a wide variety of
tactics used to enhance control over their treatment, their ability to become
pregnant through life-style changes, and their emotional responses to
infertility.

Finally, it is possible that the women who completed and returned our
questionnaire had higher control perceptions and beliefs than women who
were nonresponders. Although such a difference between responders and
nonresponders is a valid concern, there are no data to evaluate this possibility.

Control and Adjustment

Just as the women in our sample perceived more control than we
expected, they were also better adjusted psychologically than expected.
Ratings of depression were somewhat higher than those of community
samples but were much lower than the levels of depression reported by
psychiatric samples. Assessments of general life quality indicated that the
women in our sample were "mostly satisfied" with their lives. Why are
these women who have undergone years of stressful treatment and uncertainty regarding their fertility not more distressed? Many researchers
have suggested that responses to uncontrollable events depend on the
meaning assigned to them (e.g., Silver & Wortman, 1980; Taylor, 1983).
Thompson (1981) argued that the meaning assigned to uncontrollable
events may vary along three dimensions. According to Thompson, "one
important dimension of meaning [is] an assurance that one will not face an
event that is beyond the limits of endurance" (p. 98). If the event is
perceived as endurable, it will be much easier for the individual to cope.
Clearly, women undergoing IVF have decided that virtually anything is
endurable in the pursuit of pregnancy. The second dimension of meaning
is the extent to which the uncontrollable event is a means to a desirable
end. Although IVF treatment is a negative experience, it is aimed to
produce a much-desired pregnancy. The third dimension involves the

degree to which an event is perceived as planned rather than random; an event that results from an individual's plans or goals will be experienced as less stressful. Certainly a woman's inability to conceive is not part of her life plan. IVF treatment, however, is part of the larger plan for having children, and the stress associated with the treatment process may therefore be somewhat easier to cope with. By Thompson's three criteria, women undergoing IVF treatment could be expected to cope with the stress of treatment relatively well, and our data indicate that they do.

In addition to the stress of the treatment itself, women in IVF must also cope with the possibility that treatment will fail and that they will be permanently infertile. How can we explain their ability to remain psychologically well-adjusted in the face of this ambiguity? Administrators of IVF programs often report that couples seeking treatment are convinced that their own chances of conception are much higher than the reported success rates (Lasker & Borg, 1987). One study of men and women undergoing IVF and embryo transfer procedures found that all but one of 70 participants overestimated the likelihood of success of the procedures (Johnston, Shaw, & Bird, 1987). Perhaps IVF patients have not yet contemplated the possibility of permanent infertility because exaggerated optimism leads them to believe that this treatment option will provide them with the baby they desire.

Unfortunately, the success rates for IVF programs are low. Most couples will not become pregnant, and ultimately, their strong sense of perceived control will be disconfirmed. Such disconfirmation is one of the potentially negative consequences of high perceived control, and it is a major psychological risk for IVF patients. Although IVF patients may currently feel that they can influence their situation, how will they respond when they must ultimately accept a permanent loss of control over childbearing? Will they remain psychologically well-adjusted? Will their perceptions of control over other aspects of their life be altered? The ramifications of this disconfirmation of control should be of interest to both control and infertility researchers.

In addition to a possible disconfirmation of control, there may be other costs of perceived control for women undergoing IVF treatment which were not explored in our research. Psychologists have highlighted a number of ways in which control may be a mixed blessing (Folkman, 1984; Langer, 1983; Wortman, 1976). Pursuing control over one's fertility requires accepting the many negative aspects of treatment. Exercising certain kinds of control may be costly to the extent that it is inconsistent with one's personal style. For example, individuals who feel uncomfortable asking physicians questions or expressing their personal concerns may have difficulty exercising control over medical treatment. There are also potentially negative social consequences of exercising control such as the stress of infertility treatment for the marital relationship (Lasker & Borg, 1987). Finally, exercising control may require the expenditure of resources that might be needed elsewhere. The value of the time, money, and energy invested by infertile couples in the pursuit of pregnancy cannot be underestimated.

For infertile individuals, and particularly for those individuals undergoing IVF treatment, issues of control are complex and multifaceted. Perceptions of some types of control were surprisingly high and were associated with better psychological adjustment for the women in our sample. Other aspects of control, however, had little bearing on women's adjustment. Contrary to a wealth of anecdotal evidence, IVF patients did not exhibit a complete lack of perceived control or extreme levels of distress. However, the potentially negative consequences of perceived control over infertility, as well as the possible costs of infertility treatment, should not be ignored. Both control and infertility researchers, as well as health care professionals who treat infertile individuals, should recognize and explore this complexity in their efforts to understand the experience of infertility.

ACKNOWLEDGMENTS

We gratefully acknowledge the help and cooperation of Dr. Joseph Gambone of the UCLA In Vitro Fertilization Program and Elaine Ishida, R.N., of the Hoag Fertility Services Center in conducting this project.

REFERENCES

Affleck, G., Tennen, H., Pfeiffer, C., & Fifield, J. (1987). Appraisals of control and predictability in adapting to a chronic disease. *Journal of Personality and Social Psychology, 53*, 273–279.

Andrews, F. M., & Withey, S. B. (1974). Developing measures of perceived life quality: Results from several national surveys. *Social Indicators Research, 1*, 1–26.

Andrews, F. M., & Withey, S. B. (1976). *Social indicators of well-being: Americans' perceptions of life quality.* New York: Plenum.

Averill, J. R. (1973). Personal control over aversive stimuli and its relationship to stress. *Psychological Bulletin, 80*, 286–303.

Bandura, A. (1982). Self-efficacy mechanism in human agency. *American Psychologist, 37*, 122–147.

Bandura, A. (1986). *Social foundations of thought and action: A social cognitive theory.* Englewood Cliffs, NJ: Prentice-Hall.

Bell, J. S. (1981). Psychological problems among patients attending an infertility clinic. *Journal of Psychosomatic Research, 25*, 1–3.

Brehm, J. W. (1966). *A theory of psychological reactance.* New York: Academic Press.

Callan, V. J. (1987). The personal and marital adjustment of mothers and of voluntarily and involuntarily childless wives. *Journal of Marriage and the Family, 49*, 847–856.

Callan, V. J., & Hennessey, J. F. (1988). The psychological adjustment of women experiencing infertility. *British Journal of Medical Psychology, 61*, 137–140.

Dennerstein, L., & Morse, C. (1985). Psychological issues in IVF. *Clinics in Obstetrics and Gynaecology, 12*, 835–846.

Dunkel-Schetter, C., Folkman, S., & Lazarus, R. S. (1987). Correlates of social support receipt. *Journal of Personality and Social Psychology, 53*, 71–80.

Eisner, B. G. (1963). Some psychological differences between fertile and infertile women. *Journal of Clinical Psychology, 19*, 391–395.

Folkman, S. (1984). Personal control and stress and coping processes: A theoretical analysis. *Journal of Personality and Social Psychology, 46*, 839–852.

Geer, J. H., Davison, G. C., & Gatchel, R. I. (1970). Reduction of stress in humans through nonveridical perceived control of aversive stimulation. *Journal of Personality and Social Psychology, 16*, 731–738.

Hobfoll, S.E., & Lerman, M. (1988). Personal relationships, personal attributes, and stress resistance: Mothers' reactions to their child's illness. *American Journal of Community Psychology, 16*, 565–589.

Holmes, D. S., & Houston, B. K. (1974). Effectiveness of situation redefinition and affective isolation in coping with stress. *Journal of Personality and Social Psychology, 29*, 212–218.

Houston, B. K. (1972). Control over stress, locus of control, and response to stress. *Journal of Personality and Social Psychology, 21*, 249–255.

Johnston, M., Shaw, R., & Bird, D. (1987). "Test-tube baby" procedures: Stress and judgements under uncertainty, *Psychology and Health, 1*, 25–38.

Kanfer, J. H., & Goldfoot, D. A. (1966). Self-control and the tolerance of noxious stimulation. *Psychological Reports, 18*, 79–85.

Kanfer, F., & Seider, M. L. (1973). Self-control: Factors enhancing tolerance of noxious stimulation. *Journal of Personality and Social Psychology, 25*, 381–389.

Langer, E. J. (1983). *The psychology of control.* Beverly Hills: Sage Publications.

Langer, E. J., & Rodin, J. (1976). The effects of choice and enhanced personal responsibility for the aged: A field experiment in an institutional setting. *Journal of Personality and Social Psychology, 34*, 191–198.

Lasker, J. N., & Borg, S. (1987). *In search of parenthood: Coping with infertility and high-tech conception.* Boston: Beacon Press.

Mahlstedt, P. P. (1985). The psychological component of infertility. *Fertility and Sterility, 43*, 335–346.

Matthews, R., & Matthews, A. M. (1986). Infertility and involuntary childlessness: The transition to nonparenthood. *Journal of Marriage and the Family, 48*, 641–649.

McCormick, T. M. (1980). Out of control: One aspect of infertility. *Journal of Obstetric, Gynecologic and Neonatal Nursing, 9*, 205–206.

McGrade, J. J., & Tolor, A. (1981). The reaction to infertility and the infertility investigation: A comparison of the responses of men and women. *Infertility, 4*, 7–27.

Medical Research International and American Fertility Society (1989). In vitro fertilization/embryo transfer in the United States: 1987 results from the National IVF-ET Registry. *Fertility and Sterility, 51*(1), 13–19.

Menning, B. E. (1977). *Infertility: A guide for the childless couple.* Englewood Cliffs, NJ: Prentice-Hall.

Michela, J. L., & Wood, J. V. (1986). Causal attributions in health and illness. In P. C. Kendall (Ed.), *Advances in cognitive-behavioral research and therapy* (Vol. 5, pp. 179–235). New York: Academic Press.

Miller, S. M. (1979). Controllability and human stress: Method, evidence and theory. *Behavior Research and Therapy, 17,* 287–304.

Paulson, J. D., Haarmann, B. S., Salerno, R. L., & Asmar, P. (1988). An investigation of the relationship between emotional maladjustment and infertility. *Fertility and Sterility, 49*(2), 258–262.

Pearlin, L. I., Menaghan, E. G., Lieberman, M. A., & Mullan, J. T. (1981). The stress process. *Journal of Health and Social Behavior, 22,* 337–356.

Pennebaker, J. W., Burnam, M. A., Schaeffer, M. A., & Harper, D. C. (1977). Lack of control as a determinant of perceived physical symptoms. *Journal of Personality and Social Psychology, 24,* 237–253.

Platt, J. J., Ficher, I., & Silver, M. J. (1973). Infertile couples: Personality traits and self-ideal concept discrepancies. *Fertility and Sterility, 24,* 972–976.

Radloff, L. S. (1977). The CES-D Scale: A self-report depression scale for research in the general population. *Applied Psychological Measurement, 1,* 385–401.

Ross, C. E., & Mirosky, J. (1989). Explaining the social patterns of depression: Control and problem solving—or support and talking? *Journal of Health and Social Behavior, 30,* 206–219.

Rothbaum, F., Weisz, J. R., & Snyder, S. S. (1982). Changing the world and changing the self: A two-process model of perceived control. *Journal of Personality and Social Psychology, 42,* 5–37.

Rotter, J. B. (1966). Generalized expectancies for internal versus external control of reinforcement. *Psychological Monographs: General and Applied, 80*(1, Whole No. 609).

Sandelowski, M., & Jones, L. C. (1986). Social exchanges of infertile women. *Issues in Mental Health Nursing, 8,* 173–189.

Seibel, M. M., & Taymor, M. L. (1982). Emotional aspects in infertility. *Fertility and Sterility, 37,* 137–145.

Seligman, M. E. P. (1975). *Helplessness.* San Francisco: W. H. Freeman.

Silver, R. L. & Wortman, C. B. (1980). Coping with undesirable life events. In J. Garber & M. E. P. Seligman (Eds.), *Human helplessness* (pp. 279–345). New York: Academic Press.

Skokan, L. A. (1987). *The impact of perceptions of control on adjustment in cancer patients.* Unpublished Master's Thesis, University of California, Los Angeles.

Staub, E., Tursky, B., & Schwartz, G. E. (1971). Self-control and predictability: Their effects on reactions to aversive stimulation. *Journal of Personality and Social Psychology, 18,* 157–162.

Taylor, S. E. (1983). Adjustment to threatening events: A theory of cognitive adaptation. *American Psychologist, 38,* 1161–1173.

Taylor, S. E., & Brown, J. D. (1988). Illusion and well-being: A social psychological perspective on mental health. *Psychological Bulletin, 103,* 193–210.

Taylor, S. E., Lichtman, R. R., & Wood, J. V. (1984). Attributions, beliefs about control, and adjustment to breast cancer. *Journal of Personality and Social Psychology, 46,* 489–502.

Thompson, S. C. (1981). Will it hurt less if I can control it? A complex answer to a simple question. *Psychological Bulletin, 90,* 89–101.

Valentine, D. P. (1986). Psychological impact on infertility: Identifying issues and needs. *Social Work in Health Care, 11,* 61–69.

Wallston, K. A., Wallston, B. S., Smith, S., & Dobbins, C. J. (1987). Perceived control and health. *Current Psychological Research and Reviews, 6,* 5–25.

Wilson, E. A. (1979). Sequence of emotional responses induced by infertility. *Journal of the Kentucky Medical Association, 77,* 229–233.

Wortman, C. B. (1976). Causal attributions and personal control. In J. Harvey, W. Ickes, & R. F. Kidd (Eds.), *New directions in attribution research* (pp. 23–51). Hillsdale, NJ: Erlbaum.

Wortman, C. B., & Brehm, J. W. (1975). Responses to uncontrollable outcomes: An integration of reactance theory and the learned helplessness model. In L. Berkowitz (Ed.), *Advances in experimental social psychology* (Vol. 8, pp. 277–336). New York: Academic Press.

8

Cognitive Examination of Motivation for Childbearing as a Factor in Adjustment to Infertility

LESLIE F. CLARK, SUSAN M. HENRY, and DONNA M. TAYLOR

Infertility is seldom eradicated in a few months. Indeed, its current definition by medical professionals requires that the couple has been trying to conceive for one year without success prior to medical intervention. During the initial diagnosis and treatment, the couple may maintain a determined problem-solving approach, along with undaunted optimism. However, years of extended treatment and repeated failures characterize the experiences of many infertile individuals. During this time, they may confront a variety of thoughts and feelings such as anger, frustration, and despair. It is the goal of this chapter to outline the processes involved in coming to terms with such an infertility experience and the impact that it has on one's self-concept, one's goals, and one's life.

LESLIE F. CLARK and SUSAN M. HENRY • Department of Psychological Sciences, Purdue University, West Lafayette, Indiana 47907.   **DONNA M. TAYLOR,** Department of Psychology, Memphis State University, Memphis, Tennessee 38152.

OVERVIEW OF CHAPTER

This chapter characterizes the desire to have a child as a major life goal and infertility is conceptualized as an experience of goal blockage. Specifically, this chapter outlines a model of mental processes that an infertile individual may engage in while coming to terms with his/her infertility. The major point of this model is that individuals who experience prolonged infertility may undergo an examination of their beliefs, values, and goals concerning parenthood and what it means to them.

This questioning process can create a change in one's perceptions of parenthood and make clearer distinctions among different desired aspects of the parenting experience. Specific goals may be identified which promote renewed problem-solving efforts. In addition, individuals realize which aspects of parenting may never be available to them, and mourning of those lost goal objects or experiences takes place. Accepting infertility according to one infertile individual consists of " . . . the tossing off of a dream that one has dreamed for many years. And the death of that dream means finding a way to define oneself anew, to peer into the future and imagine a different self, a different life, a different family, a family of two . . . " (Cole, 1988, p. 64).

Individuals who go through this process may gain new insights into why they want to be parents. They are more aware of the parenting goals that they hold, and which ones are particularly important to them. They may gain greater perception of choice options, resulting in increased feelings of control and self-efficacy. These feelings may lead to a renewed engagement in treatment, a new decision regarding the infertility, and/or a return to pre-infertility activities. Finally, the questioning process may lead to a reordering of priorities, much like those experienced by victims of other traumatic events (Taylor, 1983). For example, some cancer victims report that the cancer led them to structure their lives around more meaningful lines (e.g., friends and family relationships) and away from mundane concerns such as housework and petty quarrels. Such a reordering of priorities among infertile individuals may enable them to see some positive aspect of their experience of infertility.

The process of examining one's values and goals does not occur for everyone experiencing infertility. Some individuals may succeed in their treatment early on and not experience repeated failures to conceive. Others may leave the question of parenting in the hands of God or fate. In particular, examination of reasons for parenting should most likely occur for couples who see the joint conception of a biological child as extremely important to them. In addition, the process, as it is described in this chapter, represents an ideal adjustment to permanent, involuntary infertility. Some individuals may begin the process, yet not be able to answer the questions they pose to themselves in a satisfactory or constructive way. Others may find that questioning their reasons for parenthood leaves them feeling guilty or uncertain as to how good a parent they might make. Finally, in some cases, an examination of one's goals and the likelihood of achieving them may lead individuals to confront an unpleasant future, resulting in a depression which may be relatively long-lasting and counterproductive to achieving conception.

INFERTILITY AND LIFE GOALS

Our thoughts and actions are guided by our goals (see Carver & Scheier, 1981; Martin & Tesser, 1989; Miller, Galanter, & Pribram, 1960). Goals are the desired outcomes we wish to achieve. Our goals are important not only for planning our behavior, but because they represent, to a large extent, our current identities and who we wish to become, our ideal selves (Higgins, 1987).

Goals are represented in our memory in a hierarchical form, with more important, general goals located at the top of the hierarchy and subgoals, those which serve as necessary steps to achieve the higher-level goal, located in lower positions on the hierarchy (Vallacher & Wegner, 1987). Achieving small goals helps us to complete larger, higher-level goals. For example, an individual may pay for a yearly medical checkup (a subgoal) in order to achieve a higher-level superordinate goal of staying healthy. Seeking to eat well and to get enough sleep each night may be other subgoals which are fulfilled in order to stay healthy.

Conception as a Major Life Goal

People are not generally conscious of all the levels of their goal hierarchies (Mandler, 1982; Vallacher & Wegner, 1987). That is, at any given moment one might not be aware of the reasons why he or she is engaging in certain behaviors (Martin & Tesser, 1989). We would like further to suggest that the goal of having children may often be an "inherited" goal. By this we mean that society has passed onto us the assumption that we will procreate, as a natural part of adulthood (Daniluk, 1988). Societal and cultural norms require that a worthwhile person engages in behaviors which show his/her normalcy and responsibility. Bearing and raising children constitute such behaviors (Tulandi, Bull, Cooke, & McInnes, 1981; Veevers, 1973). Therefore, individuals may not usually question in-depth the reasons for having children.

Even though many couples today may spend a great deal of time thinking about the decisions of when to have children and even whether to have children, this cognitive process does not prepare individuals to face the possibility of not being able to have children. Most people assume that they will be able to conceive; so infertility is met with shock and/or disbelief (Kraft, Palombo, Mitchell, Dean, Meyers, & Schmidt, 1980; Shapiro, 1982; Wilson, 1979).

For many infertile people the goal of having children is extremely important and is intricately enmeshed with higher-level goals of fulfillment and happiness in life. This would explain why threats to one's fertility can be so devastating. The combination of individuals' assumptions of their ability to conceive, along with cultural definitions tying fertility to adulthood and sexuality, means that infertility can deeply affect one's self-esteem. Indeed, many articles describe infertile individuals as experiencing damage to self-esteem (Bergin, 1986; Bernstein, Potts, & Mattox, 1985; Bresnick, 1981; Cook, 1987; Mazor, 1984; McGrade & Tolor, 1981; Skylar, 1984) as well as feelings of inadequacy and defectiveness (Berk & Shapiro, 1984; Erdwin, Small, & Gross, 1980; Mahlstedt, 1985; Walfish & Myerson, 1980). For example, some women may question their femininity because they cannot bear a child.

Infertility as Blockage to a Major Life Goal

Infertility has been described as the blockage of one or more major life goals (Daniluk, 1988; Elstein, 1975; Valentine, 1986). When goals are blocked or interrupted, individuals often find themselves thinking more about the goals themselves, along with ideas and feelings associated with those goals (Horowitz, 1982; Mandler, 1982; Martin & Tesser, 1989; Vallacher & Wegner, 1987). In fact, one of the main functions of consciousness is to rectify the disparity between one's current situation and the desired outcome of our goals (Carver & Scheier, 1981; Mandler, 1982). For example, the goal of wanting a biological child may lead an individual to seek professional treatment for infertility.

Also, individuals may be more or less aware of their low-level goals, depending upon whether they are having problems accomplishing them (Collins, 1989; Vallacher & Wegner, 1987; Wicklund, 1986). If a couple becomes blocked in their efforts to conceive they will be likely to think about how and when they are having sex, if they have chosen the right specialist, and so forth. Sometimes mental processes work toward finding new ways to achieve the goal. For example, at some point in infertility treatment a couple may seek information about adoption procedures. Other times they may need to reshape or abandon desired goals which simply cannot be achieved (Carver & Scheier, 1981; Mandler, 1987). For example, a specific treatment may be expensive or unproductive, or there may come a time when it seems best to discontinue all treatment efforts.

Ruminations in Response to Infertility

Conscious thoughts that occur from the blockage of a goal have been called ruminations (Martin & Tesser, 1989). Ruminations consist of intrusive thoughts associated with images and feelings of sharp intensity (Horowitz, 1982). For infertile individuals, ruminations may consist of repeated mental reruns of distressing events, such as a miscarriage, or the baby shower given for a pregnant friend. In addition, infertile individuals may experience distressing ruminations about their future life without children, the family gatherings that won't occur. Finally, individuals may even experience ruminations about their hypothetical child, one they fear will never exist. Ruminations have been associated with increased stress and distress (Horowitz, 1982; Silver, Boon, & Stones, 1983).

Two mental processes are thought to be responsible for the creation of ruminations related to a blocked goal. Ruminations may occur: (1) Due to associated ideas in our memory triggering off one another; and (2) because we are motivated to complete the disrupted progress toward the goal. In the first of these processes, aspects of one's infertility may pop into mind simply because the meaning of an event is associated with one's infertility somehow (see Anderson, 1983). For example, celebrating one's twenty-fifth birthday may serve as a painful reminder of a woman's infertility if her mother began to have children at this age. Environmental cues can also serve to trigger ruminations through meaning associations. For example, the aisle at the grocery store displaying baby food may be filled with painful reminders of one's own infertility.

The second source of ruminations concerns our preoccupation with uncompleted goals. That is, motivationally driven ruminations occur due to the uncompleted "task" of having a child (see Zeigarnik, 1927). For example, just *wanting* a child strongly can lead one to dream about parenting fears or to think jealous thoughts about a friend's child. When the goal is either abandoned or fulfilled, then this source of ruminative thoughts will disappear (Martin & Tesser, 1989). Rumination about abandoned goals is less frequent than ruminations about current goals (Klinger, 1975; Klinger, 1978; Klinger, Barta, & Maxeiner, 1980).

It is possible that the motivational drive to have a baby along with environmental cues which trigger ruminations can both operate at the same time to create intrusive thoughts about one's infertility. For example, many infertility patients wait for their appointments with physicians in the ob/gyn office. It is not uncommon for noticeably pregnant women to be visiting their doctors at the same time, or even new mothers visiting with their newborn infants. The motivational drive to think about one's infertility is strong when one is waiting for a doctor's appointment. Combined with the environmental cues of pregnancy and infants, the process of rumination about one's infertility becomes very likely in such a situation.

The authors would like to suggest a third source of ruminations concerning infertility. Because fertility goals are embedded with other higher-level life goals, infertile individuals may experience an invalidation of all sorts of aspects of the self (e.g., goals to be attractive, to be happy, to have a good marriage, to be a worthwhile member of society), thereby decreasing their self-worth in general. That is, individuals may see the failure of a medium-level goal (e.g., a particular treatment avenue) as the failure of a multitude of higher-level goals as well (e.g., fulfillment as a person, happiness). This leads the individual to feel that he or she is a failure in a more general sense, as a woman or man, or even as a person.

In this case, it is the perceived threat to one's highest-level goals that instigates ruminative thoughts. This feeling of failure at the highest, most general level may explain not only the ruminative or obsessive thoughts individuals experience about infertility (Menning, 1977; Valentine, 1986) but also the feelings that they are worthless and negated as a person (see the self-esteem deficits described earlier).

Given the embedded nature of the goal hierarchy concerning fertility, the individual may need to separate parenting goals from other self-strivings and expectations regarding his/her life (Cook, 1987; Menning, 1977). This may be achieved through a two-step process wherein individuals first discern what meaning the different aspects of parenting holds for them. Second, individuals learn whether it is still possible to achieve some important high-level goals which may or may not involve parenting.

QUESTIONING PROCESSES AND CHANGING ONE'S GOALS

Adjustment to traumatic events has been linked to the individual's ability to find some meaning in the event (Bulman & Wortman, 1977; Tait & Silver, 1989; Taylor, 1983; Thompson & Janigan, 1988; Silver et al., 1983). Some researchers have suggested that reaching an understanding of the event is positively related to increased adjustment, less psychological distress, and higher self-esteem (Silver et al., 1983). Others suggest that searching for meaning may not be helpful to victims. Individuals' attempts to understand why an event happened to them in particular may leave them feeling negative about themselves and the world in general (Janoff-

Bulman, 1989). Indeed, infertile individuals have been known to experience feelings of injustice (Mahlstedt, 1985). In addition, asking "Why has this happened to me?" is thought to be associated with anger (Menning, 1977; Rosenfeld & Mitchell, 1979) and depression for infertile people (Rosenfeld & Mitchell, 1979).

Victims do sometimes ask themselves "Why has this happened to me?" in attempting to cope with a stressful situation. As described above, the literature is not clear on whether such self-questioning is beneficial. We would like to propose here that infertile individuals also ask themselves a different sort of "why" question. Specifically, infertile individuals may use "why" questions to examine what it is about parenthood that makes it so desireable to them. In short, why do they want to be parents so badly? This second sort of "why" question may be quite important in an individual's adjustment to infertility.

Examination of Higher-Level Goals

Individuals who are infertile for a period of time may begin to examine why they want to have children. This may occur at various points in medical treatment as disappointments accumulate. Or couples may not engage in such examination until they are ready to terminate treatment altogether (Mazor, 1984). The questioning of the reasons for parenthood is motivated by four factors: the threat of not achieving parenthood, costs of continuing treatment, the social stigma of infertility, and the adoption process as an option. Figure 1 shows how the experience of infertility might lead an individual to question his/her goals and examine personal meanings of parenthood.

The first box in Figure 1 (Box "A") was discussed fully in the above section. Many individuals who feel thwarted in their efforts to conceive experience emotional distress (Bell, 1981; Bresnick, 1981; Harrison, 1979; Slade, 1981; Taymor & Bresnick, 1979).

The distress of the infertility experience (Box "A") may lead individuals to become more aware of how they think of parenthood and themselves as parents-to-be. In addition, the negativity of factors such as medical treatment, repeated failures to conceive, and social stigma (described in Box "E") leads individuals to: (1) Become more aware of their concepts concerning self-identity and parenthood (Box "B"); and (2) question privately held assumptions about who they are and what parenthood means to them (Box "C"). This questioning process may help individuals rethink their identity, ideal self, and the meaning that parenthood holds for them (Box "D"). Each of the negative factors in Box "E" is described in detail below.

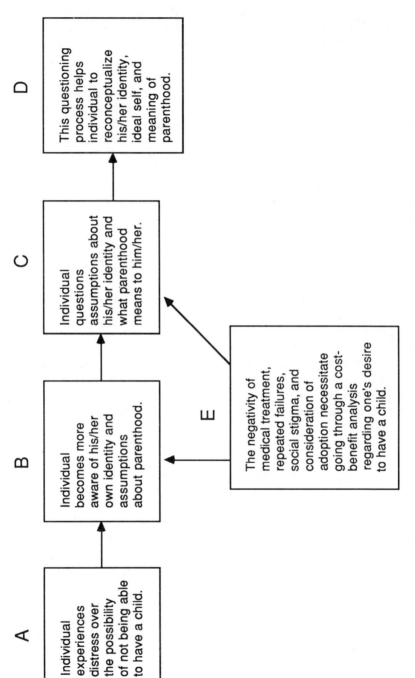

FIGURE 1. Motivations for questioning of parenthood goals and goals linked to happiness.

The nature of infertility diagnosis and treatment procedures (represented in Box "E") creates stressors (McGrade & Tolor, 1981; Menning, 1977; Slade, 1981; West, 1983). These stressors include the experience of repeated failure, negative effects of treatment, and the social stigma of being considered incapable of having one's own child. Infertile individuals report that the medical procedures themselves are intrusive and insensitive (Valentine, 1986) as well as being disruptive of their sex life (Harrison, O'Moore, & O'Moore, 1981).

In addition, individuals who suffer a major stressful event may experience the consequences of being stigmatized as victims on both personal and social levels (Janoff-Bulman & Frieze, 1983; Taylor, Wood, & Lichtman, 1983). Personal consequences of a victimizing event include an uncertain future, loss of self-esteem, applying a negative label to oneself, and a sense of loss of control (Taylor *et al.*, 1983). Social consequences of a victimizing event include the need to accept aid from others, pity, and, in some cases, blame placed upon them by others who believe in the notion of a "just world." Infertile individuals may experience some or all of these problems (see Abbey, Andrews, & Halman, this volume). The stigma of infertility, whether applied by the self or by others, may lead the individual to think about how much he/she really wants to continue trying to conceive.

Finally, considering adoption as an alternative to conception may lead individuals to consider their reasons for parenthood. Many individuals at this point experience concern over the characteristics of a nonbiological child. In addition, the infertile couple may be faced with a laborious process of searching, the evaluation of their "credentials" by social workers and adoption personnel, and other barriers to adoption. This process may lead them further to consider the underlying reasons for wanting to have a child.

All of these factors serve to focus the individual on the question of "Why am I going through all of this?" The more distress the individual experiences (Box "A"), the more preoccupied the individual becomes with thoughts about parenthood and self-identity (Box "B") (Mazor, 1984). Similarly, the more intrusive and expensive the medical treatments and the greater number of failed attempts to conceive (Box "E"), the more the individual thinks about parenthood and questions his/her desire to have a child. Finally, individuals who are more vulnerable to the effects of social stigma (e.g., who have parents and siblings who "pressure" them to have children) or who are attempting adoption are also more likely to think about and question the meaning that parenthood holds for them.

Not everyone will question why they want to be a parent. Some individuals will become increasingly committed to having a biological child in the face of these sorts of adversity. However, it is also understandable that individuals might question whether they want children at the price they are being asked to pay.

Infertile individuals can "let go" of much of the ongoing negative effects or "costs" of infertility by deciding they don't really want to have a child. Unlike cancer or rape as victimizing events, infertility is devastating precisely because the individual holds the goal of having his/her own biological child. While the harm of the past experiences with infertility cannot be undone, much of the future cost (financial and emotional), as well as some of the social stigma, may be avoided by letting go of the goal to have a biological child. This may be especially attractive because, at times, the individual may despair of ever achieving that goal.

The dilemma of being caught between goal-fulfillment strivings and acceptance of one's goal blockage or permanent infertility may be the most stressful aspect of coping with infertility (Mazor, 1979; Menning, 1980). As long as the individual holds onto the belief that they will be able to have a child eventually, they are trapped in the experience of the infertile person. The alternative to such an experience is to accept the unpleasant idea of not having one's own child. Seibel and Taymor (1982) sum up this dilemma well:

> as long as a patient is receiving medication or undergoing laboratory tests, she is usually putting aside the resolution of her fertility crisis by postponing crucial decisions about career, life plans, adoption, and personal confrontation with her childlessness. (p. 142)

In addition, Slade (1981) has speculated that the infertility experience may in part be responsible for women feeling caught between traditional and egalitarian role orientations. Infertile women have been shown to cluster around the midpoint of a role-orientation scale (traditional versus egalitarian). Specifically, Slade suggests that:

> taking a mid-range view of social roles is an effective way of coping with the uncertainty of the future. Deferring strong commitment in either direction may provide some defense against disappointment while avoiding the abandonment of hope . . . (p. 185)

Many workers in the area of infertility describe the process of individuals evaluating their motivations and reasons for pursuing parenthood (Box "C") (Adler & Boxley, 1985; Flapan & Schoenfeld, 1972; Hare-Mustin & Broderick, 1979; Kraft et al., 1980; Sawatzky, 1981). The consequences of answering "why" questions is that the individual mentally moves up the hierarchy to examine the most abstract, higher-level goals. For example, if I ask myself, "Why am I undergoing surgery?" the answer may be, "So that I can begin further fertility treatments." If I ask, "Why do I want to try further treatment?" the answer may be, "In order to get pregnant." In asking, "Why do I want to get pregnant?" the answer may be, "So that my husband and I can finally experience a family of our own."

Thinking of the goals which constitute the reasons for attempting to conceive, such as the creation of a family unit, may lead individuals to sort out various different reasons (e.g., closeness, passing on one's views on life). They may not have actually thought through some of these reasons for wanting a family before. In questioning these upper-level goals (reasons), infertile individuals will also be likely to examine personal beliefs, attitudes, and values concerning family life. Issues of what is needed for personal fulfillment, and marital fulfillment, may also be addressed. This soul-searching process may involve the simulation of various alternative futures (Taylor & Schneider, 1989) and include actual information-seeking behavior concerning parenting through different forms.

Clinicians working with infertile individuals have suggested that the identity of those experiencing infertility must undergo substantial changes. This is represented by Box "D" in Figure 1. It is thought that concepts of the self-image and sexuality must be reworked in order to become disconnected from childbearing (Menning, 1980). The authors propose that the questioning process can both prompt and help accomplish this disconnecting, through the establishment of clear and specific goals regarding parenthood and self-fulfillment.

Thus it is argued that the questioning and examination process (Box "C") leads to a reconceptualization of such concepts as the ideal self, goals for the future, and the meaning of parenthood (Box "D"). In examining what parenthood means to them, individuals may begin to realize that certain aspects of parenthood are still available to them (e.g., raising a child). Alternatively, they may decide that parenthood is not an essential aspect of their marital and personal fulfillment. They may become aware of new paths to either parenthood or other forms of personal fulfillment that they had found unacceptable or did not think of previously. Perhaps most importantly, the restructuring of one's goal hierarchy results in an "unpacking" of the major life goals concerning the self, marriage, parenting, family, and fulfillment in general. It is likely that this new goal structure will allow for paths by which the individual may still achieve happiness and fulfillment. Figure 2 presents an example of how an infertile individual's goal structure might be reworked to become less enmeshed and to carry within it more options; both for parenthood as well as for the chance to be happy and fulfilled without ever achieving parenthood.

Not everyone may succeed in finding new pathways to "happiness" that are acceptable to them. As mentioned earlier, some individuals may

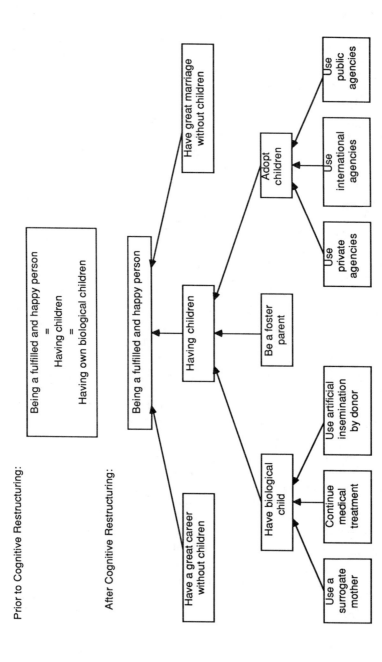

FIGURE 2. The unpacking of goals and subgoals relevant to infertility. Note: These pathways are not mutually exclusive, that is, more than one lower level goal may be achieved by an individual, and successful achievement of any lower level goals may result in achievement of the next higher level goal.

feel increased commitment towards achieving conception as a function of all the time and effort they have already invested. Because of this invested effort they may be less open to considering alternative forms of parenthood. Others may simply be unable to accept the prospect of the unpleasant possibility that they will never bear their own child.

Still others may cope with the hardships of infertility by minimizing the undesirable implications of childlessness. These individuals may never perceive their infertility as much more than a temporary setback to planning a family. Finally, there are those for whom treatment is successful after a relatively short time or adoption is seen as a favorable option immediately. For these people, a deep examination of one's parenting goals never occurs.

Finding Pathways to Achieve Newly Identified Higher-Level Goals

For those who do undertake the disentanglement of goals related to personal fulfillment and parenthood, the process may enable them to see alternative pathways towards achieving their goals. That is, once higher-level goals are clearly redefined, individuals may now begin to ask "how" questions concerning their fulfillment. "How" questions lead individuals to identify the hierarchy of subgoals that will lead to the achievement of new upper-level goals such as non-parenting options for happiness, as well as alternative options for parenting (Collins, 1989; Vallacher & Wegner, 1987).

For example, individuals attempting to conceive may examine the lower levels of the hierarchy to determine the subgoals needed to achieve the higher-level goal. Asking "How do I become pregnant?" leads to an answer of "Seek medical treatment." Asking "How do I seek medical treatment?" leads to an answer of "Find an infertility specialist," or, in other instances, "Find out what my health insurance will pay for." Answers to "how" questions for infertile people can help individuals to develop some plan of action, such as deciding upon the order of treatment procedures or how payment schedules could be arranged. Different answers to "how" questions can also serve as alternative plans which the individual is able to weigh against one another in determining the costs and benefits of each (e.g., taking a rest from treatment versus continuing a specific treatment regimen). This phase may be characterized by increased information-seeking about how to parent through alternative means as well as increased communication with one's partner concerning the acceptability of alternative options.

The individual's goal structure is now substantially less embedded and clearer, showing an increased number of new options for the individual.

Since this process of restructuring is largely a conscious one, individuals are more aware of their goals. They may feel a renewed commitment toward parenting—whether through conception of their own child or some other route (e.g., adoption). Though not necessarily a preferred route, they may also realize that they will still have hope for happiness even without ever achieving parenthood.

Mourning Irreplaceable Goals

Some goal objects cannot be easily replaced or substituted. Infertility may mean that the couple will never experience pregnancy and birth personally, that one or both members of the couple will be unable to continue their bloodline, or that even if treatment is successful, they will be unable to have more than one biological child. At the very least, infertility invariably destroys the couple's naiveté of the "miracle of conception" without medical intervention. Even for couples who terminate treatment, only to conceive on their own, the experience of infertility changes their beliefs about conception being a normal consequence of physical intercourse (Veevers, 1973).

Victims of stressful events do sometimes show dramatic changes in their basic beliefs about the world; beliefs that were unquestioned before the crisis situation arise. These changes in basic beliefs about the self and the world can endure for years after the event has occurred. Specifically, individuals who have experienced a traumatic event show decreases in the belief of the world as a just and benevolent place and negative changes in their beliefs concerning self-worth (Janoff-Bulman, 1989).

In addition to changes in beliefs, some individuals experience infertility as the death of a hypothetical child. Individuals may mourn the child that will never be. It is not necessary to experience a stillbirth or even a miscarriage to feel that a child has died (Mahlstedt, 1985; Sawatzky, 1981). For these individuals, the child that was planned for, described, dreamed about, and often even named will not be forthcoming. This can be an extremely difficult part of infertility for the individual and can place great strain on the marital relationship. The inability of others to comprehend this loss as being at the same level as death may serve to invalidate the individual's grief (Menning, 1977; Valentine, 1986). The framework proposed in this chapter argues that this experience of mourning involves the letting go of reasons for parenting (higher-level goals themselves) that are seen, at least by some individuals, as being unobtainable.

The mourning of specific unobtainable goals can be distinguished from the reactions individuals experience as a function of feeling that their uppermost goal of happiness is unattainable. Both may be thought of as grief reactions. However, the first of these entails a realistic assessment of probable outcomes. It is an important step in moving toward resolution that one comes to terms with limitations imposed by the infertility (Menning, 1977). This acceptance frees the individual to pursue goals that have some reasonable likelihood of being met with success. Grief or depression stemming from the belief that happiness itself is unattainable, on the other hand, results from the individual feeling that *all* chances for happiness have been curtailed, that all meaningful higher-level goals are out of reach. This can be thought of as the severe depression that some infertile individuals experience. While not all infertile individuals experience such depression, from a clinical standpoint it is important to understand the subset of individuals who react to infertility in such a manner.

IMPLICATIONS OF EXAMINING ONE'S MOTIVATIONS FOR CHILDBEARING AND ADAPTING TO INFERTILITY

There are several positive consequences of changing one's goal structure. These include an increased awareness of one's goals, increased options for happiness, and increased feelings of control. While changing one's goal structure forces a confrontation of what may clearly be lost, it also makes the individual more aware of what is still to be gained. Couples who opt for artificial insemination using a donor must face the realization that the child will not have the genetic makeup of the father. For some, acceptance of these losses comes more easily than to others, depending upon the meaning of achieving such goals in parenting and how invested the partners were in achieving these particular goals. On the other hand, artificial insemination means there is an increased probability of achieving pregnancy, sharing in the birth processes, and gaining a child.

Seeing new and alternative pathways to fulfilling at least some of one's goals relating to parenthood may provide a restoration of feelings of control to the infertile individual. This sense of control may stem from the perception that: (1) Additional choice options are available to them that might satisfy goals; and (2) these alternative pathways (e.g., adoption or remaining child-free) may be more feasible (or controllable). These perceptions may ease the secondary stressors associated with undergoing medical treatment, or, for some individuals, may make medical treatment unnecessary altogether.

In addition, individuals may successfully disentangle the meaning of infertility from other goals in their life. They may be freed from seeing the failure of conception as a failure to achieve happiness or maintain a sense of self-worth. Victims of traumatic life events at times emerge with a sense of self-knowledge and a reordering of priorities in their life (Taylor, 1983; Taylor & Schneider, 1989). Such individuals may shift importance from mundane daily hassles to the maintenance of successful relationships. This reconceptualization process may serve to engender new feelings of control and enhance self-esteem (Taylor, 1983).

The new views that result from a close examination of one's goal structure are likely to be accompanied by emotions such as a sense of peace, acceptance, energy, and even a renewed sense of humor (Griffin, 1983; Menning, 1980; Wilson, 1979). It is possible that the mind will "shore up" or bolster the new goal hierarchy by bringing into awareness the positive aspects of the infertility experience. This phenomenon occurs with individuals experiencing other traumatic events, such as flood victims (Taylor et al., 1983). Specifically, these individuals downplayed their victim status by highlighting the benefits of the flood (e.g., its effects in bringing people closer together). Individuals may also see the self-knowledge gained from stressful experiences as useful and important (Taylor, 1983).

Ruminations should lessen as the individuals rid themselves of the emotional investment in certain goals (see Kraft et al., 1980; Menning, 1980 on acceptance of infertility). The resolution that individuals feel about their goals and plans also allows them to invest effort in other plans and activities in their life. These efforts may bring about positive validation of the self-concept, as well as create progress towards achieving other goals necessary for personal fulfillment (e.g., education, work, time spent on personal relationships).

Figure 3 outlines the process and consequences of changing one's goal structures. Questioning one's desires for parenthood may lead to a reordering of priorities as well as new pathways to achieving happiness. These changes in beliefs and goals may increase feelings of control and allow the individual to continue pursuing other life goals as well as parenthood. In sum, the goal examination process allows individuals to regain positive feelings about themselves, the future, their marriage, and perhaps even their ability to experience parenting in some form or another. It increases one's sense of self-knowledge and control over what will happen to them. It is possible that individuals may perceive that they feel even better about themselves and their life than they did prior to experiencing the infertility.

Applications for Therapy and Social Support of Infertile Individuals

Mazor (1984) suggests that goals of infertility therapy are to help individuals: (1) Deal with the immediate frustrations of expensive, and time-consuming medical treatments; and (2) examine what infertility means to them in the context of their own life. Mazor's conclusions con-

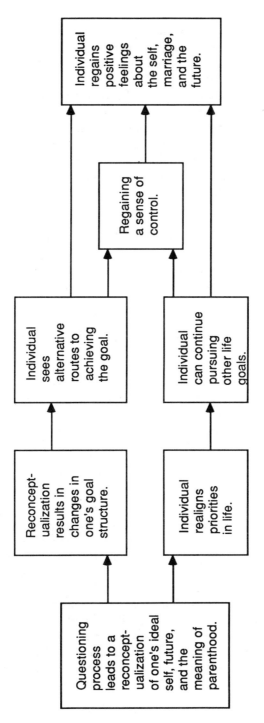

FIGURE 3. The implications of changing one's goal structure for adapting to infertility.

cerning infertility parallel those presented in the present chapter. Specifically, Mazor (1984) suggests that "Frustration in attaining that goal [of parenthood] requires significant reorganization of one's identity in relation to the self and to others" (p. 30).

According to Mazor (1984), individuals first experience a period of narcissistic injury, in which they become preoccupied with their bodies, their sexual functioning, and their infertility. Other aspects of their lives (such as work or friendships) become subordinate to treatment and conception attempts. In addition, individuals experience widespread feelings of defectiveness and low self-worth. Therapy may help individuals restore their self-esteem, regain feelings of control (e.g., over choice of doctors, or treatment decisions), as well as remind them of useful coping strategies that have served them in the past.

If a couple considers abandoning treatment, they then begin to reexamine their own feelings regarding parenthood. They grieve the loss of reproductive abilities and may mourn for the biological child they may never have. At this point therapists can help the couple put the infertility problems in the context of their entire lives. Therapists can help individuals to make the decision of how best to fulfill their creative and nurturant goals without a biological child. Mazor (1984) mentions, as the present chapter has, that at this point couples may reassess their relationships and their own self-identities.

Finally, couples may decide on alternative paths to parenthood (e.g., adoption). These paths may themselves present difficulties and a bewildering array of choices. At this point therapy can help couples to pursue alternative options, such as adoption or a new childless life-style. Mazor (1984) ends by suggesting that "Patients must prepare themselves to use resources other than reproduction in order to consolidate a comfortable identity as a middle-aged and older adult whether or not parenthood is achieved" (p. 34).

The present chapter agrees with Mazor's arguments regarding the usefulness of therapy in adjusting to infertility. Therapists can give permission to explore alternative options which individuals may otherwise feel guilty about considering. They can help individuals through questioning processes by suggesting possible reasons for parenthood or possible alternative pathways to parenting. Finally, they can make individuals aware of how much control they still have regarding parenting options, the course of their marital relationships, and their own personal identities.

The present chapter also makes some important points about the infertility experience and the roles that can be played by clinicians, health care professionals, and social network members. These points can be divided into specific aspects of infertility of which others should be aware and calls for sensitivity and caution in providing "help" under certain circumstances.

First, we need to be aware of the possible effects of prolonged infertility in terms of depression and damage to one's self-esteem. Admonishments to "stop thinking about it" or to "throw yourself into work" may be worthless and only serve to create guilt and to further a sense of deficiency. Since work productivity is often diminished, focusing the individual on work may further reduce self-esteem. In addition, avoiding thinking about infertility may be nearly impossible because individuals may have no control over the flow of thoughts (or ruminations) that enter their awareness.

Next, others need to respect the grieving process of the individual who is confronting and/or accepting infertility. It may be difficult for others to realize just how "real" the desired child may have become to the couple. Indeed, infertility may be perceived as a loss on the same level as death of that hypothetical child. In such cases it may be best to take the lead in knowing how to respond from the infertile individual himself/herself. For some, the loss is real and profound. Others should not obstruct mourning with optimism regarding future efforts. Mourning individuals may need to express their grief and have it validated by a caring, listening supporter.

Third, from time to time infertile individuals may express ambivalence regarding conception. Ambivalence may be a by-product of the questioning process itself. That is, an examination of parenting goals may lead one to consider childlessness as a life-style option. Expressions of ambivalence may also stem from the psychological "cost" of failure. Individuals may assume a posture of ambivalence as self-protection against the despair of repeated failures. At times these feelings of ambivalence may be carried over into new treatment options or the attempt to adopt a child. Health care professionals, therapists, and caseworkers should not mistakenly conclude that the couple does not want a child "badly enough." Instead, others should regard this ambivalence as a natural response to infertility. For some, a period of ambivalence may even be a necessary precursor to summoning the emotional energy for renewing their efforts towards achieving parenthood.

Finally, because infertility is a couple's dilemma, it is important to point out that the two individuals may not be coping the same or reaching the same sense of adjustment. These differences may present a source of conflict. For example, one person may see positive aspects of infertility, while the other is still mourning irreplaceable goals. It is also possible that one individual is ready to examine "how" alternative pathways can be navigated, while his or her spouse still questions "why" parenthood is important. Individuals may need help in at least acknowledging the perspective of their partner. In addition, therapists and friends should be aware that an infertile individual may find his/her partner's perspective threatening or nonconstructive. However, urging respect for each others' perspectives is important for continued communication and reducing conflict in decision-making regarding infertility.

The present model also suggests ways in which therapists and others should show caution or sensitivity in their support attempts. Specifically, others should show respect for "where" the infertile individual is in his or her thinking about infertility and parenthood. For example, suggesting alternative ways to achieve parenthood may not be useful if the individual is still asking himself/herself "why" he/she wants to be a parent. The individual may feel that a suggested option is undesirable to him/her, but may not yet be able to say *why* it is undesirable. Pressuring these individuals to consider alternatives may merely leave them feeling guilty and/or angry. Similarly, one may suggest that infertile individuals "get on with their life" at a time when they are questioning their goals or mourning a loss. Such urgings may suggest to the individual that their reactions of ambivalence/grief are abnormal (see Wortman & Lehman, 1985). Finally, discovering positive aspects of the experience is probably most useful if accomplished by the individual himself/herself. Researchers who study adjustment to difficult life events (e.g., incest), note that providing suggestions of meaning or positive aspects of the situation is rarely helpful to the distressed individual (Silver, Boon, & Stones, 1983; Silver & Wortman, 1980).

Hypotheses Suggested by the Present Framework

The present framework provides some interesting questions for future research aimed toward understanding individuals' reactions to infertility. The hypotheses posed by this model may be divided into those related to the questioning process and those related to adjustment.

In addressing the motivation for questioning, individuals who report experiencing more negative affect and stress concerning the treatment should also be more likely to report experiencing questioning activity. Individuals who report that they have questioned their reasons for wanting to be a parent will report confronting emotions of grief (such as mourning the hypothetical biological child). Some couples do experience a drawn-out process of decision-making concerning whether or not to have a child. Is prior ambivalence about having a child related to the amount and type of questioning activity individuals engage in? Are those individuals who made a conscientious drawn-out decision to have a child better off than others because they didn't merely assume they would have children, or is it more difficult for them precisely because they put so much effort into the decision only to discover their infertility? In other words, does a lengthy decision process regarding whether to have children in the first place make individuals *less* willing to consider parenting alternatives when infertility occurs? Research on these questions could be guided by the perspective of the model presented. Finally, one can ask the question of whether an individual's mental complexity and/or flexibility is related to the ability to think of alternative routes to the parenting goal.

Hypotheses also can be generated from the model to address issues regarding coping and adjustment to infertility. For example, the amount and types of ruminations concering parenthood could be related to whether the person is actively problem-solving (asking "how" questions) or questioning their goals (asking "why" questions). Also, asking "how" questions should lead to a greater number of acceptable alternative paths. In addition, the number of ways an individual perceives to obtain some form of parenting will be related to an individual's desire for certain aspects of parenthood over others (e.g., wanting to experience a nurturant role should open more alternative possibilities than wanting to pass on one's genetic structure). Because questioning is a conscious mental process, examining reasons for desiring parenthood and options for achieving some form of parenthood should increase an individual's awareness of alternative routes that are available to them. Finally, one's acceptance of alternative routes should be associated with a greater likelihood of a re-ordering of priorities, greater self-esteem, less depression, and a greater likelihood of seeing positive aspects of the infertility experience.

Other questions posed by the model concern the perseverence of treatment efforts, marital communication, and marital conflict. For example, an individual who sees alternative paths to parenthood may decide to quit treatment. For others, having additional options to pursue (e.g., adoption) may help them to continue treatment without the despair of failure weighing so heavily upon them. If one member of a couple has examined alternative options while his/her spouse is still totally committed to a biological child, communication difficulties and conflict can result. The partner who has changed his/her thinking may resent the spouse's refusal to be open to alternatives, while the spouse may feel abandoned in his/her efforts to conceive (and thus fulfill the higher-level goals in a previously agreed-upon way).

This chapter has provided a description of some of the cognitive and emotional processes individuals experience when faced with infertility. The relationships between people's goals and their responses to adversity in meeting those goals is emphasized. Infertility is experienced as the blockage of many important life goals. Coming to terms with permanent infertility may require fundamental changes in one's perceptions of what the goals are and how to achieve them. Put simply, for many infertile individuals, the degree to which they can successfully accommodate the changes imposed by such a goal blockage may well determine their successful adaptation to the crisis of infertility.

REFERENCES

Adler, J. D., & Boxley, R. L. (1985). The psychological reactions to infertility: Sex roles and coping styles. *Sex Roles, 12,* 271–278.

Anderson, J. R. (1983). A spreading activation theory of memory. *Journal of Verbal Learning and Verbal Behavior, 22,* 261–295

Bell, J. S. (1981). Psychological problems among patients attending an infertility clinic. *Journal of Psychosomatic Research, 25,* 1–3.

Bergin, M. A. (1986). Psychosocial responses of marital couples experiencing primary infertility. *Dissertation Abstracts International, 46.*

Berk, A., & Shapiro, J. L. (1984). Some implications of infertility on marital therapy. *Family Therapy, 11,* 38–47.

Bernstein, J., Potts, N., & Mattox, J. H. (1985). Assessment of psychological dysfunction associated with infertility. *Journal of Obstetric, Gynecologic, & Neonatal Nursing* (Supplement), 63s–66s.

Bresnick, E. R. (1981). A wholistic approach to the treatment of the crisis of infertility. *Journal of Marital and Family Therapy,* 181–188.

Bulman, R., & Wortman, C. B. (1977). Attributions of blame and coping in the "real world": Severe accident victims respond to their lot. *Journal of Personality and Social Psychology, 35,* 351–363.

Carver, C. S., & Scheier, M. F. (1981). *Attention and self-regulation: A control-theory approach to human behavior.* New York: Springer-Verlag.

Cole, D. (1988). Infertility tales. *Psychology Today,* 64–67.

Collins, J. E. (1989). *When the self becomes salient: Toward an integrative model of goal-directed thinking.* Unpublished manuscript, University of Illinois, Champaign-Urbana, IL.

Cook, E. (1987). Characteristics of the biopsychosocial crisis of infertility. *Journal of Counseling and Development, 65,* 465–469.

Daniluk, J. C. (1988). Infertility: Intrapersonal and interpersonal impact. *Fertility and Sterility, 49*(6), 982–990.

Elstein, M. (1975). Effect on infertility on psychosexual function. *British Medical Journal, 3,* 296–299.

Erdwin, C., Small, A., & Gross, R. (1980). The relationship of sex role to self-concept. *Journal of Clinical Psychology, 30,* 111–115.

Flapan, M., & Schoenfeld, H. (1972). Procedures for exploring women's childbearing motivations, alleviating childbearing conflicts and enhancing maternal role development. *American Journal of Orthopsychiatry, 42*(3), 389–397.

Griffin, M. E. (1983). Resolving infertility: An emotional crisis. *American Organization of Registered Nurses Journal, 38,* 597–601.

Hare-Mustin, R. T., & Broderick, P. C. (1979). The myth of motherhood: A study of attitudes toward motherhood. *Psychology of Women Quarterly, 4*(1), 114–128.

Harrison, M. (1979). *Infertility: A guide for couples.* Boston: Houghton Mifflin.

Harrison, R. F., O'Moore, A., & O'Moore, R. R. (1981). Stress and artificial insemination. *Infertility, 4*(4), 303–311.

Higgins, E. T. (1987). Self-discrepancy: A theory relating self and affect. *Psychological Review, 94*, 319–340.

Horowitz, M. J. (1982). Stress Response syndromes and their treatment. In L. Goldberger & S. Breznitz (Eds.), *Handbook of stress: Theoretical and clinical aspects* (pp. 711–732). New York: Free Press.

Janoff-Bulman, R. (1989). Assumptive worlds and the stress of traumatic events: Applications of the schema construct. *Social Cognition, 7*, 113–136.

Janoff-Bulman, R., & Frieze, I. H. (1983). A theoretical perspective for understanding reactions to victimization. *Journal of Social Issues, 39*, 1–17.

Klinger, E. (1975). Consequences to commitment to and disengagement from incentives. *Psychological Review, 82*, 223–231.

Klinger, E. (1978). Modes of normal conscious flow. In K. S. Pope & J. L. Singer (Eds.), *The stream of consciousness: Scientific investigations into the flow of human experience.* New York: Plenum.

Klinger, E., Barta, S., & Maxeiner, M. (1980). Motivational correlates of thought content. *Journal of Personality and Social Psychology, 39*, 1222–1237.

Kraft, A. D., Palombo, J., Mitchell, D., Dean, C., Meyers, S., & Schmidt, A. W. (1980). The psychological dimensions of infertility. *American Journal of Orthopsychiatry, 50*(4), 618–628.

Mahlstedt, P. P. (1985). The psychological component of infertility. *Fertility and Sterility, 43*(3), 335–346.

Mandler, G. (1982). Stress and thought processes. In L. Goldberger & S. Breznitz (Eds.), *Handbook of stress: Theoretical and clinical aspects* (pp. 88–104). New York: Free Press.

Mandler, G. (1987). Aspects of consciousness. *Personality and Social Psychology Bulletin, 13*, 299–313.

Martin, L. L., & Tesser, A. (1989). Toward a motivational and structural theory of ruminative thought. In J. S. Uleman & J. A. Bargh (Eds.), *The direction of thought: The limits of awareness, intention, and control* (pp. 226–306). New York: Guilford Publications.

Mazor, M. D. (1979, May). Barren couples. *Psychology Today,* pp. 102–104.

Mazor, M. D. (1984). Emotional reactions to infertility. In M. D. Mazor and H. F. Simons (Eds.), *Infertility: Medical, emotional, and social considerations* (pp. 23–35). New York: Human Sciences.

McGrade, J. T., & Tolor, A. (1981). The reaction to infertility and the infertility investigation: A comparison of the responses of men and women. *Infertility, 4*(1), 7–27.

Menning, B. E. (1977). *Infertility: A guide for the childless couple.* Englewood Cliffs, NJ: Prentice-Hall.

Menning, B. E. (1980). The emotional needs of infertile couples. *Fertility and Sterility, 34*, 313–319.

Miller, G. A., Galanter, E., & Pribram, K. H. (1960). *Plans and the structure of behavior.* New York: Holt, Rinehart & Winston.

Rosenfeld, D. L., & Mitchell, E. (1979). Treating the emotional aspects of infertility: Counseling services in an infertility clinic. *American Journal of Obstetrics and Gynecology, 135*(2), 177–180.

Sawatzky, M. (1981). Tasks of infertile couples. *Journal of Obstetric, Gynecologic and Neonatal Nursing,* March/April, 132–133.

Seibel, M. M., & Taymor, M. L. (1982). Emotional aspects of infertility. *Fertility and Sterility, 37*(2), 137–144.

Shapiro, C. H. (1982, September). The impact of infertility on the marital relationship. *The Journal of Contemporary Social Work*, pp. 387–393.

Silver, R. L., Boon, C., & Stones, M. H. (1983). Searching for meaning in misfortune: Making sense of incest. *Journal of Social Issues, 39*, 81–102.

Silver, R. L., & Wortman, C. B. (1980). Coping with undesirable life events. In J. Garber & M. E. P. Seligman (Eds.), *Human helplessness* (pp. 279–375). New York: Academic Press.

Skylar, B. R. (1984). Infertility: Its effect on self-esteem, marital satisfaction and locus of control orientation among men, women and marital dyads. *Dissertation Abstracts International, 45*.

Slade, P. (1981). Sexual attitudes and social role orientations in infertile women. *Journal of Psychosomatic Research, 25*, 183–186.

Tait, R., & Silver, R. C. (1989). Coming to terms with major negative life events. In J. S. Uleman & J. A. Bargh (Eds.), *Unintended thought* (pp. 351–382). New York: Guilford.

Taylor, S. E. (1983). Adjustment to threatening events: A theory of cognitive adaptation. *American Psychologist, 38*, 1161–1173.

Taylor, S. E., & Schneider, S. (1989). Coping and the simulation of events. *Social Cognition, 7*, 174–194.

Taylor, S. E., Wood, J. V., & Lichtman, R. R. (1983). It could be worse: Selective evaluation as a response to victimization. *Journal of Social Issues, 39*(2), 19–40.

Taymor, M. L., & Bresnick, E. (1979). Emotional stress and infertility. *Infertility, 2*(1), 39–47.

Thompson, S. C., & Janigan, A. S. (1988). Life schemes: A framework for understanding the search for meaning. *Journal of Social and Clinical Psychology, 7*, 260–280.

Tulandi, T., Bull, R., Cooke, R., & McInnes, R. (1981). Regrettable pregnancy after infertility. *Infertility, 4*(4), 321–326.

Valentine, D. P. (1986). Psychological impact of infertility: Identifying issues and needs. *Social Work in Health Care, 11*(4), 61–69.

Vallacher, R. R., & Wegner, D. M. (1987). What do people think they're doing? Action identification and human behavior. *Psychological Review, 94*, 3–15.

Veevers, J. E. (1973). The social meanings of parenthood. *Psychiatry, 36*, 291–310.

Walfish, S., & Myerson, M. (1980). Sex role identity and attitudes toward sexuality. *Archives of Sexual Behavior, 9*, 199–222.

West, S. (1983). Infertility-couples in crisis. *The Australian Nurses Journal, 13*, 40–41.

Wicklund, R. (1986). Orientation to the environment versus preoccupation with human potential. In R. M. Sorrentino & E. T. Higgins (Eds.), *Handbook of motivation and cognition: Foundations of social behavior* Vol. 1, pp. 64–95). New York: Guilford.

Wilson, E. A. (1979). Sequences of emotional response induced by infertility. *The Journal of the Kentucky Medical Association, 77*(5), 229–234.

Wortman, C. B., & Lehman, D. R. (1985). Reactions to victims of life crises: Support attempts that fail. In I. B. Sarason & B. R. Sarason (Eds.), *Social support: Theory, research, application* (pp. 463–489). Dordrecht, The Netherlands: Martinus Nijhof.

Zeigarnik, B. (1927). Das Behalten erledigter und unerledigter Handlugen. *Psychologie Forshung, 9*, 1–85. Translated and condensed as: (1938). On finished and unfinished tasks. In W. D. Ellis (Ed.), *A source book of gestalt psychology* (pp. 300–314). New York: Harcourt, Brace & World.

III

Current Status and Future Directions

9

Psychological Intervention and Infertility

ANTHONY E. READING

There is a long tradition of psychological intervention for individuals and couples with infertility. Some of this work has drawn upon a psychosomatic framework, suggesting that infertility stems from emotional conflicts, whereas the conceptualization of infertility as a life crisis has served as the basis for other applied work. This chapter will examine psychological interventions with infertility patients. Few empirical evaluations of psychological interventions with this patient population are available, and consequently this chapter will draw upon established theory and research from other clinical settings or populations as well as clinical observation.

ISSUES IN PSYCHOLOGICAL TREATMENT OF INFERTILE COUPLES

Several questions arise regarding psychological intervention for infertile couples. First, do infertile couples need psychological counseling? Given that some couples may benefit from intervention, what approach might staff members in infertility clinics take to provide it? What are the goals of such intervention, and what treatment approaches might be use-

ANTHONY E. READING • Center for Reproductive Medicine, Cedars-Sinai Medical Center, Los Angeles, California 90048.

ful? Consideration of each of these questions comprises the focus of this chapter.

Need for Counseling

Is infertility sufficiently distressing to warrant the provision of psychological intervention to infertile couples? As Dunkel-Schetter and Lobel document in this volume, studies in general have not demonstrated high levels of distress in infertile individuals. Although women on the average do not demonstrate clinically significant levels of general maladjustment, they may nonetheless be quite distressed about their infertility and seek counseling to aid them in coping with it. For example, in spite of normal MMPI profiles, 49% of women and 15% of men in one study (Freeman, Boxer, Rickels, Tureck, & Mastroianni, 1985) declared that infertility was very disturbing and was "the most upsetting experience of their life." Despite normal scores on psychological testing, 18% of the infertile women studied by Paulson, Haarmann, Salerno, and Asmar (1988) sought psychological counseling during their infertility investigation. A comparison of psychological test scores between this group and the remainder revealed no difference. Daniluk (1988) presented data on 63 couples attending an infertility clinic. Although average scores on measures of psychological distress and marital adjustment remained in the normal range, over 90% advocated the provision of psychological services. Shaw, Johnston, and Shaw (1988) found that 50% of couples waiting for *in vitro* fertilization (IVF) requested counseling. Baram, Tourtelot, Meuchler, and Huang (1988) found that 66% of women and 40% of men reported depression following a failed IVF treatment. Twenty-four percent of women and 13% of men felt that long-term counseling would have been helpful following unsuccessful IVF.

How does one reconcile the absence of general maladjustment in infertile samples with clinical impressions that infertility is extremely stressful and the finding that patients themselves advocate counseling? Consistent with the suggestions of Dunkel-Schetter and Lobel, a number of possible explanations arise for this discrepancy. Generally speaking, the methodologies used in most research to date may mask the complexities of the issues under study. First, infertility may be difficult only for vulnerable individuals or for those in dysfunctional relationships. Second, the measures chosen in previous research may be insufficiently sensitive to detect changes in stress levels or situationally induced sadness because most were designed to identify psychopathology in psychiatric settings. Third, respondents may tend to perceive such assessments as a form of screening and so be motivated to portray themselves in the best possible light in order to ensure treatment eligibility. Fourth, social desirability effects may be compounded by individuals' self-perceptions. For example, Mazure, De l'Aune, and DeCherney (1988) suggested that infertile couples tend to repress anxiety or stress. Using the Taylor Manifest Anxiety Scale and the Marlowe-Crowne Social Desirability Scale, they found that 18% of their sample acknowledged high anxiety and 43% had genuinely low anxiety levels. The remainder (38%) displayed the "repressor" pattern of low manifest anxiety and high social desirability scores. Fifth, the stage in treatment at which assessments are taken may influence the results achieved. When testing is conducted prior to IVF treatment, this may coincide with a peak of optimism and well-being. Studies have shown that women tend to overestimate their chances of success with IVF (Johnston, Shaw, & Bird, 1987; Leiblum, Kemmann, & Lane, 1987; Reading, 1989). Further, a self-selection factor may operate, so that only the most psychologically "hardy" engage in particularly demanding treatments. Finally, psychological reactions would be expected to vary widely depending upon individual differences in coping style and perceptions of available options.

In spite of unremarkable profiles on psychological testing, some patients clearly find infertility very distressing. Previous chapters have illustrated the types of intra- and interpersonal challenges that infertile couples may confront, including the experience of loss, frustration arising from blocked goals, and the search for a cause of their infertility. Distress arising from these issues may be exacerbated as the options for treating infertility become more numerous. Whereas biology set limits on treatment options in the past, medical advances have essentially removed those barriers. Just as a gambler feels that the next bet will be the lucky one, so the infertile couple is left with the uneasy feeling that one more try might bring its reward. The hope arising from each new medical breakthrough is a double-edged sword. It offers the promise of success, but also perpetuates the struggle. Leiblum *et al.* (1987) found that half of an IVF sample felt they had reached a resolution concerning their infertility after a failed IVF attempt. However, 90% said they would consider participating in any new reproductive treatment options that would offer a chance of pregnancy. Thus, both the issues accompanying infertility itself and those arising from the increasing array of treatments and alternatives may engender distress. Psychological intervention may benefit couples confronting these issues.

Role of Staff

A variety of medical options are available for couples undergoing infertility evaluation and treatment. The management of infertility is being consolidated into specialist centers that can provide a full range of services and specialists (U.S. Congress, Office of Technology Assessment, 1988). A number of programs provide psychological services and routinely schedule an initial consultation with a psychologist or social worker. Psychological help also can be provided by referral or offered by nursing and medical staff.

The intensive nature of infertility treatment can lead to a close relationship between staff and patient. This affords an opportunity for staff to deal with psychological issues as they arise, either through direct intervention or appropriate referral. To do this, staff must feel comfortable addressing emotional issues, understand the range of approaches available, and discriminate between issues that can be addressed in the moment and those that merit referral. Ideally, staff should have access to a mental health professional so that they can receive guidance and develop skills to prevent and deal with crises.

Staff may become invested in positive outcomes and so may share the emotional ups and downs of patients, making it difficult to give dispassionate advice. This may become a problem when couples feel they have let the staff down by failing to become pregnant or by deciding to terminate treatment. Couples also may feel unable to express their own grief because staff disappointment in a treatment failure is so obvious. Mental health professionals can be available both to provide intervention to the infertile couple and to consult with staff who inadvertently might be placing undue pressure on patients.

Treatment Objectives

Before considering psychological treatment approaches, it may be helpful to consider the objectives. In the past, therapy was often predicated on the belief that psychological factors impeded fertility. As a result, treatment methods were instituted to improve chances for conception. With improvements in diagnostic precision, it is clear that the number of cases for whom no organic cause can be found is small. This does not preclude the possibility that psychological factors have an additive effect. Psychophysiological research suggests many mechanisms by which stress may affect reproductive hormones and the immune system, as well as having local effects on uterotubal functioning (Reading, Chang, & Kerin, 1989).

Alternatively, most current psychological approaches follow from the assumption that experiencing infertility and undergoing treatment are stressful. Thus, psychological methods are used to help infertile individuals to reduce stress, enhance mood, and improve adjustment and coping surrounding infertility. Treatment objectives most likely will vary according to the couple's stage in medical treatment. Early on, issues regarding treatment decisions may be the focus, while later counseling may be concerned with the process of stopping treatment, adjusting to alternative options, or coming to terms with loss. Clinicians (e.g., Menning, 1977) have likened infertility to a grief process, implying a progression through various stages of grief. However, no research has followed infertile couples over the often-protracted course of infertility, and Wortman and Silver (1989) point out that little empirical support exists for stage models of coping with loss in general. Therefore, it is premature to advocate particular time-specific goals for psychological treatment.

Treatment Approaches

Assessment and Initial Consultation. Many programs now provide the opportunity for couples to be assessed psychologically at the time of program enrollment. Assessment at this stage is not intended to exclude participants but to ensure that other issues, such as ongoing depression or substance abuse, are recognized and effectively treated. It also provides an opportunity to prepare the couple for issues that may arise over the course of treatment and to discuss coping strategies. Regimens for high technology treatments such as IVF or gamete intrafallopian transfer (GIFT) place a substantial burden on the patient. Because these require frequent clinic visits, couples, and women in particular, may place their careers on hold in order to have the time and flexibility required. In addition, various medications may be used to suppress or stimulate ovarian functioning, and these may affect mood. During the initial consultations, psychological preparation for upcoming medical procedures may have a stress-innoculating effect (Ridgeway & Mathews, 1982).

Initial consultations also may be used to assess information processing and decision-making with regard to infertility treatments and alternatives. Because of the burgeoning number of options for attempting conception, infertile couples confront an array of complex choices. Research has demonstrated the distorting effects of motivation and emotion on information processing, which may be reflected in infertile patients' tendency to make overly optimistic estimates of success (Johnston *et al.*, 1987; Reading, 1989). Counseling may assist the couple in assessing treatment options and so facilitate decision-making.

Psychodynamic Treatment. The long tradition of psychodynamic treatment for infertility is directed at improving both fertility and overall psychological adjustment. In this context, psychodynamic therapy attempts to uncover unconscious conflicts and facilitate the process of working through unresolved emotional experiences that might impair fertility. In a study by Sarrel and DeCherney (1985), 20 couples with unexplained infertility were assigned randomly either to a psychotherapeutic interview in which psychodynamic interpretation was offered or to a no-contact control group. According to the therapist conducting the interviews, previously unrecognized psychological conflict leading to emotional stress was identified in eight of the ten couples interviewed. The most common conflicts were an abnormally close relationship between the infertile woman and her mother and unrecognized fears surrounding pregnancy. Eight of the treated couples versus two control couples reported sexual problems. After 18 months of follow-up, six of the ten interviewed couples became pregnant, compared to one of nine control couples. Treatment may have been effective by providing conditions for resolution of ongoing conflicts, in turn enhancing physiological functioning. Alternatively, relationship or sexual issues may have been addressed effectively. In addition, the intervention itself or the fact that the infertility specialist was present during the interview may have resulted in treated couples' greater persistence in medical treatment and thus higher conception rates. The authors acknowledged the exploratory nature of their study.

Relaxation and Stress Management. Relaxation and stress management techniques have been advocated by some to improve fertility. Relaxation may have the potential for dampening arousal of the autonomic and sympathetic nervous systems, which may in turn enhance fertility. O'Moore, O'Moore, Harrison, Murphy, and Carruthers (1983) administered eight sessions of autogenic training to women with idiopathic infertility. This relaxation treatment did not affect fertility outcome significantly. Beneficial effects of relaxation on fertility have not yet been demonstrated.

In recent years, interest has developed in the effects of visualization techniques on illness (e.g., Siegel, 1986). Patients often wonder what attitude to take during a treatment cycle, and some may use visualization in an attempt to improve their chances. Some couples convince themselves that they will be successful and believe that any anticipation of failure will undermine their chances for conception. During treatment they may visualize fertilization and implantation occurring. As with the use of these approaches for other conditions, there is no direct evidence for beneficial effects. In addition, it is not clear whether imagining the treatment working facilitates or hinders adjustment to the high probability of IVF failure. Visualization techniques and bolstering expectations for success may enhance couples' perceptions of control. However, if these methods are accompanied by self-blame when the desired outcome is not attained, distress may result. The professional may wish to help the couple consider the consequences of such techniques for their own adjustment.

Irrespective of its impact on fertility, stress management procedures may offer a means of coping with the stress of trying to become pregnant. By providing a mechanism for control, relaxation techniques can redirect attention from aspects of infertility that are not controllable by the couple (e.g., reproductive success). Stress management counselors can suggest additional ways to enhance control, including obtaining information, keeping a duplicate copy of medical records, and becoming an active participant in a team approach to treatment.

Cognitive Behavioral Approaches. Cognitive approaches have been used to treat depression and other problems (Beck, Rush, Shaw, & Emery, 1979) and may be helpful in issues arising from infertility. Although Dobson (1988) described over 20 different formats for cognitive-behavioral therapy, common ingredients can be discerned. These approaches assume that the ways in which one views events can initiate or maintain emotional responses to them. Beck *et al.* (1979) described the unrealistic and self-defeating cognitions that initiate or maintain depression and anxiety. The normal tendency for positive events and memories to be more accessible to awareness may be reversed in depression. Studies of depressed patients have shown a preponderance of automatic, "depressogenic" thoughts that diminish with resolution of the depression. For example, an infertile person may be convinced that "nothing will work and life will be ruined as a result." The therapist may help the person to identify such self-defeating assumptions and expectations and to replace them with self-statements that diminish distress.

Cognitive and behavioral approaches suggest that exposure of the client to the problem can be beneficial. Rachman (1980) used the term "emotional processing" to refer to the way in which emotional experiences are absorbed and so lose their disruptive effect on behavior. The central sign of unsatisfactory emotional processing is the persistence of intrusive signs of emotional and cognitive activity, such as obsessions, nightmares, and phobias. Many infertile patients complain about intrusive thoughts and preoccupation with their problem, suggesting difficulty with emotional processing. The extent of current emotional processing can be assessed with "test probes." The therapist presents relevant stimulus material (e.g., asks the infertile patient to discuss an event relevant to infertility) and assesses the evoked emotional reaction. Cognitive approaches would suggest that by getting patients to talk about their thoughts and feelings regarding infertility, the therapist also can assess clients' automatic cognitive representations of the problem. For example, reaction to the test probe might reveal accompanying thoughts which relate to past experiences of loss and failure.

Rachman suggested that emotional processing is facilitated by exposure to the source of the problem and working through it in a constructive way. Processing is impeded by avoidance, maintaining silence, and only brief exposure to the problem. In this view, emotions must be experienced to be processed constructively. The theory of emotional processing would argue in favor of expressing concerns or feelings, provided that prolonged exposure in a controlled setting is possible. With the therapist's aid, clients can identify their self-defeating automatic thoughts, and more constructive cognitive connections can be developed. In addition, fostering emotional processing might help to prevent later distress. Rather than adopting a uniformly positive outlook and denying the possibility of failure, infertility patients might adjust better to a subsequent failed outcome by expressing concerns at the outset. This opportunity to work through the implications of failure at an early stage may facilitate subsequent emotional processing.

Emotional processing may be facilitated by the degree of emotional response during a test probe (Foa & Kozak, 1986). For processing to occur, a probe must match the initial circumstance and reactions to it. This argues against attempting to remain detached during discussion of painful issues, because emotional processing may be impeded by disassociation or detachment. Patients may be concerned that distress, once elicited, will persist indefinitely. They may exaggerate the risks of releasing emotions, believing that their partners will feel let down or the doctors will see them as neurotic. They may be relieved to discover that this is not the case, but rather that negative emotions peak and subside. Rachman suggests that the neutralization of emotion-provoking stimuli may be "a matter of breaking down the incoming stimulation into manageable proportions and then absorbing it over an optimal period" (p. 58). Patients are likely to benefit from the concrete demonstration that their negative emotions do subside, as well as from attempts to counter self-defeating cognitions that accompany emotional experience.

Successful emotional processing may thus confer benefit. This suggestion is consistent with reports of increased self-esteem after coping with stressful experiences (Dienstbier, 1989) and with the reports of some infertile couples that they become stronger as a result of the experience. The emotional processing model may be useful for the therapist who is attempting to devise effective methods for helping patients deal with emotions surrounding infertility. However, it is necessary to test empirically the factors in emotional processing that are assumed to facilitate or retard adjustment (Rachman, 1980).

Whatever the origins of distress, cognitive approaches may be helpful to clarify the ways in which emotional distress is maintained or amplified by an individual's perceptions. In addition to test probes, self-monitoring or guided imagery can aid in bringing self-defeating thoughts to the individual's attention. Through this process of exposure, the individual can establish constructive interpretations. Individuals can be shown how to encode situations in new ways that are less likely to access negative memories and associations. For example, if a friend extends an invitation to a baby shower, this initially might be construed as a comment on that woman's success and the infertile woman's failure. A more helpful focus might be on the socially supportive intent of the invitation. Thus, cognitive therapy attempts to uncover and challenge rules and assumptions represented in memory, thereby disrupting the pattern of selective attention to negative information. In addition, therapy can emphasize the importance of shifting attributions regarding reproductive capacities from global and stable, which are likely to engender distress, to specific and unstable. For example, a common thought of an infertile person might be, "I can't become a parent; I'm just no good at anything important [global] and I never will be [stable]." The therapist's task here would be to help the infertile person to alter the cognitive connection between reproductive capacity and his or her other enduring abilities.

Such cognitive approaches may be combined with behavioral assignments designed to overcome avoidance behavior. Individuals may cut themselves off from activities that evoke distress, such as baby showers, parties, or other "child-oriented" events. Behavioral avoidance may generalize, starting with a specific incident and spreading to approximations of it. For example, avoiding a baby shower may generalize to avoiding contact with friends who attend it and to places where children or pregnant women are likely to be seen. Such avoidant behavior can limit sources of pleasure, distraction, and social support, thereby increasing vulnerability to depression (Lewinsohn & Hoberman, 1988). Such a pattern needs to be recognized early and treated by graded exposure to distress-provoking situations, combined with coping statements to overcome self-defeating thoughts about the situations. This might consist of establishing a hierarchy of difficulty for a series of distress-provoking situations and encouraging the person to resume each one, beginning with the least distress-provoking. Although some self-protection from painful reminders of infertility might be adaptive, more extreme forms of avoidance may confer risk for depression and anxiety.

In summary, cognitive-behavioral approaches may help the infertile couple to challenge self-defeating cognitions, facilitate emotional processing, and prevent extreme behavioral avoidance. These approaches have been demonstrated to be effective for people coping with other problems (Dobson, 1989; Emery, Hollon, & Bedrosian, 1981; Foa & Kozak, 1986), and their utility with infertile couples awaits empirical test.

Grief Management. There is reasonable professional consensus (Mahlstedt, 1985; Menning, 1977) that grief must be worked through in order to prevent persistent difficulties in functioning. These professionals suggest that if the natural tendency to avoid unpleasant feelings is heeded, the period of grief and disrupted functioning will be prolonged. One might compare the experiences of grief and phobia. Phobic reactions involve anxiety and prompt avoidance of objectively harmless situations. In the event of a loss, various objects and settings serve as reminders, and similarly may be avoided. Avoidance may prevent both resolution of the grief and extinction of phobia. Ramsay (1977) described a prolonged exposure approach to dealing with pathological grief reactions, which involved exposing the individual to reminders and stimuli associated with the loss. Sireling, Cohen, and Marks (1988) attempted to replicate Ramsay's findings by assigning patients with morbid grief to an exposure or antiexposure therapy. Both groups improved at nine months, although the improvement was more pronounced in the exposure group. It appears that continued exposure to pain or grief gradually blunts its power. However, as Wortman and Silver (1989) emphasize, clinicians should be wary of imposing unvalidated stages of grief on individuals, as if these are the norm.

Grief may occur not only in response to acknowledgment of permanent infertility, but also when any particular menstrual cycle does not bring successful conception. Grief can be triggered in response to a failed treatment cycle, particularly if the couple was convinced that pregnancy had occurred. The couple often sees the failed treatment as a lost pregnancy. Traditionally, obstetricians advised women experiencing a pregnancy loss to postpone trying to conceive again for at least six months. This allowed the couple some time to process the experience emotionally. Does a comparable recommendation apply to the infertile couple? If the couple is still experiencing grief after an unsuccessful treatment, should further treatment be deferred? Even though there may be concern over the effects of grief, couples may feel that they do not have the luxury of time to wait. Until empirical data regarding this question are available to serve as a guide, clinicians may want to discuss with the couple the emotional advantages and disadvantages of attempting treatment anew soon after a failed cycle.

Sexual and Marital Issues. Although some studies have revealed few differences between infertile and fertile couples in levels of sexual satisfaction and dysfunction (Fagan, Schmidt, Rock, Damewood, Halle, & Wise, 1986; Link & Darling, 1986), infertility is often cited as the cause when sexual problems do arise in infertile couples (Keye & Deneris, 1982). In the Keye and Deneris study, infertile women reported that their infertility resulted in loss of sexual spontaneity, poor sexual self-image, and a feeling that sex had become meaningless in the absence of an ability to conceive. It is well-known that anxiety and performance pressure disrupt the sexual response, both of which are likely to occur during sexual contact around the time of ovulation. Another common reason for sexual difficulty is inadequate or insufficient stimulation. This may occur as a consequence of sexual contact becoming focused on the goal of procreation. For example, DeVires, Degani, Eibschitz, Oettinger, Zilberman, and Sharf (1984) showed a change in the duration of sexual foreplay when couples were required to perform a postcoital test. Sexual "spectatoring," in which one carefully evaluates one's performance, also disrupts arousal. Infertile couples may be at risk for this problem, as they intently monitor their physiological responses, with the concern that their bodies are going to work appropriately. Finally, interpersonal issues can compound sexual problems. For example, if one partner experiences difficulty in performing "timed" sexual intercourse during ovulation, the other partner may believe that this signals ambivalence about starting a family.

Where sexual difficulties arise, treatment can draw upon established techniques in sex therapy (Masters & Johnson, 1970), consisting of removing performance demand, addressing resistances and impediments, reducing anxiety, using graded assignments, and enhancing the sensory experience. Counseling may enable couples to understand the reasons for a sexual dysfunction and address their fears about the meanings of such problems.

Regarding the relationship as a whole, problems can arise over decisions about treatments and alternatives, as well as over differences between partners in importance attached to various issues surrounding infertility. For example, couples may reach an impasse over decisions regarding the use of donors, what option they should pursue next, or when to stop trying medical treatments. In addition, the prolonged stress associated with infertility may create an undercurrent of disappointment and sadness, permeating the relationship and depriving the couple of opportunities for pleasure and relief.

These problems can create an overwhelming need to discuss the issues for some individuals. Yet particular patterns of discussion can simply reactivate and rehearse pain and may lead nowhere. Rather than have a cathartic effect, discussion may leave both partners feeling more distressed. In contrast to successful emotional processing, in which the exposure is prolonged and arousal kept at manageable levels, discussions are likely to be damaging when exposure to each specific topic is short and arousal is very high. As a result, avoidance behavior can develop in order to limit opportunities for discussion. In this context, stimulus-control procedures can serve a useful function by setting limits on the amount of time devoted to discussion. Providing an agreed-upon beginning and endpoint may engender a more gratifying and constructive interaction. Problem-solving and communication techniques can also be used to improve the quality of the discussion. Couples can be helped to break down issues into component parts, generate lists of options, and select one or more options that both are willing to entertain. In addition, leisure time and reinforcement should be built into the couple's schedule to offset the disappointments accompanying infertility.

Self-Help Groups. A national network of self-help groups (RESOLVE) has been established to provide an opportunity for infertile couples to share concerns, information, and support. As with other conditions, self-help groups play a valuable role in disseminating information, offering a forum for couples to exchange experiences, and allowing participants to benefit from the coping experiences of others (see also Abbey, Andrews, & Halman, this volume).

CONCLUSIONS

Psychological intervention with infertility patients can be frustrating for the therapist because the underlying problem may not be amenable to change. As with other chronic conditions, the emphasis is on enhancing effective coping and reducing the toll taken by the problem so that the affected individual can achieve a satisfying life. The changing face of medical practice is setting new psychological challenges. Technology that offers hope also confers protracted uncertainty for many couples. There is a dearth of longitudinal studies on the impact of infertility, and we have little empirical information on the differential impact of various coping strategies or psychological interventions. While such investigation is progressing, therapists may benefit from the clinical expertise of specialists in psychological intervention with infertile couples and the empirical literature on effective intervention for other clinical problems.

REFERENCES

Baram, D., Tourtelot, E., Meuchler, E., & Huang, K. (1988). Psychosocial adjustment following unsuccessful in vitro fertilization. *Journal of Psychosomatic Obstetrics and Gynecology,* 9, 181–190.

Beck, A. T., Rush, A. J., Shaw, B. F., & Emery, G. (1979). *Cognitive therapy of depression.* New York: Guilford.

Daniluk, J. C. (1988). Infertility: Intrapersonal and interpersonal impact. *Fertility and Sterility, 49,* 982–990.

DeVires, J., Degani, S., Eibschitz, I., Oettinger, M., Zilberman, A., & Sharf, M. (1984). The influence of the postcoital test on the sexual function of infertile women. *Journal of Psychosomatic Obstetrics and Gynecology, 3,* 101–106.

Dienstbier, R. A. (1989). Arousal and physiological toughness: Implications for mental and physical health. *Psychological Review, 96,* 84–100.

Dobson, K. S. (1988). *Handbook of cognitive-behavioral therapies.* New York: Guilford.

Dobson, K. S. (1989). A meta-analysis of the efficacy of cognitive therapy for depression. *Journal of Consulting and Clinical Psychology, 57,* 414–419.

Emery, G., Hollon, S. D., & Bedrosian, R. C. (1981). *New directions in cognitive therapy: A casebook.* New York: Guilford.

Fagan, P. J., Schmidt, C. W. Jr., Rock, J. A., Damewood, M. D., Halle, E., & Wise, T. N. (1986). Sexual functioning and psychologic evaluation of in vitro fertilization couples. *Fertility and Sterility, 46,* 668–672.

Foa, E. B., & Kozak, M. F. (1986). Emotional processing of fear: Exposure to corrective information. *Psychological Bulletin, 99,* 20–35.

Freeman, E. W., Boxer, A. S., Rickels, K., Tureck, R., & Mastroianni, L. Jr. (1985). Psychological evaluation and support in a program of in vitro fertilization and embryo transfer. *Fertility and Sterility, 43,* 48–53.

Johnston, M., Shaw, R., & Bird, D. (1987). Test-tube baby procedures: Stress vs. judgements under uncertainty. *Psychology and Health, 1,* 25–38.

Keye, W. R. Jr., & Deneris, A. (1982). Female sexual activity, satisfaction and function in infertile women. *Infertility, 5,* 275–285.

Leiblum, S. R., Kemmann, E., & Lane, M. K. (1987). The psychological concomitants of in vitro fertilization. *Journal of Psychosomatic Obstetrics and Gynecology, 6,* 165–178.

Lewinsohn, P. M., & Hoberman, H. M. (1988). A prospective study of risk factors for unipolar depression. *Journal of Abnormal Psychology, 97,* 251–264.

Link, P. W., & Darling, C. A. (1986). Couples undergoing treatment for infertility: Dimensions of life satisfaction. *Journal of Sex and Marital Therapy, 12,* 46–59.

Mahlstedt, P. P. (1985). The psychological component of infertility. *Fertility and Sterility, 43,* 335–346.

Masters, W. H., & Johnson, V. (1970). *Human sexual inadequacy.* Boston: Little, Brown.

Mazure, C. M., De l'Aune, W., & DeCherney, A. H. (1988). Two methodological issues in the psychological study of in vitro fertilization embryo transfer participants. *Journal of Psychosomatic Obstetrics and Gynecology, 9,* 17–21.

Menning, B. E. (1977). *Infertility: A guide for the childless couple.* Englewood Cliffs, NJ: Prentice-Hall.

O'Moore, A. M., O'Moore, R. R., Harrison, R. F., Murphy, G., & Carruthers, M. E. (1983). Psychosomatic aspects in idiopathic infertility: Effects of treatment with autogenic training. *Journal of Psychosomatic Research, 27,* 145–151.

Paulson, J. D., Haarmann, B. S., Salerno, R. L., & Asmar, P. (1988). An investigation of the relationship between emotional maladjustment and infertility. *Fertility and Sterility, 49,* 258–262.

Rachman, S. (1980). Emotional processing. *Behaviour Research and Therapy, 18,* 51–60.

Ramsay, R. W. (1977). Behavioural approaches to bereavement. *Behaviour Research and Therapy, 15,* 131–135.

Reading, A. E. (1989). IVF and decision making. *Journal of Psychosomatic Obstetrics and Gynecology, 10,* 107–112.

Reading, A. E., Chang, L. C., & Kerin, J. F. (1989). Psychological changes over the course of IVF-ET. *Journal of Reproductive and Infant Psychology, 7,* 95–103.

Ridgeway, V., & Mathews, A. (1982). Psychological preparation for surgery: A comparison of methods. *British Journal of Clinical Psychology, 21,* 271–280.

Sarrel, P. M., & DeCherney, A. H. (1985). Psychotherapeutic intervention for treatment of couples with secondary infertility. *Fertility and Sterility, 43,* 897–900.

Shaw, P., Johnston, M., & Shaw, R. (1988). Counseling needs, emotional and relationship problems in couples awaiting IVF. *Journal of Psychosomatic Obstetrics and Gynecology, 9,* 171–180.

Siegel, B. S. (1986). *Love, medicine and miracles.* New York: Harper & Row.

Sireling, L., Cohen, D., & Marks, I. (1988). Guided mourning for morbid grief: A controlled replication. *Behavior Therapy, 19,* 121–132.

U. S. Congress, Office of Technology Assessment. (1988). *Infertility: Medical and social choices,* OTA-BA-358. Washington, DC: U. S. Government Printing Office.

Wortman, C. B., & Silver, R. C. (1989). The myths of coping with loss. *Journal of Consulting and Clinical Psychology, 57,* 349–357.

10

Psychological Adjustment to Infertility

Future Directions in Research and Application

CHRISTINE DUNKEL-SCHETTER
and ANNETTE L. STANTON

In this book, we have attempted to bring together the best of stress and coping research with current issues regarding adjustment to infertility. We hope that these chapters will introduce a new theoretical tradition to research on infertility, a stress and coping framework. It is our conviction that this body of theoretical work can provide excellent direction for psychosocial infertility research in the next decade.

In this chapter, a number of the substantive and methodological issues facing researchers studying infertility will be discussed, and directions for future research and treatment offered. Infertility is a highly complex phenomenon, which increases the difficulty of building a body of scientific knowledge on this topic. It is the goal of this book, and of this chapter in particular, to illuminate the complexity of the issues and offer some solutions to those interested in psychological adjustment to infertility.

CHRISTINE DUNKEL-SCHETTER • Department of Psychology, University of California, Los Angeles, California 90024-1563. ANNETTE L. STANTON • Department of Psychology, University of Kansas, Lawrence, Kansas 66045-2160.

CONCEPTUAL ISSUES IN RESEARCH ON ADJUSTMENT TO INFERTILITY

We will discuss five conceptual issues relevant to research on adjustment to infertility: (1) Level of analysis (individuals, partners, couples); (2) conceptualizing adjustment as multifaceted and evolving; (3) positive effects of infertility; (4) gender differences in adjustment; and (5) the social context of infertility.

Level of Analysis

One can consider the issue of adjustment to infertility on three levels: the person who is diagnosed infertile, the spouse or partner of this person, or the couple who cannot conceive together. Each level of analysis warrants attention for several reasons, some of which are discussed below. Understanding individual-level adjustment is important because many forms of psychotherapy or intervention must be conducted with individuals. Sometimes the partner is unavailable or unwilling to enter couples' counseling. In other cases, infertility may evoke feelings that are tied to unique personal experiences in early development, including earlier losses. For example, an inability to conceive may evoke misplaced self-blame and guilt in someone who has been sexually abused or assaulted. Reactions to infertility that can be identified as reflecting unresolved personal intrapsychic issues would be best addressed in treatment of and research on the individual.

At present, it is unclear whether there are differences between individuals diagnosed as infertile and partners who are presumed fertile, but there are plausible rationales for expecting such differences. Although both parties are vulnerable to distress, holding oneself responsible for a fertile partner's inability to have biological children could be guilt-inducing, whereas perceiving one's infertile partner as responsible might engender anger, for example. Investigations of spouse reactions to an infertile partner are nonexistent, a gap that future research could address. Both studies of individual reactions to infertility and of spouse reactions to an infertile partner can be founded on the available stress and coping literature. Research on adjustment to the life events of one's partner, such as his or her job loss or diagnosis of heart disease, may offer valuable approaches for studying spouse reactions to infertility.

However, infertility is unusual in that it confronts the couple as a unit as well as the individuals involved. Regardless of the cause, members of the couple experience the inability to conceive jointly, and together they must make decisions about pursuing treatment, seeking alternatives such as adoption, or choosing not to have children. Thus, research on life events that affect couples as a unit is relevant to studying adjustment to infertility. For example, studies of parents of terminally ill children may be of value (Adams, 1979; Chesler & Barbarin, 1987). Like infertile couples, these parents experience a loss that entails gradual adjustment. Events occurring for couples such as having a handicapped child, divorce, or the sudden death of a family member, although less analogous to infertility, may be relevant nonetheless. Thus, past research on these events (e.g., Benson & Gross, 1989; Lehman, Wortman, & Williams, 1987) is worth considering as it pertains to understanding adjustment to infertility.

In addition, work on marital distress is pertinent to infertility. Because infertility poses threats to the couple's joint goals and plans, it may disrupt marital functioning and cause significant marital distress. Studies of couples' reactions to infertility are complicated by the fact that assessment tools and statistical techniques for studying couples in general are still under development. However, much progress is being made in both theory and research on couples that can inform infertility research (e.g., Fincham & Bradbury, 1990; Huston & Robins, 1982; Kelley, Berscheid, Christensen, Harvey, Huston, Levinger, McClintock, Peplau, & Peterson, 1983; Kenny, 1988; Rusbult, Johnson, & Morrow, 1986).

To summarize, infertility represents goal blockage for the couple as well as the individuals involved. Each partner responds to it in light of his or her own vulnerabilities, psychological resources, personal predispositions (e.g., beliefs and attitudes) and so forth. In turn, the reactions of each individual affect the functioning of the couple as they face decisions regarding what to do in seeking to be parents. To gain a greater understanding of adjustment to infertility, researchers must study the interrelationship of the couple as a unit and of each individual's role within it.

Conceptualizing Adjustment as Multifaceted and Evolving

A problem that plagues stress and coping research is that of defining successful adjustment. This issue faces infertility researchers as well. Is an infertile woman with considerable emotional distress less successfully adjusted than an infertile woman whose medical condition is the same but who experiences less distress? Is it maladaptive to become severely depressed for a period of time if one later returns to, or exceeds, earlier levels of functioning? Is an infertile man who refuses to adopt a child, despite his strong desire to have one, less well-adjusted than a man who agrees to pursue adoption with his partner? These and similar questions emerge when the issue of adjustment is addressed.

To date, the most common indicators of adjustment in the literature on infertility are emotional distress and psychiatric symptomatology. One way to define adjustment is to posit that levels of symptoms or distress above norms or cutoffs for psychiatric samples indicate problems in adjustment. However, as many researchers have pointed out, high distress, at least temporarily, may be reasonable in coping with a major loss (Wortman & Silver, 1987). The more appropriate indicator of maladjustment would seem to be consistently high distress over a fairly long period of time without any indication of reduction, particularly if such distress impedes functioning in one's central roles.

Moreover, other facets of adjustment seem equally important. For example, permanent loss of self-esteem, or stable feelings of helplessness and lack of control in multiple domains of living, may be signs of maladjustment. Persistent problems in social relationships or chronic marital strain may also warrant attention as indicators of difficulties in adjustment. Thus, infertility researchers must conceptualize multiple facets of adjustment, and assess them in single studies, to determine the extent to which each facet is affected by the experience of infertility. As stress researchers have frequently noted, an individual may be well-adjusted in some respects and poorly adjusted in others. Moreover, some aspects of adjustment may require the trade-off of others. For instance, managing emotional distress may interfere with effective action or problem-focused coping (Carver, Scheier, & Weintraub, 1989). In the case of infertility, stressful treatments may be discontinued in order to alleviate or control the emotional distress they cause.

McEwan, Costello, and Taylor (1987) investigated dimensions of adjustment in 62 women and 45 men who visited a Canadian infertility clinic. Nine measures were analyzed to develop three components of adjustment. They were emotional and social adjustment (combined), sexual adjustment, and alcohol consumption. This approach represents a step in the right direction for infertility researchers, although the particular measures used may not have been comprehensive enough and, ideally, a larger sample would be used for factor-analytic procedures. With the use of additional measures, it is likely that emotional and social adjustment would be distinguished. In addition, the exact nature of the third factor is unclear and requires follow-up.

The stress and coping framework underlying this volume conceptualizes adjustment to stress as multifaceted, varying over time, and as sometimes involving compromises. Lazarus and Folkman (1984) distinguish the effects of stressful situations as either immediate or long-term. Long-term effects are in three categories: (1) Morale or well-being; (2) somatic health/illness; and (3) social functioning. A response to stress that involves increased use of substances, such as alcohol or drugs, may provide benefits to morale but accompanying risks to somatic health and possibly to social functioning. Although this response may assist in immediate adjustment (i.e., reduce anxiety), it may have detrimental or no effects on later adjustment.

The effects of infertility may be conceptualized within these three categories. Most infertility research to date is on morale or well-being as measured by indicators of emotional distress, self-esteem, or loss of control (see Dunkel-Schetter & Lobel, Chapter 3). Virtually none of the existing research has investigated somatic health changes in infertile individuals, although the chronic nature of the stress involved is likely to have somatic effects. Although some infertility research has examined effects on social functioning (Abbey, Andrews, & Halman, Chapter 4), in-depth investigations of social effects of infertility over time are not yet available.

In summary, it is recommended that infertility researchers be more cognizant of the complexities involved in defining adjustment to stress, specifically with reference to infertility. It is suggested further that a multidimensional approach like that of Lazarus and Folkman (1984) be adopted. Researchers also must remember that infertility may have distinct effects on different dimensions of adjustment and that these effects may change over time. Finally, investigators are encouraged to study dimensions of adjustment not emphasized in past research, such as somatic health and social functioning.

Positive Effects of Infertility

One dimension that models of adjustment to stress tend to overlook is that of the positive or beneficial effects. This may be because many forms of stress have few or no positive effects. Also, the extent of positive effects may vary greatly between individuals as a function of their coping mechanisms and coping resources. For infertility, a significant amount of evidence suggests that there are perceived positive effects of the experience for many individuals and couples. Perhaps most common are reports of positive effects on the marital relationship (Daniluk, 1988; Hearn, Yuzpe, Brown, & Casper, 1987). Past research on parents with a chronically ill child has shown that a stress like this can strengthen or weaken a marriage (Chesler & Barbarin, 1987; Masters, Cerreto, & Mendlowitz, 1983). Thus, evidence is already available to suggest clearly that some people can grow from adversity (see also Collins, Taylor, & Skokan, 1990). Yet research on infertility has never focused on this aspect.

Potential positive effects of adverse events are difficult to examine because social desirability may be involved in self-reports. Perhaps more significant is the issue of whether positive effects really occur, or if the self-reports reflect adaptive cognitive coping techniques. While this may not be possible or necessary to determine, further consideration of these issues is worthwhile. An emerging tradition of work on adaptive illusions (Taylor, 1983; Taylor & Brown, 1988) provides a basis upon which to formulate hypotheses and to design investigations on possible positive effects of infertility among individuals.

Gender Differences in Adjustment

Few results from research on reactions to infertility have been replicated (Dunkel-Schetter & Lobel, Chapter 3). The one finding that is observed somewhat consistently is that men and women differ in the intensity of their reactions to infertility, with women experiencing more distress (Daniluk, 1988; McEwan et al., 1987; O'Moore, O'Moore, Harrison, Murphy, & Carruthers, 1983; Platt, Ficher, & Silver, 1973) and other adverse reactions (Freeman, Garcia, & Rickels, 1983) than men. Also, some of the chapters in this book indicated women's greater propensity to express distress regarding infertility (Abbey et al.; Stanton), greater use of behavioral self-blame (Tennen, Affleck, & Mendola), and greater willingness to seek social support (Abbey et al.; Stanton) and to view their social interactions regarding infertility more positively (Abbey et al.) than men. In addition, Stanton (Chapter 5) reported gender differences in coping and infertile individuals' tendency to endorse the perception that the sexes cope differently (see also Stanton, Tennen, Affleck, & Mendola, in press).

Not all past studies on infertility have revealed gender differences, but sufficient evidence of them exists to merit follow-up. A flaw in past infertility research is that not all studies that have sampled men and women report the results of tests for gender effects on psychological responses. A further problem is that women with suspected or diagnosed infertility are studied much more often than infertile men. Since it is possible that infertile men are equally distressed and since infertility affects equal numbers of men and women, it is important to increase the number of studies available on men and to report tests of gender differences when men and women are studied. Further investigations might seek not only to document definitively the dimensions on which infertile women and men differ, but also to shed light on the underlying mechanisms.

Several plausible explanations, not mutually exclusive, exist for gender differences in psychological reactions to infertility. First, more infertility treatments exist for women than for men. Related is the observation that women initially seek treatment for infertility more often than men. Further, women carry responsibility for monitoring their menstrual cycles and ovulation which involves considerable time and inconvenience, whereas men generally have less responsibility, even when the male is the infertile partner. Thus, the "average" infertile couple may be one in which the woman is undergoing diagnostic procedures, treatment, or menstrual cycle self-monitoring, and the man is less involved in fertility pursuits. Most tests of gender differences have not controlled for amount of time devoted to fertility diagnosis and treatment, a factor that may underlie differences in distress.

It is also important to compare couples in which the woman has been diagnosed infertile to couples in which the man has been diagnosed. Few studies have attempted to untangle effects of gender from effects of diagnosed infertility. Chapters in this volume by Stanton and Tennen *et al.* report tests for effects of which partner was diagnosed in samples of couples and found no differences in psychological distress. However, the sizes of the subgroups of men and women with diagnosed infertility were not large in either study. McEwan *et al.* (1987) also addressed this issue and found that women were more distressed than men when the cause of the couple's infertility was unknown. In future studies of men and women with diagnosed infertility and their partners, it is advisable to include groups of couples with no known cause of infertility and with both partners infertile for comparison purposes.

Other possible underlying factors in gender differences in reactions to infertility are gender differences in the value or importance of parenting and in coping. It is necessary in developing an understanding of reactions to infertility, and specifically gender differences in those reactions, to consider the importance individuals place on parenting as a life goal or aspect of identity (Clark, Henry, & Taylor, Chapter 8). Presumably, individuals who value parenting highly will be more distressed if they are infertile than those who do not. To the extent that traditional sex roles dictate that women should value parenting, and are inadequate if they do not become mothers, gender differences in reactions to infertility may reflect this socialized difference in the importance of becoming a parent.

A related factor to consider is sex-role traditionalism. Because motherhood is a central aspect of traditional female roles, one would expect that more traditional women experience more distress over inability to conceive than less traditional women. Furthermore, to the extent that fertility is important in traditional male sex roles, a similar difference may exist between more traditional and less traditional men. Untangling gender differences in sex-role traditionalism and strength of desire to be a parent from gender differences in distress remains a challenge for infertility researchers.

The Social Context of Infertility

Some life stresses are more socially stigmatizing than others. AIDS today is a highly stigmatizing and stressful condition (Herek & Glunt, 1988). Ten years ago, cancer was similarly stigmatized (Wortman & Dunkel-Schetter, 1979), although this is not as true at present. An often overlooked aspect of infertility is that, for many reasons, it is a highly stigmatizing condition. First, infertility is not very well understood by the public. Myths exist about it, such as the belief that adoption will increase the likelihood of conceiving, or that high degrees of masculinity and femininity are associated with being more fertile. Facts about infertility are not well disseminated, nor is there much public education on this health problem.

Second, there is a veil of secrecy surrounding infertility—people don't talk openly about their infertility problems with others very often. In addition, information that a couple is unable to conceive is considered very private and embarrassing. The degree of secrecy involved probably reflects in part that infertility involves sexual behavior. Many individuals are not comfortable discussing sex with families and friends. Discussions of infertility can make them vulnerable to comments or suggestions regarding their sexual behavior. The secrecy surrounding infertility may also reflect the fact that couples fear negative social reactions from social network members, such as jokes or unwanted advice. In order to avoid these, the couple may refrain from discussing their inability to conceive with others.

There are probably other complicated reasons why infertility occurs within a social context of misconceptions, myths, stigma, and secrecy. Only one study has investigated this aspect of adjustment to infertility (Miall, 1986) apart from the chapter by Abbey et al. in this volume. Yet, the social context of infertility is certain to pose barriers to successful adjustment for couples and individuals. Social acceptance and support are valuable assets in adjusting to stress (Cohen & Syme, 1985; Cohen & Wills, 1985; House, Umberson, & Landis, 1988; Sarason & Sarason, 1985). The absence of these resources may make infertility a compounded stress event, not only one of personal loss, but also one of social victimization. Negative social reactions such as derogation, avoidance, or rejection which co-occur with a number of life events may be an additional source of stress. Work on negative social reactions to victims provides theoretical premises for studying these issues in infertility (Bennett Herbert, & Dunkel-Schetter, in press; Wortman & Lehman, 1985). Research of this kind promises to improve the social circumstances faced by infertile individuals, particularly if it can serve as a basis for public education and destigmatization of this disorder.

METHODOLOGICAL ISSUES IN RESEARCH ON ADJUSTMENT TO INFERTILITY

The issues discussed in this section are: (1) The need for theory; (2) sampling and generalizability; (3) research designs and analyses; and (4) assessment issues and problems.

The Need for Theory

A problem that characterizes most of past research on psychological reactions to physical illness and medical treatment in general is that it has been atheoretical. With the exception of investigations based on stage theories of adjustment, this applies to psychosocial infertility research as well. Use of existing theories from psychology to formulate hypotheses and to design studies would expand the horizons of infertility research and offer more grounded approaches to understanding the effects of infertility. Because the value of theory in scientific research is well established, we will not expand on this point, but rather discuss some examples of how specific theories may apply to infertility. By doing so, it is hoped that the meaning of the term "theory" in this context can be demonstrated and the value of theoretical approaches to research explicated.

Several of the chapters in this book adopt theoretical perspectives as frameworks in the manner we are recommending. Stanton (1991), for example, uses the Lazarus and Folkman (1984) framework to study coping and appraisal in infertile couples. This broad and comprehensive framework has much to offer infertility researchers. Not only does it provide a method for conceptualizing long- and short-term effects of stress, but the model also distinguishes causal antecedents and mediating processes. Although specific hypotheses are sometimes difficult to formulate based on the model, it provides a basis for designing infertility models and a framework for operationalization of variables. Other stress and coping theoretical frameworks that might be useful include those by Hobfoll (1989), Pearlin (Pearlin, Menaghan, Lieberman, & Mullan, 1981), and Moos (Moos & Billings, 1982; Moos & Schaefer, 1986).

Further examples of the use of theory in infertility research are the chapters by Tennen et al., Abbey et al., and Campbell et al. These chapters utilize theoretical work on control, cognitive appraisal, social support, and causal attributions to develop hypotheses. Although no single theory is used in any of these investigations, the integration of several past approaches served as the basis for these authors to develop their individual foci. The chapter by Clark et al. also illustrates the application of theory to infertility research. In this case, theory and research from social cognition are utilized to pose hypotheses and develop a model of cognitive restructuring following permanent involuntary infertility.

Many traditions of research not covered in this book provide theoretical bases for enriching the study of adjustment to infertility. For example, there are many theories about grieving and bereavement that have not been applied to infertility. As Dunkel-Schetter and Lobel (this volume) describe, infertility is a threat initially for most and, for many, that threat is gradually transformed into a loss. The work of Weiss (1988), Parkes (1972, 1988), Stroebe and Stroebe (1987), and others (Hansson, Stroebe, & Stroebe, 1988) on bereavement and adjustment to loss has clear applicability to studies of that subset of individuals for whom infertility represents a permanent loss.

The term "theory" should not be confused with having a formal, causal model. Theoretical perspectives on the processes of adjustment to stress are not always grand, macroscopic, or causal theories. Major theoretical frameworks are very useful, yet they do not always specify all the intricacies of how the variables in the model interact or operate over time to produce effects. Mid-range theories, in contrast, provide more specific or finer-grained analyses of the interrelationships of variables and their effects. Theoretical work on cognitive adaptation (Taylor, 1983), the self (Cantor, Markus, & Niedenthal, 1985), self-regulation (Carver & Scheier, 1990), commitment (Brickman, 1987), social support (Thoits, 1986), attachment (Bowlby, 1973; Cohen, 1974; Shaver, Hazan, & Bradshaw, 1988), and on many other topics may offer valuable insights to infertility researchers. It is hoped that at least some of this wealth of theory existing in psychology will be thoughtfully applied to the study of infertility in the future. Comparative tests of hypotheses and theories are recommended, as well as tests of hypotheses drawn from individual theories.

As described in the first chapter of this book, the most dominant theories of adjustment to infertility are stage theories that posit a set sequence of emotional reactions and a final stage of resolution, one viewed as adaptive. Landmark work on stages of response to major losses has documented that stage theories are not well substantiated empirically, and that models of individual variation in emotional response seem more appropriate (Silver & Wortman, 1980; Wortman & Silver, 1987). In light of this, it would be useful for longitudinal studies to test stage theories of adjustment to infertility. However, it does not seem advisable to test these models exclusively. Research designs might be developed to test simultaneously hypotheses derived from stress and coping theories and from stage models of adjustment. Also, studies of infertile individuals long after they have been through the experience (i.e., 2 to 10 years) would be valuable in indicating the extent to which emotional "resolution" occurs and to investigate long-term or permanent effects.

Sampling and Generalizability

Studies of infertility to date have not been strong with respect to sampling procedures. Examination of the methods of studies reviewed by Dunkel-Schetter and Lobel in an earlier chapter of this volume indicates that little attention is paid to representativeness of sampling and to qualifying conclusions correspondingly. Perhaps the biggest problem with these studies is the frequent use of IVF patients and infrequent discussion of the unusual self-selected nature of this group (see Campbell *et al.*, Chapter 8, on this issue). IVF patients do not represent infertility patients as a whole. Thus, investigators must move beyond studying this readily available and cooperative group to the study of other less accessible but equally important groups. Not only should users of other medical treatments for infertility be studied, but those who do not seek services should receive attention also. Hirsch and Mosher (1987) found several infertility-related and demographic differences between users and non-users of infertility services. At present, we know little about the psychological status of those who do not pursue medical options.

In general, sample characteristics should become a greater focus in psychosocial infertility research. Medical characteristics such as duration of infertility, diagnosis and treatments for infertility, and whether infertility is primary or secondary are potentially relevant factors influencing psychological reactions. Studies must either sample homogeneously on these dimensions, or sample heterogeneously enough to allow for powerful tests of these variables. Since infertility is such a diverse category of disorders, differences in psychological adjustment among infertile subjects with different medical characteristics may be as critical as differences between infertility and other life stresses. Thus, medical variables must be taken into account more fully in future studies.

Sociodemographic characteristics of subjects also must receive more attention. The majority of investigations to date have included white, middle-class women being treated in private practices or exemplary university infertility programs. Infertility is of high prevalence in minority groups and occurs disproportionately in lower socioeconomic-status individuals in the United States, as described in the first chapter of this book. In addition, a good deal of infertility treatment occurs in public clinics. These factors must be considered in sampling and in drawing conclusions. Achieving a full understanding of the effects of infertility necessitates more diversity in samples and more attention to differences among subjects in social class, ethnicity, education, income, and gender. In particular, there are virtually no studies of infertility in black or Hispanic groups and they are very much needed.

Finally, the usual standards for rigorous survey research with respect to sampling should be applied to infertility research. Sampling should be systematic as much as possible, response and refusal rates should be accurately recorded, and biases in sampling should be estimated. In medical settings, patients are often missed or removed from the study for various reasons, thereby introducing possible sampling bias. It is important to track these occurrences and to consider sources of bias, then to limit conclusions appropriately. Psychosocial infertility research has progressed sufficiently that the representativeness of samples and the generalizability of the results are now essential to consider. Future reviews of this body of research might seek to distinguish studies on the basis of the sampling procedures of the samples and the extent to which the results have been shown to generalize to various subgroups of the infertile population.

Research Designs and Data Analysis

At this stage of knowledge, certain research designs seem clearly superior to others for studying infertility. Two recommendations follow from the research in this book. First, there has been very little longitudinal research on adjustment to infertility, yet longitudinal research can add immeasurably to the knowledge we have gained from cross-sectional designs. Most of the pressing research questions concerning changes over time, for example, can be addressed only with longitudinal studies. It is recommended that future studies on adjustment to infertility assess multiple indicators of adjustment on multiple occasions over a number of years. Such studies would help greatly in understanding the process of adjustment to infertility.

Second, control groups continue to be helpful in distinguishing which effects accompany infertility specifically and which are not unique. Only infertility-specific effects help to clarify the unique characteristics of this particular disorder. Although the use of control groups is recommended, the choice of what type of groups to use should be undertaken carefully. By choosing particular groups, an investigator may be able to distinguish distinct effects of various aspects of infertility. For example, infertile individuals might be contrasted with individuals who adopt, who choose childlessness, and who already have a child in order to untangle the effects of infertility from those of childlessness. Attention must be paid to purity of control groups also. For example, individuals who have a child cannot have experienced infertility earlier.

It is not clear that control groups need be of the same size as infertile groups, that they must be studied at every point in time longitudinally, or that every measure must be administered to control subjects. A potentially useful design is one in which a large sample of infertile individuals is followed longitudinally with multiple assessment instruments, with smaller control groups studied at the outset and end of the study using a more limited assessment package. In short, innovative variations of clinical research designs may offer value to infertility researchers at this time at a manageable cost.

Clearly, attention to sample size and statistical power is needed in planning infertility research. Larger samples not only afford better power to detect effects if they exist (i.e., reduced likelihood of Type II error), but they also permit more sophisticated multivariate data analyses that may be appropriate. For example, structural equation modeling has not been utilized yet in infertility research although it may be useful in understanding the simultaneous effects of several factors in predicting adjustment. With the advent of longitudinal case-control designs with large and representative samples, our understanding of infertility will be much enhanced.

Assessment Issues and Problems

Most of psychological infertility research to date has utilized self-report instruments. Therefore, the discussion here concentrates on these methods of measurement. There are two basic approaches to the systematic assessment of psychological effects of infertility through self-report. One approach is to utilize available instruments that assess the effects of other life events and stresses. The second approach is to develop multiple-item quantitative indices specific to infertility. Past research has utilized both approaches. Most of the chapters in this book employed standard scale measures such as the SCL-90-R (Derogatis, 1977), but a few involved the design of measures unique to the study of infertility, such as Abbey *et al.*'s fertility-problem stress measure and Stanton's measure of infertility distress. A combination of these two general approaches is recommended because each has advantages and disadvantages.

The advantage of using standard scales is illustrated in the chapter by Dunkel-Schetter and Lobel wherein the interpretability of the results of studies on infertility is discussed. Scales with known reliability and validity and with available norms for normal and psychiatric adult groups are attractive with respect to drawing conclusions specific to infertility. In choosing among the scales that fit these criteria, researchers may benefit by using certain scales across studies in order to replicate and extend results. When different instruments are used, divergence of findings is more difficult to explain. On the other hand, it would be unwise for all researchers to adopt certain instruments to the exclusion of others at this stage in our knowledge.

The chief disadvantages of standard scales are that they may be inappropriate, impractical, or incomplete for infertility research. For example, some instruments such as the MMPI may seem offensive to infertile subjects and may require careful prefacing. Others may be impractical simply because of length, method of administration, or match with the education or language of the population. Many instruments have not been developed for general population studies and are therefore not useful in urban public clinic settings where level of education and fluency vary. Clearly, care should be taken in considering the appropriateness of the selected scales for the particular population studied. Moreover, standard scales should not be used at all costs. If one does not exist to measure a particular theoretically important concept, new items must be developed instead.

The advantage of developing measures for studies of infertility is that they can be tailored specifically to the targeted populations, and they can include all theoretically and clinically important dimensions. At this stage of infertility research, there is a risk of missing important aspects of subjects' experiences unless we design new measures to supplement standard scales. These measures can be piloted to weed out problems that accompany instrument development, such as poorly worded or redundant items and response option problems. Even with careful piloting, however, new measures may have poor reliability, questionable validity, and there is no basis for comparison of scores to other groups or studies. For these reasons, they are best combined with standard scales in almost any design.

In addition to the use of standard scales and new measures specific to infertility, researchers should include open-ended questions in their protocols to the extent that time permits, in order to supplement quantitative assessment tools. By allowing subjects to answer questions on the concepts of interest in their own words, open-ended questions can provide further information, such as insight into the obtained results and ideas for additional hypotheses.

These assessment recommendations are not only geared to infertility research; they apply to most stress and coping research endeavors. When hypotheses are being both generated and tested, as in psychosocial research on infertility at present, a combination of assessment approaches is ideal. At earlier or later stages of our knowledge on a topic, different assessment methods might be recommended.

As this area of research expands, it would be useful to add to the repertoire of assessment techniques applied. For example, observational measures might be collected, such as techniques for observing and recording interactions of infertile partners with each other or with medical practitioners. It would also be useful to measure stress physiologically. For example, the effects of infertility on cardiovascular, immune, and endocrine functioning could be assessed. Emerging work on the effects of stress in pregnancy on physiology and birth outcomes suggests that it plays an important role in some reproductive outcomes (Lobel, 1989). In addition, research is in progress on stress as a barrier to conception (Edelmann & Golombok, 1989; Giblin, Poland, Moghissi, Ager, & Olson, 1988; Harrison, Callan, & Hennessey, 1987). However, as we discussed in Chapter 1, there are drawbacks to psychogenic approaches. In particular, investigators of psychosocial contributors to infertility must be cautious not to overinterpret results or to blame the victim. Given these caveats, it is useful to examine physiological changes over time in infertile individuals who are chronically stressed and any role these changes may have in decreasing the likelihood of conception.

IMPLICATIONS FOR TREATMENT AND INTERVENTION

In Chapter 9, Reading discussed general issues in psychological intervention with infertile couples. In this section, we focus on several clinical issues generated specifically from the research and discussion in this book. Three issues and their clinical implications are highlighted: (1) Diversity in reactions to infertility; (2) risk factors for distress in infertile individuals; and (3) intervention issues regarding partners coping with infertility. Finally, we suggest directions for clinical research and intervention in infertility.

Diversity in Reactions to Infertility

As Dunkel-Schetter and Lobel indicated in this volume, much variability exists in the reactions of individuals to infertility. This observation carries several clinical implications. First, infertility will result in marked distress for some people, and the availability of psychological support for this group is essential. The need for intervention is not necessarily exclusive to those with clinically significant levels of psychological symptomatology, however. As Paulson, Haarmann, Salerno, and Asmar (1988) demonstrated, approximately half of a group of infertile women who sought counseling did not evidence clinical maladjustment. Thus, those who offer medical services for infertility might best serve their patients by providing psychological assistance and resources to all who enter the service. Despite this recommendation, the assumption that everyone who is infertile will require psychological counseling is unwarranted. Some individuals will need little or no formal support, others may benefit from a support group or informal assistance, and still others may require individual or couple therapy to cope with the rigors of the infertility process.

A second clinical implication that follows from the observed variability in response is that, when an individual or couple does seek therapeutic intervention, clinicians would do well to assess the particular areas of impact of infertility for the individual client. No one particular issue has emerged in past research as the most salient or challenging for most infertile couples. Rather, individuals are likely to differ markedly in their experience of the specific aspects of infertility that carry the greatest threat. For example, the most distressing aspect for some might be the threat to their expectation that parenthood would comprise their primary life activity, whereas others might fear abandonment by their partner in response to infertility. Helping clients to identify the most difficult aspects of the experience can render more manageable what initially might seem overwhelming. This delineation of specific areas of impact can then serve as a framework for organizing a collaborative plan to address specific difficulties.

Finally, the demonstrated diversity in reaction to infertility reminds clinicians that there is no one "correct" way to react to or cope with this problem. At this point there is little evidence that those experiencing grief over infertility or other losses go through a predictable sequence of emotional reactions. Although there are good reasons to believe that personal self-disclosure and emotional expression may facilitate adjustment to traumatic events in general (Pennebaker, Hughes, & O'Heeron, 1987; Pennebaker, Kiecolt-Glaser, & Glaser, 1988) and to infertility specifically (Menning, 1989; Reading, Chapter 9), invariably encouraging such expression may not be in the best interests of particular clients. Some might respond more favorably to a problem-solving approach, for example, and others might need help in moving from emotional expression to developing ways to lessen the power of those emotions and to enhance choice and control in their lives.

If therapists' expectations regarding the most appropriate reactions to infertility and their sequence are translated to the client into prescriptions for acceptable responses, this may only hinder the therapeutic process. Greater assistance may be provided to clients by carefully assessing the client's levels of distress, identifying the primary contributors to that distress, and tailoring interventions for particular domains of psychosocial functioning. This is not to suggest that commonalities in reactions to infertility do not exist or that we should abandon attempts to construct normative frameworks for understanding adjustment to infertility. Rather, we are recommending that, at the current state of knowledge, assumptions regarding predictable or appropriate patterns of adjustment to infertility are a poor basis for therapy. Instead, we encourage clinical assessment and therapeutic acceptance of diversity in reactions to infertility, similar to that which might be provided to victims of other negative events.

Risk Factors for Distress in Infertile Individuals

Although no single pattern of adjustment to infertility appears normative, authors of the previous chapters have identified several factors that might render particular infertile individuals and couples more vulnerable to distress. By assessing these factors, the clinician may be able to identify those who are most at risk for adjustment difficulties. Interventions can then be targeted toward these individuals and to issues that are most problematic. Factors that appear promising as risk factors for distress in infertile individuals are: (1) Expectation that parenthood will fulfill high-level goals; (2) preoccupation with a search for causes of infertility; (3) low perceived personal control; (4) coping with infertility through avoidance; and (5) low satisfaction with spousal and general social support. Some of the clinical implications of each of these will be highlighted.

A first factor that warrants clinical examination is the infertile person's goal structure. As noted by Clark and colleagues in Chapter 8, infertile individuals expect parenthood to fulfill particular goals. Those for whom fertility is synonymous with high-level goals of happiness, fulfillment, or maturity, for example, might be particularly vulnerable to distress. This suggests that therapeutic goals might include enabling clients to examine these higher-order goals, identifying alternate paths to fulfillment, and perhaps mourning the loss of unattainable goals.

As Tennen and colleagues pointed out in Chapter 6, infertile couples are similar to others who experience negative events in that they often search for explanations for their experience. These researchers found that individuals attributed their infertility to a variety of factors, including biomedical causes, their own behaviors, and chance. Greater endorsement of causal explanations was related to greater distress, whereas the absence of causal attributions was associated with less distress. More intense preoccupation with the cause of infertility, then, may render one vulnerable to distress. Although pursuit of the medical cause of infertility can lead to effective treatment, a cost associated with such a causal search is that it is disruptive emotionally. Thus, the clinician might want to explore the various advantages and disadvantages of engaging in such a search with clients experiencing infertility. Similarly, the pros and cons of reaching particular conclusions regarding the causes of infertility might be examined.

The issue of control also provides a potentially productive point of therapeutic intervention. Although the three chapters in which control was examined (Campbell *et al.;* Stanton; and Tennen *et al.*) assessed somewhat different facets of the construct and results were not completely consistent, all suggested that low perceived control is associated with greater distress. As Campbell and colleagues found, perceptions of control surrounding infertility and the impact of these perceptions on distress vary as a function of the particular domain of control examined. Clinically, one might ask the question, "Control over what?" What can the infertile couple control in their lives? What issues are beyond their control? Again, separating this issue into its components might help the infertile couple to distinguish aspects of the situation that are controllable from those that are not and to see that all control is not lost. A goal of therapy could be to examine how one's sense of control can be realistically enhanced. Generating mechanisms for bolstering control, such as obtaining information, communicating assertively with medical personnel and significant others, and focusing on other roles where the opportunity for control is great may aid those whose sense of control is compromised.

Even when a couple is informed that the reproductive technology they are electing has a very low rate of success or that they are permanently infertile, they may be reluctant to give up hope that they will conceive and that they can control the reproductive outcome. At these times the clinician may be called upon to help the couple develop a realistic assessment of control over reproductive outcomes so that they can make informed choices or move on to concentrate on potentially more productive life pursuits. This may entail helping the couple to revise their assumption that all important outcomes are under their own control, to change their notion that permanent infertility comprises a personal failure, or to give up the belief that their only route to happiness is to have a biological child.

Among the diverse coping mechanisms used by those who are infertile, coping through avoidance is associated with distress for both men and women (Stanton, Chapter 5). Avoidance may contribute to distress because it impedes the grief process, restricts engagement in potentially rewarding activities, or involves behaviors such as drinking or binge-eating. Alternatively, experiencing substantial distress might lead to actions designed to avoid that distress. In addition, women's coping through accepting responsibility and men's confrontive and self-controlling coping may prove problematic (Stanton, Chapter 5). Alternatively, both Tennen *et al.* and Stanton found that citing the benefits of infertility or otherwise appraising it positively enhanced well-being. Clinicians may find it useful to administer one of the scales developed to assess coping, to assess the effectiveness of the strategies employed, and to aid the client in trying out and practicing new coping skills, along with evaluation of their success. In this regard, past intervention research involving coping skills with other populations may be instructive (e.g., D'Zurilla, 1986; Heppner & Hillerbrand, 1991; Strentz & Auerbach, 1988).

It should be noted that the consequences of naturally electing a particular coping method may be quite different from those that result when the coping strategy is prescribed therapeutically. For example, self-generated positive aspects of infertility might be beneficial to the infertile person, but encouragement by the clinician to focus on the positive might be ineffective and perceived as insensitive. Rather, the clinician may wish to help the client develop an open-minded approach to generating and experimenting with possible coping mechanisms. A support group setting also can promote creative generation of coping alternatives.

Finally, the impact of the social context on the infertile person's adjustment deserves therapeutic attention. As Abbey *et al.* (Chapter 4) demonstrated, lower satisfaction with social support and greater interpersonal conflict with the spouse were related to lower perceived marital quality. Clearly, professionals should assess the relationship quality of the infertile person whether or not both members of a couple seek counseling. Identified areas of marital conflict, such as those involving infertility-related decision-making, discrepant communication styles, and sexual difficulties can be addressed through established couples' therapy techniques (Jacobson & Gurman, 1986). Whether or not the individual seeking to become a parent is in a well-functioning relationship, identification of ways to enhance social support more generally may be useful. National or local support groups such as those run by RESOLVE can be invaluable in this regard. Some specific targets for intervention with the couple are outlined in the next section.

Although this section has focused on a few specific factors that render the infertile person vulnerable to distress, several other personal and social variables deserve clinical attention as risk factors as well. For example, these include but are not limited to the infertile client's premorbid characteristics, such as the individual's own parenting and family history, religious attitudes regarding family issues or the meaning of infertility, and personal gender schemas. We also wish to note that assessment and intervention aimed at specific risk factors should not preclude a concomitant focus on the individual's strengths. Some infertile clients are so preoccupied with personal deficits and losses that they are taken aback when a clinician asks them to discuss their positive attributes or their prior successful coping efforts. Identification of these characteristics can inform current coping attempts. Further, maintaining an explicit focus on personal strengths can help individuals live with infertility as one aspect of their lives rather than as their sole focus.

Intervention Issues Regarding Partners Coping with Infertility

We noted previously in this chapter several gender differences in the experience of infertility that emerged from the research reported in preceding chapters. How these differences are perceived by couples may certainly influence their relationship functioning. Consistent with Stanton's (Chapter 5) finding that infertile men and women believe that the sexes cope differently with infertility, couples may demonstrate a tendency to magnify their differences and neglect their similarities. How each partner interprets perceived differences also has interpersonal consequences. In their review of attributions in marriage, Bradbury and Fincham (1990) concluded that spouses who make attributions for their partner's behaviors that cast them in a negative light are more likely to be dissatisfied with their marriages. For example, spouses in distressed marriages tend to view their partners' motivations as selfish and their behaviors as negatively intended. Thus, an infertile woman might view her partner's seeming stoic acceptance of their status as indicating that he cares little about becoming a parent or about her. The professional working with the infertile couple might assess how each partner views the other and how each interprets any perceived differences. Discussion of these perceptions might help to pinpoint where real differences lie and to establish the mutual goals that exist for the couple. Such discussion could lead to the development of methods by which to address differences and to pursue shared aims.

This is not to suggest that a therapeutic goal is to remove conflict on all issues surrounding infertility for the couple. In fact, Gottman and Krokoff (1989) recently found that although disagreement and exchanges of anger were related to concurrent marital dissatisfaction, these indicators of conflict engagement predicted *increased* marital satisfaction over a three-year period in a community sample of couples. Marital deterioration, in contrast, was predicted by defensiveness, stubbornness, and withdrawal from interaction. Although not without controversy (Gottman & Krokoff, 1990; Woody & Costanzo, 1990), the authors speculated that conflict-avoiding couples may be at risk for dissatisfaction in the long run. Applied to infertility, these results suggest that couples should be encouraged to maintain open discussion with each other on issues surrounding infertility, even when conflict results. A focus on the couple's mutual goals and on the other partner's perspective can help to minimize defensiveness. Avoidance of the painful issues surrounding infertility is tempting for many couples. However, engagement with the partner, even if that entails conflict, may yield more respect for the other's perspectives and better adjustment in the long run.

Directions for Clinical Research and Intervention in Infertility

Contributions to this volume have generated many ideas for therapeutic interventions that might aid the couple in coping with infertility. These techniques await empirical test by clinical researchers. As Reading noted in Chapter 9, very few studies have assessed the value of supportive interventions with infertile individuals. Questions regarding every aspect of effective treatment remain. Which kinds of interventions most effectively decrease distress? When is an intervention best directed toward the individual, the couple, or groups of infertile people? Do components of effective treatments vary as a function of characteristics of the infertility experience, such as length of time infertile and probability of pregnancy? When should professionals be involved in psychological intervention and when is peer support more effective? Must grief be expressed and processed in order to attain psychological resolution of infertility? It is important to identify the most effective strategies to aid those who are coping with infertility.

We are just beginning to understand the predictors of successful adjustment to infertility, and intervention studies must be carefully designed in order to address these questions and the others that we face. The best design for such studies involves random assignment of infertile individuals or couples to treatment and control conditions. Ideally, designs will also include some consideration of factors that might moderate the effects of treatment (e.g., infertility duration) and assessment of treatment efficacy in multiple domains of functioning (e.g., marital functioning, individual well-being). Short of this, quasi-experimental research designs with rigorous evaluation procedures can be conducted.

Other areas of intervention also hold promise. For example, sexually transmitted diseases are a frequent and preventable cause of infertility (U.S. Congress, Office of Technology Assessment, 1988). Effective primary prevention programs designed to decrease disease transmission could do much to curtail fertility problems (Leiblum, 1988). In addition, treatment for infertility often necessitates interaction with a variety of health care professionals. The literature on improving physician-patient communication (e.g., Hays & DiMatteo, 1984) can guide interventions designed to enhance communication regarding infertility in the medical setting. In all cases, models for conducting methodologically and conceptually sophisticated intervention studies are available to inform the researcher. Researchers who conduct such studies will perform a valuable service for those who confront infertility.

CONCLUSIONS

In this chapter we have attempted to highlight a number of the issues involved in research with and intervention for those who experience infertility. Recommendations have been offered to those interested in undertaking future investigative or intervention activities. We hope that the complexities of the problem and the rigor required for future contributions are not daunting to those with an interest in infertility. Although there are challenges ahead, the rewards promise to be equal or greater.

The aim of this book as a whole has been to engender enthusiasm in the reader about the study of infertility. As we hope the book has demonstrated, this topic offers rich opportunities to researchers and practitioners. Building a stronger scientific knowledge base and developing potent psychological services targeted to each subgroup of the infertile population are among the major challenges that lie ahead.

Stress and coping research can contribute substantially to the quality of these endeavors. For example, the large body of work existing on stress and stress management has not been applied to infertility until quite recently. In general, a stress and coping perspective can improve the theories, methods, and applications that exist in the study of infertility. However, integrating research on infertility is not a unidirectional process. We hope that the analysis of research problems concerning infertility included in this chapter proves useful to researchers studying other target groups who are experiencing stress. In addition, results from studies of infertility can offer insights and new understanding to stress and coping researchers. Further, programmatic efforts to provide services for infertile couples and individuals may inform program development for other stressed groups. For example, well-designed interventions for infertile partners may be instructive in counseling efforts for couples who lose a child in an accident or to illness. Other specific groups to whom infertility programs might apply include parents experiencing sudden infant death syndrome and couples who experience repeated miscarriages. A reciprocal process of learning and exchange of information with research on stress and coping generally is much more valuable than scientific and professional efforts directed toward a singular problem or stressor.

We hope that the chapters in this book provide clear direction for the implementation of a stress and coping perspective in infertility research. It has been our intention to stimulate research in particular, but also program development. We have much to learn about psychological adjustment to infertility, and there is much to contribute. A stress and coping perspective can guide efforts to develop our scientific knowledge of individuals who confront the challenges of infertility. The content of this book and the empirical research to come should be the basis of efforts to provide effective aid to infertile people. By concerted clinical and research efforts, we believe much can be done for the significant number of individuals and couples who face the stress of infertility.

REFERENCES

Adams, D. (1979). *Childhood malignancy: The psychosocial care of the child and his family.* Springfield, IL: Charles C Thomas.

Bennett Herbert, T. L., & Dunkel-Schetter, C. (in press). Determinants of negative social reactions to victims of life events. In L. Montada, S. H. Filipp, & M. J. Lerner (Eds.), *Life crises and the experience of loss in adulthood.* Hillsdale, NJ: Laurence Erlbaum.

Benson, B. A., & Gross, A. M. (1989). The effect of a congenitally handicapped child upon the marital dyad: A review of the literature. *Clinical Psychology Review, 9,* 747–758.

Bowlby, J. (1973). *Attachment and loss.* Vol. 2. New York: Basic Books.

Bradbury, T. N., & Fincham, F. D. (1990). Attributions in marriage: Review and critique. *Psychological Bulletin, 107,* 3–33.

Brickman, P. (1987). *Commitment, conflict and caring.* Englewood Cliffs, NJ: Prentice-Hall.

Cantor, N., Markus, H., & Niedenthal, P. (1985). On motivation and the self-concept. In R. M. Sorrentino & E. T. Higgins (Eds.), *Handbook of motivation and cognition* (Vol. 1). New York: Guilford.

Carver, C., & Scheier, M. (1990). Principles of self-regulation: Action and emotion. In E. T. Higgins & R. M. Sorrentino (Eds.), *Handbook of motivation and cognition* (Vol. 2). New York: Guilford.

Carver, C. S., Scheier, M. F., & Weintraub, J. K. (1989). Assessing coping strategies: A theoretically based approach. *Journal of Personality and Social Psychology, 56,* 267–283.

Chesler, M. A., & Barbarin, O. A. (1987). *Childhood cancer and the family.* New York: Brunner/Mazel.

Cohen, L. J. (1974). The operational definition of human attachment. *Psychological Bulletin, 81,* 207–217.

Cohen, S., & Syme, S. L. (Eds.). (1985). *Social support and health.* Orlando, FL: Academic Press.

Cohen, S., & Wills, T. A. (1985). Stress, social support, and the buffering hypothesis. *Psychological Bulletin, 98,* 310–357.

Collins, R. L., Taylor, S. E., & Skokan, L. A. (1990). A better world or shattered vision? Changes in perspective following victimization. *Social Cognition, 8,* 263–285.

Daniluk, J. C. (1988). Infertility: Intrapersonal and interpersonal impact. *Fertility and Sterility, 49,* 982–990.

Derogatis, L. R. (1977). *SCL-90-R: Administration, scoring and procedures manual—I.* Baltimore, MD: Clinical Psychometrics Research Unit.

D'Zurilla, T. J. (1986). *Problem-solving therapy: A social competence approach to clinical intervention.* New York: Springer.

Edelmann, R. J., & Golombok, S. (1989). Stress and reproductive failure. *Journal of Reproductive and Infant Psychology, 7,* 79–86.

Fincham, F. D., & Bradbury, T. N. (Eds.). (1990). *The psychology of marriage.* New York: Guilford.

Freeman, E. W., Garcia, C. R., & Rickels, K. (1983). Behavioral and emotional factors: Comparisons of anovulatory infertile women with fertile and other infertile women. *Fertility and Sterility, 40,* 195–201.

Giblin, P. T., Poland, M. L., Moghissi, K. S., Ager, J. W., & Olson, J. M. (1988). Effects of stress and characteristic adaptibility on semen quality in healthy men. *Fertility and Sterility, 49,* 127–132.

Gottman, J. M., & Krokoff, L. J. (1989). Marital interaction and satisfaction: A longitudinal view. *Journal of Consulting and Clinical Psychology, 57,* 47–52.

Gottman, J. M., & Krokoff, L. J. (1990). Complex statistics are not always clearer than simple statistics: A reply to Woody and Costanzo. *Journal of Consulting and Clinical Psychology, 58,* 502–505.

Hansson, R. O., Stroebe, M. S., & Stroebe, W. (Eds.). (1988). Bereavement and widowhood [Special issue]. *Journal of Social Issues, 44*(3).

Harrison, K. L., Callan, V. J., & Hennessey, J. F. (1987). Stress and semen quality in an in vitro fertilization program. *Fertility and Sterility, 48,* 633–637.

Hays, R., & DiMatteo, M. R. (1984). Toward a more therapeutic physician-patient relationship. In S. Duck (Ed.), *Personal relationships 5: Repairing personal relationships* (pp. 1–20). London: Academic Press.

Hearn, M. T., Yuzpe, A. A., Brown, S. E., & Casper, R. F. (1987). Psychological characteristics of in vitro fertilization participants. *American Journal of Obstetrics and Gynecology, 156,* 269–274.

Heppner, P. P., & Hillerbrand, E. T. (1991). Problem solving training: Implications for remedial and preventive training. In C. R. Snyder & D. R. Forsyth (Eds.), *Handbook of social and clinical psychology: The health perspective.* New York: Pergamon Press.

Herek, G. M., & Glunt, E. K. (1988). An epidemic of stigma: Public reactions to AIDS. *American Psychologist, 43,* 886–891.

Hirsch, M. B., & Mosher, W. D. (1987). Characteristics of infertile women in the United States and their use of infertility services. *Fertility and Sterility, 47,* 618–625.

Hobfoll, S. E. (1989). Conservation of resources: A new attempt at conceptualizing stress. *American Psychologist, 44,* 513–524.

House, J. S., Umberson, D., & Landis, K. R. (1988). Social relationships and health. *Science, 241,* 540–545.

Huston, T. L., & Robins, E. (1982). Conceptual and methodological issues in studying close relationships. *Journal of Marriage and the Family, 44,* 901–925.

Jacobson, N. S., & Gurman, A. S. (Eds.). (1986). *Clinical handbook of marital therapy.* New York: Guilford.

Kelley, H. H., Berscheid, E., Christensen, A., Harvey, J. H., Huston, T. L., Levinger, G., McClintock, E., Peplau, L. A., & Peterson, D. R. (1983). *Close relationships.* New York: W. H. Freeman.

Kenny, D. A. (1988). The analysis of data from two-person relationships. In S. Duck (Ed.), *Handbook of personal relationships* (pp. 57–78). New York: Wiley.

Lazarus, R. S., & Folkman, S. (1984). *Stress, appraisal, and coping.* New York: Springer.

Lehman, D. R., Wortman, C. B., & Williams, A. F. (1987). Long-term effects of losing a spouse or child in a motor vehicle crash. *Journal of Personality and Social Psychology, 52,* 218–231.

Leiblum, S. R. (1988). Infertility. In E. A. Blechman & K. D. Brownell (Eds.), *Handbook of behavioral medicine for women* (pp. 116–125). New York: Pergamon.

Lobel, M. (1989). *Prenatal contributers to adverse birth outcomes: Applying a biopsychosocial model.* Unpublished doctoral dissertation, University of California at Los Angeles, Los Angeles, CA.

Masters, J. C., Cerreto, M. C., & Mendlowitz, D. R. (1983). The role of the family in coping with childhood chronic illness. In T. G. Burish & L. A. Bradley (Eds.), *Coping with chronic disease* (pp. 381–407). New York: Academic Press.

McEwan, K. L., Costello, C. G., & Taylor, P. J. (1987). Adjustment to infertility. *Journal of Abnormal Psychology, 96,* 108–116.

Menning, B. E. (1989). *Infertility: A guide for the childless couple* (2nd ed.). Englewood Cliffs: Prentice-Hall.

Miall, C. E. (1986). The stigma of involuntary childlessness. *Social Problems, 33,* 268–282.

Moos, R. H., & Billings, A. G. (1982). Conceptualizing and measuring coping resources and processes. In L. Goldberger & S. Breznitz (Eds.), *Handbook of stress: Theoretical and clinical aspects* (pp. 212–230). New York: Free Press.

Moos, R. H., & Schaefer, J. A. (1986). Life transitions and crises: A conceptual overview. In R. H. Moos (Ed.), *Coping with life crises: An integrated approach* (pp. 3–28). New York: Plenum.

O'Moore, A. M., O'Moore, R. R., Harrison, R. F., Murphy, G., & Carruthers, M. E. (1983). Psychosomatic aspects in idiopathic infertility: Effects of treatment with autogenic training. *Journal of Psychosomatic Research, 27,* 145–151.

Parkes, C. M. (1972). *Bereavement.* New York: International Universities Press.

Parkes, C. M. (1988). Bereavement as a psychosocial transition: Processes of adaptation to change. *Journal of Social Issues, 44*(3), 53–65.

Paulson, J. D., Haarmann, B. S., Salerno, R. L., & Asmar, P. (1988). An investigation of the relationship between emotional maladjustment and infertility. *Fertility and Sterility, 49,* 258–262.

Pearlin, L. I., Menaghan, E. G., Lieberman, M. A., & Mullan, J. T. (1981). The stress process. *Journal of Health and Social Behavior, 22,* 337–356.

Pennebaker, J. W., Hughes, C. F., & O'Heeron, R. C. (1987). The psychophysiology of confession: Linking inhibitory and psychosomatic processes. *Journal of Personality and Social Psychology, 52,* 781–793.

Pennebaker, J. W., Kiecolt-Glaser, J. K., & Glaser, R. (1988). Disclosure of traumas and immune function: Health implications for psychotherapy. *Journal of Consulting and Clinical Psychology, 56,* 239–245.

Platt, J. J., Ficher, I., & Silver, M. J. (1973). Infertile couples: Personality traits and self-ideal concept discrepancies. *Fertility and Sterility, 24,* 972–976.

Rusbult, C. E., Johnson, D. J., & Morrow, G. D. (1986). Impact of couple patterns of problem solving on distress and nondistress in dating relationships. *Journal of Personality and Social Psychology, 50,* 744–753.

Sarason, I. G., & Sarason, B. R. (Eds.). (1985). *Social support: Theory, research, and applications.* Dordrecht, Netherlands: Martinus Nijhoff.

Shaver, P., Hazan, C., & Bradshaw, D. (1988). Love as attachment: The integration of three behavioral systems. In R. J. Sternberg & L. Barnes (Eds.), *The psychology of love* (pp. 68–99). New Haven, CT: Yale University Press.

Silver, R. C., & Wortman, C. B. (1980). Coping with undesirable life events. In J. Garber & M. E. P. Seligman (Eds.), *Human helplessness: Theory and applications* (pp. 279–340). New York: Academic Press.

Stanton, A. L., Tennen, H., Affleck, G., & Mendola, R. (in press). Coping and adjustment to infertility. *Journal of Social and Clinical Psychology.*

Strentz, T. A., & Auerbach, S. M. (1988). Adjustment to the stress of simulated captivity: Effects of emotion-focused vs. problem-focused preparation on hostages differing in locus of control. *Journal of Personality and Social Psychology, 55,* 652–660.

Stroebe, W., & Stroebe, M. S. (1987). *Bereavement and health.* Cambridge, England: Cambridge University Press.

Taylor, S. E. (1983). Adjustment to threatening events: A theory of cognitive adaptation. *American Psychologist, 38,* 1161–1173.

Taylor, S. E., & Brown, J. D. (1988). Illusion and well-being: A social psychological perspective on mental health. *Psychological Bulletin, 103,* 193–210.

Thoits, P. A. (1986). Social support as coping assistance. *Journal of Consulting and Clinical Psychology, 54,* 416–423.

U.S. Congress, Office of Technology Assessment. (1988). *Infertility: Medical and social choices,* OTA-BA-358. Washington, DC: U.S. Government Printing Office.

Weiss, R. S. (1988). Loss and recovery. *Journal of Social Issues, 44*(3), 37–52.

Woody, E. Z., & Costanzo, P. R. (1990). Does marital agony precede marital ecstasy? A comment on Gottman and Krokoff's "Marital interaction and satisfaction: A longitudinal view." *Journal of Consulting and Clinical Psychology, 58,* 499–501.

Wortman, C. B., & Dunkel-Schetter, C. (1979). Interpersonal relationships and cancer: A theoretical analysis. *Journal of Social Issues, 35,* 120–155.

Wortman, C. B., & Lehman, D. R. (1985). Reactions to victims of life crisis: Support attempts that fail. In I. G. Sarason & B. R. Sarason (Eds.), *Social support: Theory, research, and applications* (pp. 463–489). Dordrecht, Netherlands: Martinus Nijhoff.

Wortman, C. B., & Silver, R. C. (1987). Coping with irrevocable loss. In G. R. VandenBos & B. K. Bryant (Eds.), *Cataclysms, crises, and catastrophes: Psychology in action* (pp. 189–235). Washington, DC: American Psychological Association.

AUTHOR INDEX

Page numbers in italics refer to works cited in the References.

223

SUBJECT INDEX

Stress *(cont.)*
  infertility-treatment-related, 165
  in-vitro-fertilization-related, 152
  long-term effects, 200–201
  marital life quality and, 78
  measurement scale, 72–73
  ovulation effects, 7
  physiological measurement, 210–211
  during pregnancy, 211
  psychological adjustment to, 10–12
  self-esteem and, 190
  social support and, 72–73, 78, 79, 82
  spermatogenesis effects, 7
  suppression of, 185
Stress management, 186, 188–189

Testes, biopsy, 20
Testolactone, 24
Testosterone, as male infertility treatment,
    24

Tubal abnormalities
  diagnosis, 21–22
  treatment, 24–25

Ultrasound, transvaginal, 20
Uterus, endometrial biopsy, 20

Varicocele, treatment, 24, 74
Vasography, 22
Vesiculography, 22
Victimizing events
  goal reordering following, 171–172
  infertility as, 165, 166
  worldview effects, 170
Visualization techniques, 188–189
Vitamins, as male infertility treatment, 24

Worldview, in infertility, 35, 170

Zygote intrafallopian transfer, 26